DP/12

Edward Bond

Plays: 9

Innocence, The Balancing Act, Tune, A Window, The Edge

Edward Bond was born and educated in London. His plays include *The Pope's Wedding* (Royal Court Theatre, 1962), *Saved* (Royal Court, 1965), *Early Morning* (Royal Court, 1968), *Lear* (Royal Court, 1971), *Bingo* (Northcott Theatre, Exeter, 1973), *The Sea* (Royal Court, 1973), *The Fool* (Royal Court, 1975), *The Woman* (National Theatre, 1978), *Restoration* (Royal Court, 1981), *Summer* (National Theatre, 1982), *The War Plays* (RSC at the Barbican Pit, 1985), *In the Company of Men* (Paris, 1992; RSC at the Barbican Pit, 1996), *Coffee* (Rational Theatre Company, Cardiff and London, 1996; Paris, 2000), *The Children* (Classworks, Cambridge, 2000), *The Crime of the Twenty-first Century* (Paris, 2001), *Born* (Avignon, 2006), and seven plays which were toured by Big Brum Theatre-in-Education: *At the Inland Sea* (1995), *Eleven Vests* (1997), *Have I None* (2000), *The Balancing Act* (2003), *The Under Room* (2005), *Tune* (2007) and *A Window* (2009). He is also author of *Olly's Prison* (BBC2 Television, 1993; first staged by the Berliner Ensemble, 1994), *Tuesday* (BBC Schools TV, 1993), *Chair* (BBC Radio 4, 2000; first staged Avignon, 2006), and *Existence* (BBC Radio 4, 2002; first staged Paris, 2002).

* Also available as a Methuen Drama Student Edition

EDWARD BOND

Plays: 9

Innocence
The Balancing Act
Tune
A Window
The Edge

with an introduction by the author

Methuen Drama

METHUEN DRAMA CONTEMPORARY DRAMATISTS

1 3 5 7 9 10 8 6 4 2

This collection first published in Great Britain in 2011 by Methuen Drama

Methuen Drama, an imprint of Bloomsbury Publishing Plc

Methuen Drama
Bloomsbury Publishing Plc
50 Bedford Square, London WC1B 3DP
www.methuendrama.com

Copyright © 2011 Edward Bond

Introduction copyright © Methuen Drama 2011

Edward Bond has asserted his rights under the Copyright, Designs and
Patents Act, 1988, to be identified as the author of these works

ISBN 978 1 408 16063 3

A CIP catalogue record for this book is available from the British Library

Available in the USA from Bloomsbury Academic & Professional,
175 Fifth Avenue/3rd Floor, New York, NY 10010
www.BloomsburyAcademicUSA.com

Typeset by Country Setting, Kingsdown, Kent
Printed and bound in Great Britain by CPI Group (UK) Ltd, Croydon CR0 4YY

Contents

Edward Bond
Chronology

Play	*First performance*
The Pope's Wedding	9.12.1962
Saved	3.11.1965
A Chaste Maid in Cheapside (*adaptation*)	13.1.1966
The Three Sisters (*translation*)	18.4.1967
Early Morning	31.3.1968
Narrow Road to the Deep North	24.6.1968
Black Mass (*part of* Sharpeville Sequence)	22.3.1970
Passion	11.4.1971
Lear	29.9.1971
The Sea	22.5.1973
Bingo: Scenes of Money and Death	14.11.1973
Spring Awakening (*translation*)	28.5.1974
The Fool: Scenes of Bread and Love	18.11.1975
Stone	8.6.1976
We Come to the River (*music* H.W. Henze)	12.7.1976
The White Devil (*adaptation*)	12.7.1976
Grandma Faust (*Part One of* A-A-America!)	25.10.1976
The Swing (*Part Two of* A-A-America!)	22.11.1976
The Bundle: New Narrow Road to the Deep North	13.1.1978
The Woman	10.8.1978
The Worlds	8.3.1979
Restoration	21.7.1981
Orpheus (*music* H.W. Henze)	2.11.1981
Summer	27.1.1982
Derek	18.10.1982
After the Assassinations	1.3.1983
The Cat (*music* H.W. Henze)	2.6.1983
Human Cannon	2.2.1986
The War Plays	
Part I: Red Black and Ignorant	29.5.1985
Part II: The Tin Can People	29.5.1985
Part III: Great Peace	17.7.1985

Jesus and Hitler Wept

During the Murdoch scandal there was a discussion on a BBC news programme. The financial corruption and its reach into national institutions shocked the speakers. They were naive. All big-business financial dealings are corrupt and corrupting. It comes to light only when the legal old-boy–old-girl network breaks down. The BBC speakers went on to deplore the closing of the *News of the World* – a fine paper, they said, that had exposed corruption and scandal and was the voice of the working class. I first read it when I was thirteen. It educated me in one swift act of disillusion. Not because it was salacious and pornographic and wallowed in human filth and misery. I knew about all that, I had grown up in the most vicious of all wars. It was the righteous tone in which it clothed its leering prurience. It was not the voice of the working class but the baying of a mob. The judgement expressed on the BBC went unchallenged. The heads nodded earnestly.

Faced with such moral opacity I will not argue a case but state the obvious. Society is held together and driven by its culture. When vast business organisations and the accumulation of vast fortunes dominate society, so that the whole of its existential dynamic derives from this, then those organisations and fortunes own society and everything in it – and above all its culture. The culture holds the whole thing together and makes it work. This is corrupt not only because it leads to pitiful poverty, but even more because it corrupts the most profound of things: the way in which we know ourselves. In day-to-day life self-consciousness is the same as culture-consciousness. We become the culture in which we live. And because of that, because it is our way of life, it passes in the mind almost without notice. Culture creates the means by which it is itself measured and when it is trashed it trashes us.

These vast corporations survive by making profits: the law is the survival of the richest. Yet it is all based on illusion. Money makes nothing, it is not even a raw material. It is absolutely the one value that has no value in itself. Yet it has a relentless dynamic. Where does it come from? It is parasitic on all other social and personal forces. It is a parasite that forms its host. It does this by turning all the host's other forces and values into their opposites – and the function of the host becomes to keep the parasite alive. This is a new dynamic in history, an unprecedented change of course. In the past, history transcended itself. By surviving the past's chaos, reaction, conflicts and suffering we strengthened our creativity. We made the past a beautiful grave out of which we came alive. Bit by bit we made our culture the means not just of surviving but of understanding ourselves better. Our culture began to know us. Now that is changing.

Because we live in extreme contrasts it's easy to find evidence that what I have just written is not so. In the fifties when Prime Minister Macmillan armed the country with nuclear super weapons (in politics there are always good reasons for doing the wrong thing) Bertrand Russell said this made him more evil than Hitler. Russell was in his nineties and his 'cultural self-consciousness' was formed in an earlier age. He saw what the newer culture could not. But the bombs were not used, and compared to Belsen what are a few thousand deaths in the World Trade Center? But there is a difference. Society knew what Hitler was and how to remove him. It was as obvious as a fire in the top of a block of flats. Our problems are out of sight in the building's foundations and we do not know how to deal with them. Our culture, entangled in the ramifications and complexities of daily survival, prevents us seeing them. We are being destroyed even more by our successes than by our failures. We do not, to give one example, see the connection between super-finance and science – not in the peripheral matter of funding but in the fundamentals of culture. The *News of the World* had *prevented* its readers from understanding the causes of crime and the origins of violence. It replaced the dignity of justice with the lubricity of revenge – and that is perhaps the greatest of cultural crimes. As corrupt culture destroys human values, it trivialises and dehumanises our whole society, including science.

Many scientists now see us as maladapted animals who like to read the *News of the World*, as genetic-things to be tampered with. To corrupt culture is to corrupt people. Under the pressure of future catastrophe politicians could use science to re-engineer the human self to save it from itself (in politics there are always good reasons for doing the wrong things). It would be the grandiose 'final solution' of the human dilemma, the completion of Hitler's euthanasia programme. This won't happen because before it could evolution would extinguish us in one final human agony. But it allows us to see without reservations the extent of our problem. Murdoch and the other geniuses of super-finance are – it is not enough to say 'are *in effect*' because we are intellectually responsible for our emotions – a burden on civilisation. They are more evil than Hitler. And this brings us to drama.

*

Culture is society's self-consciousness. Its assertions and rifts resemble those of the human self. Human life is derived from the effects of many forces, which you could call the life forces – material, economic, emotional, imaginative, dreams, the state, law, family, time, mortality, anxiety, ideology, reason, pleasure, pain . . . together they have the urgency of a landslide. We live by organising these life forces into a practical and conscious self. We can do this only by dramatising their inter-relationships. And as culture creates its own means of knowing itself, so does the self. This is the paradox I am writing about in this introduction. How can the means of measurement measure itself? It can't, and the consequence is unavoidable: we cannot know our self any more than a stone can know itself. Humans can't be reduced to a taste in clothes or food or to their biology or genes – because then they would have no means of measurement and it would be as if we were being measured by the dead. The stone cannot know itself because it is 'dead', we cannot know ourselves *because* we are alive. We are a chaos driven by the fierce wind of time, but our problem is not the pathos and contingencies that this causes – that would be merely the random play of the life forces. The problem is how do we organise these forces into a practical and conscious self? How does the human measure, know, itself? There is a litmus test for this question: why is Auschwitz wrong? It's startling to realise that neither religion nor science can say why. If God says it, it's just the word of The Big Person, but that is just a bigger measure, and it becomes so big that reality falls between the calibrations of the measure and it cannot measure anything – it is the problem of how could eternity be made of time. Science's answer is 'ask your genes' – which means no more than 'ask the stone'. Genes do not give answers because they cannot ask questions. There must be a fully human reason why Auschwitz is 'bad' or the answer is reduced to ideology, which is another Big Thing: and then Auschwitz is all right so long as it destroys the right people or enough people to destroy all opposition, and so on. The survival of the fittest means only the survival of the fittest to survive. So make your Auschwitzes efficient and fit for their job. Then *why* is Auschwitz wrong?

Once – in say Roman times – the venom Auschwitz made physical would not have been wrong and it may not be in the future. We do not make ourselves human *by* giving the right answer, we give the right answer because we *are* human. And the only way we have of making ourselves human is drama. We are the dramatic species. Drama works by changing the means humanness has of measuring itself. Reason can't do this, that was Brecht's fallacy. He was caught in a *News of the World* trap, the ambiguity of human values. The *News of the World* subverted the morality it claimed to protect and Brecht corrupted the politics he claimed to promote. Stalin did not know how we create our humanness. He gave Marxism its current intellectual frustrations and made it politically impotent perhaps for generations. Yet Brecht supported Stalinism even after Stalin had crowned Marx with a halo of shit. He should have written plays that made that impossible, instead they are Gulag kitsch. Brecht's influence is one reason why there is now no political theatre. He castrated it and what passes for political theatre is the voyeurism of eunuchs watching sex.

Theatre is not drama. Drama is political, theatre is not. The need for a new drama is urgent. Here I will sketch out what I've written at length in other places. Our culture is increasingly pessimistic about us and the future. The power of technology magnifies the effects of our historical limitations and science has legitimised the theological doctrine of original sin. It says we are born animals and must be strenuously socialised. Scientists are almost forced to do the reactionary work of theologians, instead of being their intellectual opponents, because of the ambiguity in our culture. Drama is the struggle with this ambiguity. To understand this we must begin with its origin in the new-born infant, the neonate, perhaps in its first days or first few hours. The playwright's skill is to put himself in the minds of those he writes about, the characters, as if he were inside their self-consciousness. This intuition is an insight which scientific investigation cannot have because it must be objective. But the most practical objectivity is found in subjectivity. It's why Freud said that he followed in the footsteps of writers.

*

What happens in the neonate's mind? We need to be Copernicus looking at the sun – everything about the neonate is contrary to expectations, nothing is what it seems. The neonate doesn't know it is in the world, it thinks it *is* the world. It has no concept of 'exterior'. It sees things around it, but 'around' is (as yet) 'in' it. It smiles at and touches the exterior, but for it exterior is interior, just as when you dream of what is outside you the dream is in you. The neonate is the whole of reality, and it misses the point to say of *its* reality. Of course genes prime us to relate to the exterior – when a puppeteer animates the puppets on the end of the strings he does not think they are animating him. But the neonate could not distinguish between the reality of itself and the reality of the puppets, and neither puppets nor genes could enlighten it. The neonate must itself realise the distinction by an act of consciousness – and to preserve its monadic generality I will call such an act an 'intellectism'. Until the neonate does this it is what Leibniz called a 'monad' – a world completely enclosed in itself with, Leibniz says, no window on the world outside it. The neonate–monad *is* the world – and the world, the whole of being, is synonymous with its consciousness: what is measured and the means of measuring are one and the same. And so the neonate *is, to itself, reality.* The neonate is conscious only of the reality that is it. In its later life the world will be outside it. Its consciousness will retain its own reality but it knows there is an autonomous reality outside it of which it is only part. The neonate is like a stage but the stage is the audience. You must be Copernicus to understand this, to understand yourself and even to understand anything that is human. It is strange – but this Copernican reality endures in you and without it the concept and experience of drama would be impossible. The sun cannot get outside the sun to see itself – translate this to consciousness and it is the sun that is looking at Copernicus.

The neonate *is* the world. It has no 'intellectism' of time and space. The relations between its mind and its felt body are vast and cosmic, it *is* infinity and eternity. This vastness experiences pleasure and pain. And as the neonate *is* the world, the world will be in pleasure or pain. And as the neonate *is* its consciousness, reality will now be pleasure and now pain. Later an adult will seek pleasure and avoid pain (however you experience these things, they have the same ambiguities as values, and for the same reason) but the neonate cannot do this because it is the world and the world, reality, cannot avoid itself. There is nowhere else for it to go to seek pleasure or avoid pain. The world-neonate, reality, is in cosmic pain at birth and after: so consciousness is in pain. The neonate has no knowledge of cause and effect but pain is itself the consciousness that pain should not be and so, at one and the same time, the neonate is conscious of this and of the pain that *it is* – and this is the origin of human consciousness: consciousness is responsibility. Not just for the pain but that 'it should not be'. They are the same thing. At first this is responsibility for the self – but at this stage self and world are one and so consciousness of the self is responsibility for the world. This makes us human. In the infant affect and reason, cause and effect, moral-is and moral-ought, altruism and egotism are the same – the neonate has no duality, it is 'one'. The responsibility is not an attitude that consciousness adopts, the responsibility is innate in consciousness itself – it is the reality that consciousness is always conscious of as itself. It is how the self creates itself and the actor must retrace this process in creating a character. Now if you go back to the list of life forces that form us you can see that what orders them into the coherence of a human being is responsibility for the world. This is the human imperative that later haunts us in the vicissitudes of corrupt and unjust society. The responsibility is the infant's radical innocence and that is the human imperative that makes the self responsible for the care of the world. In the adult it becomes the imperative for justice and pain and pleasure become the Tragic and the Comic. Without the Tragic we cannot be human and could never make a just society. The Tragic hero and heroine are radically innocent. When the infant leaves the drama of the monad-world and enters society the self takes its radical innocence with it (or you might just as well say that radical innocence takes the self with it). We relate to society's practical exigencies and to historical injustice – but as we take our radically innocent self with us we remain our own 'opposite'. Drama continually repeats this founding process. Justice is a matter of community but humanness is always possible for the single self, it may be glimpsed in euphoria and it is sometimes shockingly near in repression and despair.

Consciousness gives the self the imperative, the need, to seek the just world but the infant enters unjust society. That is the human paradox that creates the ambiguity of values. The injustice is institutionalised in culture. Culture decides what justice is but all its laws are unjust because they maintain unjust society. It's why values change their meaning. To survive in this society we create a new social self and our old, radically innocent self becomes our own 'opposite'. We make the adaptation in different ways and different degrees, and often these are led by our position in society. Historically social inequality originated in scarcity and our natural vulnerability. But the momentum of history turned this shared organisation into injustice and the institutions of repression and power. Injustice maintains itself by ideology and, finally, by political and economic violence. Ideology is more complex and subtle than violence. It creates a culture to occupy the gap between the social self and its 'opposite' self (which for simplicity I've called radical innocence). The gap is actually the site of human reality. How is this? The self is in social reality but is also its own 'opposite', which it created in infancy. The 'opposite' is the imperative for justice, but as justice has no natural description society decrees what justice is. To do this its description must occupy the gap between the two selves – occupying it, that is, with its own version of reality. The gap is first opened when the infant enters society and finds that it is not in its first (ontological-monad) world but in our existential social reality. It learns that reality has different forms. The gap is the site of imagination – which is why fiction is not fiction but the site of human reality. The 'opposite' confronts the social self because for the 'opposite' it's as if in society 'reality' was in pain, and when it does this it is confronting the distortions of injustice with its own radical innocence. This is the logic of imagination and as it confronts injustice with justice it is also the logic of humanness. Drama is this confrontation – drama takes place in the gap, in imagination, but it is human reality. The logic of imagination and the logic of drama are one. Drama is not an event in fiction but the necessary turmoil in reality. Because, in the way I have described, in the neonate reality and consciousness are one, they must endure to be so in the 'opposite' – we are in reality because we are conscious and reality is this turmoil. It makes us the dramatic species. Historically this process also gives ideology its power: injustice occupies the gap as ideology – it is the way the social self sees the world and so the way it sees itself. It is its self-consciousness. Notoriously ideology in the forms of religion and patriotism becomes belief: it is the way self-consciousness sees itself – as if it were the way reality sees itself. It distorts the measure of humanness. It is why both Jesus and Hitler wept.

How can the 'opposite', the site of radical innocence, accept this corruption of its imperative? I shall describe only the extreme instance, because it illustrates all possible degrees of corruption. The human self is radically innocent, its innocence is the means by which it knows the world and is responsible for it – so it must seek justice. Then how can it accept injustice and live in it? Imagination must be corrupted by culture. The self becomes the enemy of its own 'opposite' – it takes revenge on itself. It is as if the imperative to be human becomes the need to be inhuman – and the unjust man turns on himself with rage. He does this with the absolute force of reality – he hates himself. His own 'opposite' torments him – and he turns his rage on others to punish them for the torment he causes himself and to relieve himself of the pain of the torment. All injustice is revenge and has the need to rage and destroy. If to prevent himself being destroyed by his own rage he contains it within malice and cynicism and extends its scope through bureaucracy, it becomes even more destructive. Revenge is never satisfied. There are never enough victims to be sent to Auschwitz. All reactionary politics, from Fascism to paternal conservatism, are forms of revenge and overt or incipient violence. The unjust are constantly reminded of their injustice in the images of poverty and its slums, in suffering, destitution and despair, in the living-bones of the starving and the rags of the dead. They see it because sight was the neonate's first language. The spoken texts of drama are the eyes speaking. Drama takes place in the gap that is the site of imagination and as such is the profoundest form of reality. It is a tragedy when one man dies but when the Tragic hero dies all men die – the Tragic hero or heroine dies so that humanness lives.

*

The difference between theatre and drama can now be understood. Whether theatre is comic or serious it is fundamentally ludic, a game. It tries to put on the shoes without taking them out of the box. It doesn't seek for order in the life forces. Without the comic society would be inhuman, but it has its time and place. It's comic to slip on a banana skin but not if you break your neck and the starving child who slips on the banana skin eats it. Theatre avoids the human problem in the gap. It serves ideology. Even agitprop is theatre on the same level as light entertainment. It may tell audiences what to do and encourage them to believe that they are able to do it. But there are other means of doing this more effectively. It does not change its audience because it cannot change the means by which humanness measures and knows itself. Theatre carves the Comic out of the Tragic, drama carves the Tragic out of the Comic. The Comic avoids the ultimate seriousness of being human: that the self and not authority gives itself its responsibility.

Drama repeats the first act of creation in which the self created itself in the neonate. It did this when exposed in itself to pleasure and pain. But the self was not the random experience of these effects. It is also the 'intellectism' in which it discriminated between their meanings to itself. This is why humanness cannot be reduced to the genetic. The 'intellectism' is an 'aware discrimination' and after it consciousness must always observe itself. The neonate needed to be at home in the world but it *was itself* the world and so responsible for the world – its consciousness was not just of feelings, sensations, emotions and affects, but, now, of reality and in reality of the logic of necessity. It is this logic which gives us human responsibility – it is not that we are victims of fate but are, on the contrary, responsible for necessity. Necessity is hideously transparent, it is the death of gods. Tragic heroes and heroines see this and it makes the problem of humanness clear to them. Greek drama reached this understanding in Euripides. Human consciousness is conscious of this necessity and so the necessity is part of the self – and ultimately this is what makes us responsible for reality. The neonate's experiences are cosmic, as if of a volcano that was aware of itself – but they are not overwhelming because human experience bears the laws of necessity, and human frailty even in the infant becomes the site of the laws of necessity. They create the logic of reality which sustains our consciousness.

This logic emerges in the turmoil of social affairs and takes human form, and then the Tragic hero and heroine see that human necessity is justice.

*

The self's care of the world, of reality, is this necessity of justice. The infant's drama later becomes the stage for human catastrophe. It's as if for an audience each drop of blood, each agony, offence, each footfall in Auschwitz, were on the little stage before them. But the neonate's origin of the self is closer even than that: reality is consciousness. What is on the stage is not fiction but reality because it is the 'opposite' self that ideology seeks to corrupt, and which you may learn to ignore as if you had died and casually pushed aside your own corpse to get on with the business of making money and living. Every drama has a centre in which justice and radical innocence confront corruption and revenge. The power of drama is that this centre is also in us, the audience. We may become fiction because we look away, and then we are as empty as unread books or unperformed plays – but our opposite will torment us for doing this. Drama is reality not merely in the sense of 'what really happened' but reality itself in which we are responsible for the meaning of what happens.

The interpretation of every line, event and even every gesture and expression must pass through the play's centre. The centre itself makes this possible but the production must know the centre's seriousness, its meaning – not hide it in abstract effects which however powerful they may be are only theatre. How does the play finally arrive at its centre? It enters the extreme event – and this repeats the extreme experience of the neonate. The extreme is the site of 'accident time'. Accident time is a common biological effect that occurs in accidents in everyday life. It is a time of extreme concentration. In it things may move with great speed but may (and usually do) seem to be slow. It is not cinematic slow motion – which is theatre that draws attention to the motion itself but not to what is happening. Accident time in a street accident is a matter of life and death, it allows the mind to see how it might escape from the accident and survive. In dramatic accident time the self sees the whole human situation in an event and understands its meaning. It sees beyond the ideological screen. And as in the neonate, it is without the dualities of egoism and altruism, of moral-is and moral-ought – they are the same, as in perfect justice. It sees with the logic of imagination, which is radical innocence's way of seeing – it sees the 'invisible object'. But only the actor, not the text, can make the invisible object visible or be the invisible object. Drama is the art of acting. The text may produce the situation of the extreme event but the actor must enter it. And when he or she does, the invisible object is made visible. What the object is depends on the situation and its relation to the whole site. It can be anything – the face or the back of the head or an object that is pointed to. If the actor knows the play's centre he or she may find the invisible object anywhere in the text – then the extreme would be the relation between the play and the actor's psyche. Greek drama defined the extreme situations so exactly that the actor's mask could become the invisible object and then when the audience looked at the mask they saw themselves. The invisible object makes the play's centre objective and you recognise it because you yourself are the centre – really, you create the invisible object and the actor's creativity is empty without your creativity. To create the invisible object you use the same creativity you used to create yourself in the neonate. The creation has the logic of necessity. This is not a reversal to infancy because now your life bears all the weight of the damaged world. It's as if the infant lends its strength to your frailty. In the invisible object you see your 'opposite'. However outré or recherché the characters or the drama, the drama comes from your life and you are at its centre. How could you possibly be Hamlet or Antigone – or Medea or Macbeth? It is written that both Jesus and Hitler wept.

   Finally we can understand the site and boundary of drama. The site is not the set, which may be realistic, symbolic and so on – the site is in the human self, the site of the contradictions and conflicts that I have described. But the self is in society, which is also a site of the self – and so drama has a physical space, the stage. The stage is the site of the self-and-society, of social and political contingencies and necessities but also of the conscious self. In contemporary theatre the stage is not a site in this sense. Instead it is taken over by sets which bind it to the incidental and reduce reality to the realistic. Greek and Jacobean stages were the sites of self-and-society because the architecture structurally reproduced the topography and interior levels of the self and society. The stage replicated the social and subjective structures. Reality was a house and drama showed the people living in it, it did not obscure reality with realism or the symbolic. Modern dramatists must learn how to write the missing stage-site into the text. The total site, the stage-site and the self-and-society site, contains all that is relevant to humanness. 'Site' is an immense tool of drama. Here I can make only a few points. An object or action may change its meaning and value when its place on the site is changed. A simple example: the meaning of Yorick's skull is changed if it's in the grave or Hamlet's hand. Hamlet holds his own mortality. So perhaps the way he puts the skull back in the grave will be an invisible object, or perhaps it will be the way he brushes dust from his hand. When a baby is stoned to death in a pram the meaning of the whole site changes.

Drama is situated on the boundary between society and self, because that is where we make our practical humanness. It is also the maelstrom where ideology distorts and corrupts. Imagination in the gap is the means for understanding the site, and when drama creates the logic of imagination it changes the meaning of (and on) the site. How is this done? Drama is possible only because the self is torn by its 'opposite' – otherwise there would just be suffering. The rage that stones the baby repeats the baby's own radically innocent rage at the pain of the world – and this is the rage that makes us human. Drama uses the creativity with which the neonate created itself. From this comes the vital difference between acting and enacting. Acting is theatre and mimics reality, enacting is drama because it uses the processes with which the neonate created itself and its reality – and so enacting changes reality. Reflection and argument may change the appearance of what happens but they cannot undo corruption and are corruptible themselves. They leave the site unchanged. Drama does not argue a case or use force but changes reality, changes the measure by which we know ourselves and create our reality The problem is not which to change first, the self or society – they create and change each other. Only drama can penetrate this mutual creation and change the meaning of values. It is our only barrier against barbarism. So drama raises the most serious questions. The question 'Who is doing what?' can be answered only when its situation on the site is known. *Nothing is obvious. An act itself has no meaning, it does not give us its meaning – we give it its meaning.* The problem of meaning is that the site presents itself as the means of measurement. Historically that is ideology's power. So we *have* to change the meaning of society. If we destroy drama and its power to do this we could not know ourselves. If modern media – say the Murdoch press – trivialise or debase us by destroying the logic of imagination we will not be human and there are no gods left to save us. I cited the stoning of the baby because it produces the absolute seriousness of the Tragic which ultimately defines our humanness. It's the subject of my plays. I'll end this point by saying only that when the cattle arrived at the slaughterhouse they heard the butchers mooing. It is written that both Jesus and Hitler wept. So *why* is Auschwitz wrong?

*

The Greeks were the first democracy not because they founded a public legislature but because they founded drama. The assembled citizens made the laws and administered them in their law court. But the laws were unjust – all social laws are unjust because society is unjust. So they created drama to find justice. Their drama used the means I've described to create humanness on the boundary between society and self, between social self and its 'opposite'. Because the Greeks were collectively responsible for the burden of democracy they looked with unprecedented closeness at the extremes of the human paradox. Their theatre was so swept up in the astonishing rapture at what doing this released that it created the basis of all future drama. Our civilisation is based on it. But its great period lasted scarcely more than a human lifetime. It was too radical to survive in the primitive social organisations of its time. The simplicity that made it destroyed it. We have to instal its simplicity in our complexity. Greece ruined itself in civil wars and later Roman violence was free to colonise everything it could lay its hands on or its soldiers tread on. But because the 'opposite' cannot be colonised by ideology, however subtle, Rome sustained its violence by replacing the stage with the arena. It ruled by bread and revenge. This conflicted with the human imperative and the solution of Christianity was inevitable – because although the values and meanings of humanness are in themselves ambiguous their relations are logical and theoretically simple. Christianity was both tragic and grotesque. What the Greeks said was fiction the church said was real – it twisted the meanings to change the values. It secured its millennial flash of freedom by repression – the church is a prison in which the self's 'opposite' lies in manacles. The gods of Greek drama are stage fictions but the God of Christianity is real. There is an almost hermetic correspondence between Greek drama and Christianity. It's seen most clearly in the central story. In Greek drama Oedipus resists his father and kills him to possess his mother; in Christianity the father kills the obedient son and the mother is a virgin untouched by either of them. In Greek drama fiction enacts the logic of imagination to give humanness the power and authority to change reality. Christianity replaces the logic of imagination with the bureaucratisation of brute facts – ultimately it tries to bureaucratise the human 'soul'. This is Christianity's prison. Antigone shows why it must fail. To be ironic, fiction is always more real than what reality is becoming. Christianity is crammed with ambiguities from the human paradox – for instance in the *Bacchae* Dionysus–Christ is the God that destroys the prison. The human paradox – the working of imagination in the gap – is relentless: it means that values must change as their situation on the site changes and this changes the meaning of the site. As it is, Christianity's manipulation of the human paradox was profound. It stabilised society, made the organisation of practical creativity possible and lasted until reason killed God and science carried out a post-mortem on him. Now it has reverted back to fiction but without the logic of imagination. It has becomes a lie and only fanatics believe lies. What becomes of the violence that is incipient in it, in all religion? Those who once would have been the victims of its inquisition become the inquisitors – the fanatics and terrorists.

*

Human beings are more inventive than creative. For generations history 'creeps' forward till new technologies destroy social relations and make them impractical. Clearly Jacobean London and fifth-century Greece were such times. Then history didn't creep forward but played leapfrog. It was frightening but liberating. It created drama that entered the extremes of existence – between the grinding of the tectonic plates of society and self – and created a new reality and a new way to be human. It made huge problems bearable even by human frailty and we still live from what it gave us. Our age is a time of even greater change, centuries seem crammed into a few years. It too should be frightening but liberating. Instead there is chaos and irritable boredom relieved in street riots. Our social relations are unworkable, the gap between rich and poor widens and we become more unjust. And because all injustice is held together by the violence, the government replaces justice with revenge. (This is not always done cynically. The owners of the *News of the World* probably believed it was the voice of morality speaking for the common good.) To cling to its veneer of scientific modernism the government constantly tries new ways to reform offenders and reduce crime. The only way to reduce crime is to make society more just. Why is something so obvious not seen? We have already met the answer.

Society knows itself only through its means of communication. Our 'media age' and its vast media technology are

dominated by the press and its relentless outpouring of news.
We ought to be more informed than at any other earlier time,
should know ourselves better and be able to create a culture
that made the culture of Greece with its slavery, simple
economy and elementary science seem primitive. But we do
not create the modern heirs of Oedipus and Antigone, or
Hamlet and Lear, the fictions that still breathe in us. Instead
we have the *News of the World* and its vicious mix of hate and
sentimentality, puritanism and lewdness, the triviality of its
celebrities and the futile battles of millionaire footballers.
This is Murdochery, the culture of Murdoch, and it survives
the end of the newspaper. Murdoch is not its origin or sole
contemporary source, he did not intend or foresee it and
he may be its greatest victim and we may even have had to
create him before he could destroy us – it comes to the same
thing and so the name is apt. The Murdoch media are an
unelected NGO with no responsibility but to make money.
Money is the parasite that drives our society and gives it its
frantic energy. Murdoch is the one person who controls the
parasite. He does it not on the money market but by combining
the parasite with the communication of information. This
corrupts all society's institutions because to survive they need
money and to make it they must enter the Murdoch culture.
The combination of money and media is *totally* corrupting.
It's why Murdoch's organisation could buy police and
politicians and he could set up his market stall in No. 10.
Murdoch owns our culture – TV, radio, sport, all the means
we have of knowing ourselves, the art that is now trash and
the chemical taxidermy of animals, hypnotic mass music and
its festivals, and even Hollywood–Bollywood – films have their
own culture of vigilantism-and-soft-Fascism but what makes
it acceptable is the corruption of the rest of culture. It taints
everything. When the ship sinks everything sinks with it.

Its most corrosive effect is on drama. It has destroyed it.
We live in one of those seldom crises that define an epoch.
In the past they turned themselves into the overwhelming
outbursts of creativity that produced giants who bent reality
to serve the human purpose. Now all the richness of drama

that I've been describing is thrown away and its responsibility for the future abandoned. History is waiting at the door and our National Theatre, the RSC, the Royal Court, all the main established theatres, are reduced to serving one furtive, scurrying little man who made himself the master of the parasite. It should be said again and again and again: it is a catastrophe.

Edward Bond
August 2011

Note on Punctuation

Each character in these plays produces his or her own punctuation. It is part of their reality. It belongs to them as much as their actions and their transcribed demotic speech. They could not speak if the writer did not respect this. They are fictions but they have the reality of drama and so their actual tears are shed and their laughter released by the audience. There is nothing mystical or aesthetic about this. In the shared mind of the reader and the characters it is as actual and immediate as the dust and rain in the streets.

Reading a play invokes – raises – the characters from the page. The reader is not interpreting an idea but creating a character. The characters become the reader's reality as much as, or more than, they do the spectator's in the theatre. The reader performs and is enacted or is as still born as the uninvoked page.

An empty page is a blank face. When it bears print the reader reads the page just as we read the faces of those we talk with and listen to. The page speaks the words, the punctuation is the expression on the speaker's face: the twitches, the tensions, the frowns, the passivity, the physical effort of speaking in tense situations – the punctuation marks imprint all this on the face of the page. It is the same with the elisions. A character hides his face and another says 'Look – 'e's 'id 'is mug' – when the reader sees these empty spaces he is looking into the whites of the speaker's eyes and *sees* the tension in his thought.

Punctuation may lie. According to the situation it must be dangerous or reassuring. Forcing the characters into academic printing correctness would destroy them and betray the reader. It would corrupt reality.

Innocence

Part Five of

The Paris Pentad

Author's Note

Innocence is the fifth and last play in the series originally called *The Colline Pentad*, after the theatre for which they were written to be staged by its Artistic Director Alain Françon. Only the first three plays were staged there before Alain Françon left to stage the two remaining plays elsewhere in Paris. It seems appropriate to rename the series *The Paris Pentad*.

The plays proceed through time from the Second World War to the year 2077. They concern the problem of creating humanness in a time when its existence is threatened. This is also the subject of a parallel series called *The Birmingham Plays*. These plays were written for Big Brum Theatre-in-Education and were first staged for younger audiences but are also intended for older audiences.

Apart from *Innocence*, the plays in this book belong to *The Birmingham Plays*. The plays of *The Paris Pentad* are *Coffee*, *The Crime of the Twenty-first Century*, *Born*, *People* and *Innocence*.

Part One: Fen

Part Two: House

Characters

Son
Brother
Treg
WAPO 3
WAPO 4
WAPO 5
WAPO 6
WAPO 7
WAPO 8
Silhouette Soldier
Minty
Stewart
Woman
Ancient Crone
Grace
Village Woman

Brother and Silhouette Soldier must be played by the same actor.

Ancient Crone and Village Woman must be played by the same actress.

Minty and Stewart may be played by WAPO actors.

Part One: Fen

One

A clearing in the fen. Night. A storm has passed and circles in the distance.

Woman *is alone. Her clothes are dark: slacks, overcoat, boots. They were once decent but are now soiled and tattered. A dark grey backpack. In each hand she carries an identical stout plain brown-paper carrier bag with a tough cord handle the same colour as the paper. The bags bulge at the bottom.*

She is weary but intense. She is still – then she walks a few steps. Stops. Hesitates. She stands the first carrier bag upright on the ground. Turns. Holds the handles of the second carrier bag together with both hands. Raises the second carrier bag. Lowers it. Waits. Returns to the first carrier bag. Picks it up. Holds a carrier bag in each hand. Walks a distance. Stops. Puts the second carrier bag on the ground. Walks away. She holds the handles of the first carrier bag in one hand. Suddenly stops. Turns to stare back at the second carrier bag. Looks away.

Woman (*to second carrier bag*) Nails in water.

She stands the first carrier bag on the ground. Walks a few steps towards the second carrier bag. Stops between the two carrier bags. Her face is dry. She passes a hand over it as if she wiped away tears. Lets her empty hands hang at her sides. She goes to the first carrier bag. Picks it up. Walks to the edge of the clearing. Stops. Still. Goes out left. The second carrier bag stands upright on the ground.

Pause.

Ancient Crone *comes on from the back. She and her clothes are dirty. Long grey matted hair. Face and hands bony and thin. A long raincoat. One side is partly torn away. It flaps when she moves. Muffler. Rags tied to her feet with string.*

She has been watching **Woman**. *She goes cautiously left. Looks off till she is sure* **Woman** *has gone. Turns back towards the second* *carrier bag. Searches the ground. Finds a jagged stone. Takes a dirty string from her pocket. Ties one end through a waist-high buttonhole of the raincoat. Goes to the second carrier bag. Opens the top.*

Ancient Crone (*fingers to her mouth. Drools*)   Ooosh.

She holds the stone and string over the bag as if showing them. Reaches into the bag. Takes out a baby swaddled in grubby white. Ties the loose end of string to the swaddling over the belly.

Ancient Crone (*titter*)   Oow. – The things yer ain know! Got all that t' learn yer!

Woman *comes back.*

Woman   Give me that.

Ancient Crone   Yer –

Woman   Give me that.

Ancient Crone   Mine. Yer left it.

Woman   Forgot. Come back t' –

Ancient Crone   Left it before. Watched yer for days. Always leave it.

Woman   Give me. Give it.

Ancient Crone   Come back t' see if 'n animal got it. 'Oped yer find a little 'eap a' chew bones. Then yer ain 'ave t' come back no more. (*To baby.*) She ain touch yer never again.

Woman   Give me.

Ancient Crone   What use 're yer t' it? I pity yer. Skin 'n bones! Cant feed two. (*To baby.*) Twice nothing is less than nothing.

Woman   I manage –

Ancient Crone   Yer dont! Drag it round 's if the world's a graveyard 'n yer lookin for a empty 'ole t' bury it in. (*Slashes the string in half with the stone.*) 'S mine now! (*Titters. To baby.*) The wound talks. Thass called pain.

Woman   Give me it.

Ancient Crone   Cant. I'd feel what yer felt when yer left it. What's the use us both sufferin? (*Raises the stone over the baby.*) Shall I kill it? –

Woman   No – no –

Ancient Crone   If it could talk it 'a say yes! Get the sufferin over – why leave it t' later? (*To baby.*) Ain kill it. Little babies 'ave t' wait their turn – take their place in the queue. (*Raises the stone over the baby.*)

Woman   Dont –

Ancient Crone   Scratch! (*She cuts the baby's forehead.*) Scratch its 'ead so it knows it's mine!

Woman (*grabbing at the swaddling*)   Dont – !

Ancient Crone   Look – she strip yer naked 'n starving a' the cold. A scratch! Yer 'urt it more when yer give it yer tittydug! Yer taste more bitter 'n my stone. See! – lines on its 'ands. Thass the wounds yer give it when yer bore it. (*Cuts the baby's forehead.*) Scrape it deeper – teach it the world its born in.

Woman (*huddles into herself*)   Sorry – sorry – kept yer if I could –

Ancient Crone *starts to walk away. Stops and turns back to* **Woman**.

Ancient Crone   Never wanted one a' these till the soldiers come. (*To baby.*) Thass 'ow stories start now. 'One day the soldiers come.' They burnt the street. Took the women. Little girls. Ask the mother who the man was. Ain say. (*To baby.*) More silent 'n yoo – 'n yer ain got language. The kid slep on the kitchen chair. Flies crawlin on its face like letters tryin t' spell a name. Yer see that when soldiers come. If the flies'd spelt the man's name the soldiers 'd still done what they did. They 'anged it. First they try it with a rope. Too thick for its little neck. It fell through the noose on t' the ground it'd never walk on. Yer notice them things when the soldiers come.

Then they try a skipping rope. Still too big. So they 'ang it on a bit a' string an' it was dead. (*She pulls her raincoat round her with a simple ceremonial gesture.*) Its mother never spoke. The squeak come from the chair. The soldiers left – went 'untin in 'er silence. The soldier 'oo did the 'angin kep it on the string. Tied it t' the end a' 'is gun. Took it everywhere. Kid jiggin on the string. Thass when I wanted one a' me own t' play with. Followed 'im. Kep out a' sight. Till the baby turn t' bones 'n the soldier was blew up 'n the bones turn t' bits a' shrapnel. Luck 'ave it – I saw yer in the fens. Yer put yer kid down. Come back. Pick it up. Put it down. Yer ain suffer. The woman 'oo never spoke suffered – 'ave t' study 'ard t' suffer like that. (*Points to second carrier bag.*) Ain leave yer rubbish. (*Harsh.*) Ain want nothin a' yourn.

Woman *picks up the bag. Goes out left.* **Ancient Crone** *tucks the baby under her arm – she doesn't know how it should be held.*

Ancient Crone (*watching*)   See 'er off . . .

She goes off at the back.

Two

A clearing elsewhere in the fen. Grey dawn. On the ground two backpacks, a sack and a few boxes bound with carrying ropes, some loosened. A few utensils by the boxes.

Woman *sleeps wrapped in a groundsheet.* **Brother** *takes things from the sack and puts them in his backpack. He is methodical and neat. He half-stops – his hands move more slowly and he stares at* **Woman**. *Has she moved? He goes back to his packing as before. He takes a plate, mug, jug, knife and fork – all metal – from a box and puts them in his backpack.*

Woman *stands, slowly and mechanically, not as if still partly asleep but like a cold machine setting into motion. Her back is bent. She does not look at* **Brother**. *She goes out of sight to urinate. She comes back.*

Woman (*stops*)   Why yer up early? (*Fear.*) See somethin? (*Goes a little way up. Looks off.*) Nothin there. (*Turns back to* **Brother**. *He takes a jumper from the sack. Puts it in his backpack.* **Woman** *is mystified.*) What yer doin? – Yer goin! – Where yer – ? (*Shock.*) Yer pack! – Y'ain comin back! Goin while I was – ! Yer cant! Yer will come back? O God what shall I – ? (*Snatches the jumper.*) Mine! Stealin! (*Snatches things from his backpack.*) Mine! (*Throws the things aside.*) Yer cant go! O God I wake up 'n yer – ! Tell me what yer – ! Yer want someone t' be – we'll find someone – I'll 'elp yer t' – If there was someone I'd be glad – yer need someone t' – (*Goes to get food from a box.*) Eat! – Cant go on yer own. Yer ain 'andle people. Ain know what they mean when they say. (**Brother** *picks up the things* **Woman** *scattered. Neatly puts them back in his backpack. She holds food in her hand. Watches him.*) . . . No. Ain that. Want what's out there – where it's empty. Ain come back – else yer ain slink off while I slep. . . (*Pleads.*) Please please. Cant bear it if yer . . . (*She watches* **Brother** *fastening his backpack. Flat, colourless, quick.*) Where was it when I was 'appy – before the carryin everythin from place t' place – when I was 'appy with meself before yer was born – with 'appy people? – dont grudge me that because yer never 'ad it – yer take it from me if yer go – (**Brother** *finishes. Her voice becomes hoarse.*) If I was 'n animal yer'd 'ear it cry 'n stop – I say words so yer dont 'ave t' listen . . . (*Her voice becomes normal.*) I knew the day 'd come when yer go.

Brother *doesn't look at* **Woman**. *He shoulders his backpack and goes out right.*

Woman   Why do I say all that? Useless. I'm tired a' livin in this place. Waste. Rubbish. Dirt. All I got left now.

Brother *comes back.*

Woman   Yer come back t' me!

Brother *goes straight to her. Clenches his fist. Punches her once violently full in the face. She falls over. Turns immediately and goes out right without looking at her.*

Woman (*feels her face*) 'E – 'e – ! (*Looks at the blood on her hands.*) Broken me . . . (*She stands. Goes unsteadily towards the boxes. Something on the ground catches her eye – she picks up a spoon. Holds it awkwardly in her outstretched hand. Tries to call.*) Spoon.

Three

A **WAPO** *deserters' camp in another fen clearing. Right, an unseen swamp. Day.*

The only path from the fen ends up left at a lookout post. Right, a heap of gear – boxes, canvas carriers, a portable field kitchen, water containers. Further right, **WAPO 3** *lies unconscious on a groundsheet. He has been shot in the stomach. The* **WAPO**s *wear assorted bits of uniform and civilian clothes.*

Son *is downstage. He cleans his weapon. His balaclava is pulled down to cover his face. He sees through eye-slits.* **Treg** *is at the lookout post. His balaclava is rolled up so that his face is bare.*

Son *goes towards the lookout post but stops short. Looks off left.*

Son (*gestures with his head to* **WAPO 3**) Give 'im a look.

Treg *goes to* **WAPO 3**. *Stoops over him. Goes to the gear. Picks up a water bottle. Starts to unscrew the top.*

Son No.

Treg Give 'im water.

Son No.

Treg (*still unscrewing the cap*) Tried t' talk. Give 'im water – 'e could say what 'appened. Ain say much when 'e's dead.

Son No.

Treg (*to* **WAPO 3**) Water? (*Silence. Tips water on a rag.*) Wet 'is face.

He wipes **WAPO 3**'s *face with the wet rag. No response. He removes blood-soaked rag from* **WAPO 3**'s *wound. Pads it with the soaked rag. Stares at* **WAPO 3**. *Silence.* **Son** *makes a half-gesture to someone approaching on the path. Comes down to his weapon. Jerks his head to send* **Treg** *back to the lookout post.* **Son** *cleans his weapon. Pause.* **WAPO 4** *comes in. He is the youngest of the* **WAPO**s.

WAPO 4 (*to* **Son**)   Nothin. – 'E alright? (*Goes to look at* **WAPO 3**.) Wish we could do somethin.

Son (*to* **Treg**, *not answering* **WAPO 4**)   Water'd finish 'im off. Stomach wound.

WAPO 4   Ow long's it take?

Treg   Got what 'e deserve. Rattin on 'is mates t' –

WAPO 4   'E ain!

Treg   Why 'e take the grub with 'im if 'e's comin back?

WAPO 4   Bribe the civvies – they tell 'im where the army's movin.

Treg   Rattin on 'is –

WAPO 4   Not on 'is mates!

Treg   Thass what we did – bunk off the army.

WAPO 4   Different. They ain mates. When they start fightin theirselves – if we stayed we'd be dead. Least out 'ere we got a chance.

Treg   Then why's 'e take –

WAPO 4   Dunno, dunno, do I! (*Goes left. Starts to change his clothes. Looks across at* **Son**.) If 'e said why 'e was goin 'e'd a bin stop. Ain mean 'e rat on 'is mates. (*Takes off his boots. Nods at* **WAPO 3**.) Tongue stickin out. (*Wrings socks.*) Mud stinks like dead man's puke. Ain bin dry for weeks. Stuck 'ere. Water be over our 'eads before the army finish us off. Should we push 'is tongue back? So 'e can breathe better. (*Steps into one boot. Hops to* **WAPO 3**.) Tongue's movin.

Treg (*goes to look at* **WAPO 3**)   Tryin t' speak.

WAPO 4   Oceans a' water. 'E smell it 'n 'e cant drink.

Son *goes up towards the lookout.*

Treg (*to* **WAPO 3**)   Can yer 'ear?

WAPO 4   Ought 'a stick 'is tongue back.

Son   Cover 'im.

WAPO 4   'E ain dead –

Son   The sheet. They're comin.

WAPO 4   They got someone?

Son   Ain let 'em see 'im yet.

Treg *goes back to the lookout.* **WAPO 4** *hops on one foot. Picks up the groundsheet. Trips on the edge. Falls across* **WAPO 3**.

WAPO 4   Ow! What the bloody – ! Gerroff! (*Pushes* **WAPO 3** *away. His hand slides on* **WAPO 3**'s *wound.*) What the bloody – ! (*Stands. Throws the groundsheet over* **WAPO 3**.)

Son   Shutit!

WAPO 4 (*sees the blood on his hand*)   Urgh! (*Wipes his hand on the ground.*) 'Is bloody blood-shit on me 'and! (*Pulls his balaclava down to cover his face. Kicks* **WAPO 3**'s *boot.*) Shat yer stinkin shitty blood on me!

Son (*to* **WAPO 4**. *Not shouting*)   Wrap it.

Son *goes to his weapon. Pause.* **Brother** *comes on at the lookout.* **WAPO**s 5 *and* 6 *follow just behind him. Their balaclavas mask their faces.* **WAPO 5** *holds his weapon in both hands.* **WAPO 6** *carries* **Brother**'s *backpack.*

WAPO 5   'Idin under the big dike.

Son (*glances up, goes on cleaning his weapon*)   Just with 'is-self?

WAPO 5   Yeh.

Son   No one bin with 'im?

WAPO 5   No sign a' no one recent. Grass under water.

Son (*peers down the barrel of his weapon*)   'Is luggage?

WAPO 5   Quick shuffties. Nothin.

Son   'Ave a proper look.

WAPO 6 *rolls up his balaclava into a hat. Empties* **Brother***'s backpack on the ground. Spreads it with his boot.*

WAPO 6   Jist civvie gear.

Son (*blows speck of dust from his weapon*)   Shoot 'im.

Brother *takes one step back.* **WAPO 5** *raises his weapon. Does not cock it or aim.*

Son (*to* **Brother**)   Drop yer weapon in the drink, that it? (**Brother** *stares at him.*) Yer up t' somethin. Thass why yer try t' do a runner. (*As if contradicting him.*) O yes yer did. I said shoot 'im – yer took a step back.

WAPO 5   Right.

Son   On my patch that qualifies as attemptin escape. Ain run if yer ain got nothin t' 'ide. What yer up to? (*Silence.*) Shoot 'im. (**WAPO 5** *aims at* **Brother**.) 'Old it. (*To* **WAPO 4**.) Yer turn. (*To* **Brother**.) Yer ain object do yer? (**WAPO 6** *sniggers. To* **WAPO 4**.) Shoot 'im.

WAPO 4 *aims his weapon at* **Brother**. *Raises his head to look across to* **Son**.

WAPO 4   Shall I drop 'im 'ere – or where 'e fall straight in the splash so we ain 'ave t' lug 'is carcase out?

Son *puts a hand on* **WAPO 4***'s weapon. Pushes the barrel down.*

Son (*deadly serious*)   Wrap it. Never joke when yer killin someone. Never. Serious when yer die. Always. Yer could be stood where 'e is t'morra. (*Goes to* **Brother***'s gear. Stares down at it. To* **WAPO 4**.) Yer think I was jokin when I said 'Yer ain object'. No. I was thinkin whass in 'is 'ead. If I knew it'd 'elp. (*He gives a snatch of laughter – shows his teeth. Serious again.*) I was thinking a' us. (*Looks down at the gear. Raises his voice to* **Brother**.) No mates? Out 'ere on yer own? Where yer goin? Oo yer meet up with? (*No answer.*) Ain got t' give 'im the word if yer oblige me a bit. This is my patch. I'm lord 'n everythin else 'ere. My little bit a' world. My little bit a' sky. (*The* **WAPO**s *watch* **Brother** *and* **Son**. *To* **Treg**.) Watch the path. Yer lookout. (**Treg** *goes back to the lookout.*) I'll count t' ten. Then 'e'll shoot. I ain count loud. That'd make it easy. Count in me 'ead. Matter a' fact I already bin started. Guess what number I reach?

Pause. In the silence **WAPO 4** *raises his weapon to aim at* **Brother**. **WAPO 3** *splutters a low cough.* **Treg** *and* **WAPO**s 5 *and* 6 *look towards* **WAPO 3**. *Pause.* **Son** *goes to him.*

WAPO 4 (*still aimed, dances a little shuffle*)   Ain I dolly in one boot!

Son *looks down at* **WAPO 3**. *Then looks across at* **Brother**.

Son   Little boy done a runner away from 'ome? Out on 'is own. Got loss. – Yer 'idin somethin. I can tell. I'll 'ave t' know everythin in the end. The longer I wait the bigger yer little secret gets. (*To* **WAPO 5**.) Gob must be block. Wash it out.

WAPO 4 *lowers his weapon.*

WAPO 5 (*to* **Brother**)   Walkies, sonny.

WAPOs 5 *and* 6 *take* **Brother** *out by the lookout.* **Son** *goes back to* **Brother**'s *clothes. Stares down at them. Listless.* **WAPO 4** *puts on his other boot. Goes up to the lookout. Looks off. No sound comes from outside.*

WAPO 4 (*sudden laugh*)   Whey-hey! Ain 'e splash! (*Shouts over-loudly to* **Son**.) Like a whale doin 'ip-'op. (*Turns back to look left.*) Ain 'e splash!

Son (*picks up the jumper from* **Brother**'s *gear*)   This fit yer?

WAPO 4 *goes to* **Son**. *Takes the jumper.*

WAPO 4   Yeh! Do that colour! 'E brung any socks? (*Finds socks.*) Great! (*Puts down his weapon. Sits on ground. Kicks off boots. Puts on socks.*) Ow look! – bin repair. (*Shouts off.*) Ask 'im if 'e does stitchin! Save 'is life if 'e does stitchin.

Son *goes to lookout. Looks off. Short pause.*

Son   Bring 'im back. (*To* **WAPO 4**.) Get yer weapon. Ain a dress shop.

Son *comes down.* **WAPO 4** *picks up his weapon.* **WAPO**s 5 *and* 6 *come on by the lookout. They push* **Brother** *in front of them. He is drenched in watery mud.* **WAPO 5** *has been splashed.*

Son   I got up t' seven. 'Oo was yer goin t' meet? (*No answer.*) Yer was goin somewhere – pack spare socks. When I say ten yer dead. Reckon yer dead now corpse – 'cept for the details. They ain count out 'ere. Yer dug yer own grave while yer kep me waitin. – If yer talk I could give yer another life.

WAPO 5   Bastard drench me.

Son   Can 'e see? (*Goes to* **Brother**. *With a finger wipes mud from his right eye and flicks it to the ground. Does the same to his left eye. Stands closer to him.*) I can smell yer eyeballs. See me face in 'em. Yer ain got mates comin. Ain got mates. No one go with yoo. Tell from yer face. Never seen a face as empty as that. Man from nowhere. Only way yer goin is down.

Son *goes to* **Brother**'s *gear. Tears a strip from a shirt and holds it out.* **WAPO 6** *takes it. He and* **WAPO 5** *turn* **Brother** *round and take him out by the lookout.* **WAPO 4** *goes up to watch. Silence.*

Treg   Water ain bother 'im. They live in it out 'ere. Break 'is back, then 'e talk. Say more 'n ow! (*He goes to the WAPO gear. Starts to pack.*) Git pack. Move out.

Son   Leave that.

Treg   Should a' move already. (*Nods to* **WAPO 3**.) 'E ain commit hari-kari – someone shot 'im. (*Nods in direction of* **Brother**.) Now 'im wanderin round out there – somethin's goin on.

Son   Leave it.

Treg   Yer wan a' risk losin our gear? All we got?

Son   We go out – what we run into? 'E could 'ave mates out there. (*Nods at* **WAPO 3**). 'E aint know we got 'im. Show 'im when 'e ain expectin – that'll make 'im talk.

WAPO 4   Could pack ready. Case we 'ave t' move sudden.

Son (*ignores* **WAPO 4**)   . . . Place stinks like a snake's armpits.

Treg *goes up to the post. He holds a container in his hands.*

Treg (*calls off*)   'Old 'is feet in the air – keep 'is 'ead under water – 'n kick 'is belly 'ard! That'll make 'im swaller.

He watches in silence. Then he takes the container back to the gear and starts to fill it.

Son   I said leave it.

Treg   Git ready. 'E ain –

Son   Leave it. Yer know 'im? Know what's in 'is 'ead? P'raps 'e ain scared – ain talk just out a' provocation: ain care if 'e ain alive s' long as we're dead. We go out there 'n 'e's got 'is mates waitin.

WAPO 4   Yer said 'e ain got mates?

Son   Ain yer got *no* balls in yer brain?

Treg   We sit in this graveyard 'n wait t' be shovelled.

Brother *walks in on his own. He is drenched in mud. His eyes are blindfolded with the strip of shirt. His hands are not bound – he holds them in front of him as he feels his way.* **WAPO 4** *picks up his weapon. He loosens the safety catch.* **Brother** *hears this. Stops abruptly. His hands motionless in front of him.* **WAPO**s **5** *and* **6** *come on.* **Son** *gestures to* **WAPO 5**. *He gestures back 'nothing'.*

Treg   Ought a' pack – ready t' move out if –

Son (*hisses through teeth*)   Shutit! (*Goes halfway towards* **Brother**.) I know 'oo yer are. Not all I'm goin t' know. 'Ad someone 'ere

before yoo. 'E talk. Yer tell me the rest. Where was yer goin?
Oo yer meetin? Oo fix it? (*Silence.*) Ten. (*Silence.*) Ten. Ten.
(*Silence.*) But I left a number out. Cant make a mistake if I'm
goin t' kill yer – wouldnt be right. 'Ave t' count again.

Brother *sinks to the ground.* **Son** *stares down at him.*

WAPO 5 (*to* **Treg**)   Should keep pack anyway. Discipline.
Spread out like a 'orehouse.

Son (*to* **Treg**)   Watch! I posted yer lookout! Dont just let 'em
come – send out invitations!

Treg *doesn't move.* **WAPO 6** *goes up to the post to keep watch.*

Son (*to* **Brother**)   I left out six. Six 'n yer shot (**Brother** *turns
away.*) Dont turn yer back on me!

He jerks **Brother** *to his feet. Pushes him to* **WAPO 3**. *Throws
him to the ground. Pulls the groundsheet away.* **Brother**'s *hands go
halfway to his blindfold.*

Son (*raging*)   No no no no! – ain 'ave t' see! Touch 'im! (*Pulls
the sheet away from* **WAPO 3**.) Feel it! (*He pushes* **Brother**'s *hands
onto* **WAPO 3**'s *chest.*) Use yer 'ands! (*Walks away. Tries to control
himself.* **Brother**'s *hands pull back.*) Out! Out! Touch! (*Goes to*
Brother. *Grabs his hands. Presses them on* **WAPO 3**'s *face.*) Feel it!
Feel it! Get yer fists on 'is – ! Thass 'is eyes! Thass 'is gob! Got
it? (**WAPO 3** *is jerked aside.*) 'E knows yer! Look! – 'e's turn
away! – Shrink when yer! – Knows yer smell! – Yer stink a' 'is
death! (*To* **WAPO 3**.) Bite 'im, bite 'im – 'e kill yer! (*Goes away.
Tries to control himself.*) Stink a' 'is – I can smell it 'ere!

WAPO 4 (*to* **WAPO 6**, *showing*)   Socks bin repair.

Treg *goes to the WAPO gear. Starts to fill a crate with things.*

Son (*gestures at* **Brother**)   Pathetic! 'E ain feel! 'E'd slide 'is
bloody 'ands down the side of a mountain rather 'n feel that!
Yer kill 'im!

WAPO 5 (*to* **WAPO 6**)   The others should be back. Whass
keeping 'em?

Son (*goes to* **Brother**, *raging*)   Remember? Yer kill 'im! Put
yer 'ands – put yer – 'ands – ! (*He puts* **Brother**'s *hands round*
WAPO 3's *neck.*) throttle 'im! – tighter! Remember that! Yer –
(*He goes to* **Treg**. *Takes the crate from his hand. Throws it aside. Goes
back to* **Brother**.) Remember? (*To* **WAPO 3**.) Look! – 'e's got
'is 'ands on yer – ! (*To* **Brother**.) 'Oo was yer sent t' meet?
(*Stands. Looks down at* **Brother**. *Stunned. Low.*) I see. Wont say.
Six. Yer still ain know 'im? (*Tries again.*)Try ! – put yer 'ands in
'is – (*Grabs* **Brother**'s *hands. Puts them in* **WAPO 3**'s *wound.*) Put
yer 'ands – dont be afraid – put yer 'ands in 'is wound – if yer
grab in there yer'll find the – shot – yer – proof yer shot 'im –
'Ave a good whoorl round in – grab 'is – (**Brother** *tries to slide
away.* **Son** *jerks him back to* **WAPO 3**.) – guts – yer slippery –
blood – (*Takes the wadding from* **WAPO 3**'s *wound.*) – smell it! –
taste it! – 'ave a gargle in 'is blood! (*Slaps the wadding across*
Brother's *face. To* **WAPO 3**.) Look at 'im! The shite 'oo shot
yer! No – cruel t' make yer look at 'im while 'e's alive 'n yer
'arf aint! (*He pulls the groundsheet over* **WAPO 3**.) Too late. . .
(*Walks away with the wadding in his hands.*) . . . bin six long ago . . .
could wring the rag out . . . ain decent yer live while 'e's dyin
. . . yer dead before 'im – 'e'll 'ear the shot that ends up in yer
'ead. . .

WAPO 4 (*with the torn shirt*)   Tore the shirt. Ruined.

Son   . . . 's only right . . . somethin must still be right even if
the world's fell apart . . . (*To the* **WAPO**s.) 'N yer want t' pack
'n go out t' 'is cannibals?

Son *goes to* **WAPO 3**. *Drops the bloody wadding on the groundsheet.
Pulls* **Brother** *up. Takes him to a space clear of the others.*

Son (*to* **WAPO 4**)   Finish it. Kill 'im.

WAPO 4 *gets his weapon.* **Son** *walks away while* **WAPO 4** *aims.*
Son *stops abruptly.*

Son   Did 'e – ? (*To* **WAPO 4**.) Wait. (*Hesitates. Looks at*
WAPO 3.) Did 'e speak?

WAPO 5   'E's too –

Son   Shutit! (*Goes to* **WAPO 3**.)

WAPO 5   – far dead t' speak.

Son   I thought 'e – . When I moved 'im – might 've woke 'im so 'e . . . (*Lifts* **WAPO 3**'*s groundsheet*.) Muffle under the . . . (*Stares at* **WAPO 3**.)

WAPO 4   Do I?

Son (*ignores* **WAPO 4**)   If we knew! (*Covers* **WAPO 3**. *To* **WAPO 5**.) Did 'e run when yer saw 'im on the dyke?

No answer.

Treg   Take yer balaclava off.

Son (*goes to* **Brother**'*s gear. Squats to examine it more closely*) Trash tell yer nothin. Could a' come from anywhere. (*Goes to the WAPO gear. Picks up water bottle. Loosens cap. Doesnt drink.*) Kick the shit out a' 'im 'n 'e'll tell yer anythin. Might as well tell ourselves. (*Holds the water bottle. Goes to* **WAPO 3**. *To* **Treg**, *as he looks down at the groundsheet.*) What?

Treg   Take it off.

Son (*still looking down at groundsheet*)   When 'is 'ands touch 'im 'is eyes move as if 'e saw . . . (*To* **Treg**.) Why?

Treg   When yer kill someone yer always 'ave it on.

WAPO 6   I wan' t' know why we ain pack. Ain do no 'arm.

Treg   Someone else do it, yer still 'ave it on.

Son   Yer on watch.

Treg   Take it off.

Son   Watch was an order! I sent 'em on reccy. Yer 'ad it cushy. Still ain do it. Wander round like a fart lost in a thunderstorm.

Treg (*to* **WAPO**s)   Yer lads get it pack ready. Jus' *that* – ain mean we 'ave t' –

Son   Leave it! – We 'ad one mutiny in the army. They end up killin theirselves. We might as well a' stayed if we're goin t' do the same. 'E say pack! – Whass 'e say next? (*To* **WAPO 5**.) Take 'is weapon. – Yer under arrest.

Treg   Arrest! 'E thinks 'e's runnin court martials! I wan' 'a know whass goin on. Take yer balaclava off. – Why dont 'e?

Son   We stick t' the rules. Ain a mob a' –

Treg   No rules 'ere. Lot a good they done the army! – Rule said keep yer nut 'id so yer cant be pick out later. Ain apply 'ere. Take it off. (*To* **WAPO**s.) Does e' put 'is gloves on t' shit?

Son (*low, almost calm*)   The thinkin was – be'ind it – yer kep yer face 'id so yer werent one a' the crap on the street no more – yer 'ide it t' show yerself 'n yer mates we're a different sort – cut off – or we couldnt do what we 'ave to. We wear it out a' respect for life 'n death – or we reach the bottom a' the pit. It's 'oo we are – (*Points to his balaclava.*): this.

WAPO 6   Ain follow that.

Son   Just do it. (**WAPO 3** *twists sideways. They look at him for a moment but then turn back to each other.*) Or yer end up like that.

WAPO 4   Cant yer take if off t' satisfy 'im – 'n put it on again when I done it – 'n we can carry on like it was before?

Son   'E'd still wan' a pack.

Treg   No. Take it off – when the lads see yer can make the gesture we know yer still got enough grip t' be in charge.

Son *goes to* **WAPO 3**. *Puts his arm under his shoulders. Tilts him up.*

Son   Look – tears. Cryin cause 'e's dyin – so we can row? (*He turns* **WAPO 3** *to face* **Brother**. **Brother** *has covered his face and head with his hands and arms.*) Was it 'im 'oo shot yer? We 'ave t' know 'oo 'e is. Look – I give yer water – drink it for yer mates even if it kill yer – (*Puts water bottle to* **WAPO 3**'s *mouth.*) Let it go down – (**WAPO 3** *retches mechanically.*) 'Is teeth tryin t' bite the water . . .

Brother *has wandered to his gear. Gropes. Picks up a piece of clothing. Mutely holds it out to the* **WAPO***s. Picks up another piece of clothing. Offers a piece in each hand. The* **WAPO***s barely notice him – they watch the* **Son**.

Son   Water's trickling out 'is – 'e's pissin through 'is belly . . . (*Lowers* **WAPO 3** *to the ground. Screws the top on the water bottle. Places it upright on the ground. Weary.*) The sky's a butcher's shop. (*To* **Brother**.) Yer lived long enough. I'll shoot the marrow out yer bones.

Son *goes for his weapon.* **Brother** *stands holding the two offerings.* **Treg** *goes to him and pulls the blindfold from his eyes. Blinks.*

Treg   Take yer balaclava off so 'e gets a proper see.

Son *goes to* **Brother**. *Tears the things from his hands and throws them down. Aims.* **Treg** *stands in front of* **Brother**.

Treg   Take it off.

Silence.

WAPO 6 (*waves. Calls. Jubilant*)   Wha-hey! – They're comin!

Son *shoots* **Brother** *– one shot. He falls immediately.*

WAPO 6   They got a woman!

Son (*to* **WAPO 4**)   Cover 'em! (*Points to* **WAPO 3** *and* **Brother**.) 'Im! – 'im! Cover 'is gear! Cover it! Cover yerself! Show nothin! Everythin 'id.

WAPO 4 *covers* **WAPO 3**, **Brother** *and his gear. The* **WAPO***s except* **Treg** *pull down their balaclavas.* **Son** *sits and cleans his weapon.*

Son (*touches the hot barrel*)   Tsssss . . .

Pause.

WAPO*s* **7** *and* **8** *come on at the lookout. They bring* **Woman***. Their balaclavas are down.* **WAPO 7** *holds his weapon ready in both hands.* **WAPO 8** *pushes the* **Woman** *before him. She is blindfold and has no backpack.*

Son   On 'er jack?

WAPO 7   Was when we got 'er. (*To* **WAPO 5**.) Get anything?

WAPO 5   One.

WAPO 8   That the shot?

WAPO 5 *grunts*.

WAPO 7 (*looks towards* **WAPO 3**)   'E – ?

WAPO 5   Not yet.

WAPOs **7** *and* **8** *go to the gear*. **WAPO 7** *gets water for himself and* **WAPO 8**. *They drink*. **Woman** *stands isolated*.

Son (*to* **Woman**)   What yer up to?

Woman *turns uncertainly towards* **Son**.

Son   Yoo.

Woman   Nothin.

Son   Where yer from?

Woman   Live 'ere.

Son   'Oo with?

Woman   Meself.

Son   Out 'ere on yer own?

Woman   They left when the water come up.

Son   Yoo stayed? Why? (*No answer.*) Where's yer stuff? (**Woman** *gestures vaguely off.*) Ow long yer bin 'ere?

Woman   Long time.

Son   Ain believe it. Go mad out 'ere on yer own. 'Oo yer with?

Woman   No one.

Son   Warn yer. We'll find 'em. Aint on yer own now. (*Nods to* **WAPO**s.)

WAPO 6   Sir.

WAPO 4   Sir.

WAPO 7   Sir.

WAPO 5   Sir.

WAPO 8   Sir.

Treg (*hesitation*)   Yeh.

Woman *sits down.*

Son (*cleans weapon*)   'S all simple – *is* if yer co-operate. Know more about yoo 'n yer know yerself. Got a witness. Someone's done somethin. Ain told yer. Gone off on the next job. Left yer t' carry the can. (*No answer. He doesn't look at her.*) Yoo 'ear? Better start thinkin a' yerself while yer still got a 'ead t' think with. (*No response.*) One day out 'ere the ground'll open up 'n the sky fall in it. (*No response. He stops cleaning his weapon. Looks at her. To* **WAPO 7**.) Yoo 'it 'er face?

WAPO 7   No.

Son   'Oo did yer face?

Silence.

Woman   Sorry. Forgot yer was there. Yer ask me . . .?

Son   Forgot?

Treg   Takin the piss.

Woman   I was thinkin – why should I live? What can I do now? Go 'n it's over.

Son (*to* **WAPO 5**)   Take 'er out.

WAPO 5 *hauls* **Woman** *up.* **WAPO 7** *kicks her legs away. She falls.* **WAPO 5** *hauls her up again.*

Woman (*weary*)   Yer waste yer time if yer try t' 'urt me. Got more bruises inside 'n yer 'ands can give me.

Son (*violent*)   Take 'er out!

Woman   I'm sorry for yer. I can 'ear yer torment in yer voices. Yer should go in the water. All a' yer. Be finish then.

Son   Take 'er out! (**WAPO**s 5 *and* 6 *start to take* **Woman** *out.*) Yer tell me yer forget? Y'ain *know* yet! If I let yer live the next arf 'our yer'll learn 'oo *I* am!

WAPOs 5 *and* 7 *take* **Woman** *out.*

Son (*to* **Treg**: *low, violent*)   I ain know the meanin a' the word enemy till yer teach me. (*Jumps up. Goes to the lookout. Calls.*) Bring 'er back!

WAPO 8   They ain 'ad time t' –

Son (*calls*)   Bring 'er back!

WAPO 5 (*off*)   We ain started!

Son (*calls*)   I wan' 'er 'ere! – Finish it! Wastin time!

Treg   This ain right! We ought a pack. Should never 'a bin –

Son   Shutit! I say balaclava – yer dont! Show 'er a 'uman face 'n wonder why she aint talk!

Treg   She ain see! She's blindfold!

Son (*mutters*)   . . . If thass a 'uman face . . .!

WAPOs 5 *and* 7 *bring* **Woman** *on. Her clothes are wet but scarcely muddied.*

WAPO 7   Take 'er – bring 'er back . . . !

Son (*to* **Woman**)   Yer wan t' die! I'll give yer a 'and! – when *I* say! (*Pulls the blindfold from her eyes. Rams it in her hand .*) Now – where's yer mates? 'Ad someone! They 'it yer face!

Woman   No one . . .

Brother's *body lies under a groundsheet between* **Son** *and* **Woman**. **Son** *goes to* **WAPO 3** *and lifts the groundsheet from his head.*

Son   Look!

Woman (*shocked. Wails weakly*)   Ah! Cover me eyes with the –
(*She fumbles to press the blindfold on her eyes.*)

Son   My mate lyin there! Me respect lyin there!

Woman   'Is mate?

She goes slowly to **WAPO 3**.

Son   Ain shot in the 'ead! – in the gut where it 'urts! Yer
wan' a be dead? 'E's young – wanted t' live! – Look! – 'is gut!

Woman *reaches* **WAPO 3**. *Stares – points at him with her finger.*

Woman   Thank God. (*Walks away.*)

WAPO 8   She's mad.

Son   Thank God? Bitch! She said thank God! Bitch!

WAPO 8 *takes off his balaclava.*

Treg   None a' this –

Son (*puts his arms under* **WAPO 3**'s *armpits. Hoists him till the tips
of his boots are touching the ground*)   Thank God for this?

WAPO 3's *head is bent back. A curious thin scream escapes from his
mouth and spirals into the air.*

Treg   None a' this ain necessary! (*To* **WAPO**s.) Take yer
covers off! Uncover it! All day we bin waitin! Got two. What
d'we know? Nothin! 'Cause it ain in order! Take 'em off!
(**WAPO**s **6** *and* **7** *take off their balaclavas.*) We'll all end up stuffin
our guts back! Take it off! – (**WAPO 5** *takes off his balaclava*.) –
so we can see what we're doin!

WAPO 4 *takes off his balaclava.*

Son (*embracing* **WAPO 3** *to stop him falling. To* **Treg**)   Yer
show 'er their faces so she thinks we ain 'er killers Yer give 'er
a *licence* t' say thank God! – Blood pour out a' 'im 'n 'e cant go
– can feel 'is 'eart knockin against me 'and – (*He lowers* **WAPO
3** *to the ground.*) Yeh. The day's gone – the best part's over – 'n
we're nowhere. – Only we wont run wild out there – stay 'ere

where it's safer. In the mornin it could be different – may be time t' go then – She's mad. Nothin t' tell.

Treg   Then kill 'er.

Son (*to* **WAPO 4**)   I promised yer a turn.

WAPO 4 *gets his weapon.*

Treg (*to* **Son**)   Yoo do it.

Son   I 'ave. When I said. Cant take 'is turn away from –

Treg   Yoo do it.

Son   Is that what yer think? – I killed all me life.

Son *goes to* **WAPO 4**. *Wearily puts out his hands for his weapon.* **WAPO 4** *takes a step back.* **Son** *makes a small polite gesture of dismissal. Goes to the gear to pick up his weapon.*

Treg   Take it off.

Son *stares at* **Treg**. *A metallic clash:* **WAPO***s collectively release their safety catches.* **WAPO 3** *twitches at the sound and starts to stand. He faces away to the water on the right. The others dont notice him.*

Son (*walks away, holding his weapon*)   I give in t' yoo – the lads are lost. (*To* **WAPO***s.*) Good as dead.

Treg (*joins the other* **WAPO***s. Begins to jeer*)   'E cant. Yer see. 'E cant. Ain natural. Ain fit t' give orders. 'E's yers lads. I give 'im t' yer. What yer wan' a do with 'im?

Son *goes towards* **Treg**. *The* **WAPO***s raise their weapons.* **Treg** *darts for his weapon – grabs it, half drops it, steps back among the* **WAPO***s, aims at* **Son**. **WAPO 3** *turns his head sightlessly towards them.*

WAPO 5   Take it off.

Son   Take it off? (*He takes off his balaclava. Holds it up for a moment. Throws it contemptuously at* **Treg**.) Yer little runt.

Son *turns to face* **Woman**, *aimed at her. There is a scar on his forehead.*

Woman   My son.

She is still. Bends to peer closer. Moves towards him as if pushed by a little puff of wind.

Woman   My son.

WAPO 6   Why she − ?

WAPO 7   My son.

Woman (*not answering*)   Scar.

WAPO 8   . . . She's mad.

WAPO 5   . . . (*Half laugh.*) 'S try-on! − I 'eard a' dodgy capers − ! (*Aims at* **Woman**.) I give 'er a son!

Treg   No. Stop. Wait. Wait. (*To* **WAPO 6**.) Watch. Keep watch. − What − what is it? (*To* **WAPO 6**.) Watch!

WAPO 6 *goes half way to lookout. Looks off. Turns back.*

WAPO 8   Why she say that?

Treg *takes* **Son**'*s gun from him. He doesn't resist.*

Treg (*to all the* **WAPO**s)   Wait! − (*To* **Woman**.) Why yer say that?

WAPO 8   She said scar.

Treg (*to* **Son**)   That why she's still alive? That why we're 'ere? We learnin somethin at last?

WAPO 5   She's mad − give 'er the −

Treg   I said let's go on − dry ground 'igher up. 'E said no − stop in this swamp. 'Oo is 'e?

WAPO 5 (*to* **Son**)   D'yer know 'er?

WAPO 3 *has started to move slowly left towards the lookout.*

Son (*realises he is disarmed*)   Me weapon − ?

WAPO 7   Chriss. Chriss. Chriss. The land's gone – towns fallin in t' the water – wind's tore the rocks t' shreds – now 'e's 'er son! We got a' go! Should a' stay with the army 'n done the killin not come 'ere 'n be killed.

Son   Kill 'er. We can settle *that*. (*Looks round.*) Me weapon –

Treg   No. She's got 'a say now. (*To* **Woman**.) 'Ow's 'e yer son?

WAPO 3 *knocks over the water bottle.*

WAPO 4 *sees* **WAPO 3**. *Points. The* **WAPO***s turn to look at* **WAPO 3**.

WAPO 4   'E's comin t' tell us –

WAPO 3 *half-totters, half-drifts towards them.*

WAPO 7 (*staring at* **WAPO 3**)   Ask *'er* what 'e – ! – I knew 'e wanted t' say –

Treg   Shush! Shush! Let 'im.

WAPO 7 (*reaching out to take hold of* **WAPO 3**)   What did yer want t' –

WAPO 4 (*panic*)   No no. Ain touch. Yer kill 'im!

WAPO 3 *passes through the* **WAPO***s without seeing them and goes on towards the lookout.*

WAPO 4 (*staring at* **WAPO 3**)   Why dont 'e say? Why ain 'e tell us? (*Terrified whisper to* **Son**.) Yer shouldnt 'a pick 'im up so all 'is blood fell out on the – why ain 'e say? (*To* **WAPO 3***'s back.*) What we done t' be shat on in this shit place – ?

WAPO 7   Scar.

Treg   Let 'im go – 'e wants t' show us somethin's out there –

WAPO 3 *goes out left. The* **WAPO***s start to follow him. They hold their weapons at the ready.*

Treg (*gives* **Son***'s weapon to* **WAPO 4**)   Yoo stay. Watch 'im. Nail 'im on that spot.

WAPO 8 (*turning back*)   Ain goin there.

Treg   Move! Wan' us all dead?

The **WAPO***s go out.* **WAPO 4** *is left with* **Woman** *and* **Son**.
He holds two weapons, his own and **Son**'*s.* **Son** *goes to* **WAPO 4**.
Reaches for his weapon.

WAPO 4   No. Dont. – Leave me alone – dont wan' t' use it
on –

Son   Yer alright. Nothin'll 'appen 'ere.

WAPO 4   Yer shouldnt a' pick 'im up –

WAPO 5 (*off*)   Na! – keep 'im off the –

WAPO 4   – 'n all 'is blood fell on –

WAPO 6 (*off*)   Whass 'e tryin t' –

Son (*takes his weapon from* **WAPO 4**)   Go or yer'll miss it.

WAPO 4 *goes out left.*

WAPO 5 (*off*)   Grab 'im or 'e'll – look! – what the –

WAPO 6 (*off*)   Stop! – the bugger's – look!

Son *doesn't look at* **Woman**. *He picks up his balaclava and covers
his face with it.* **WAPO 4** *comes on at the lookout to check on* **Son**
and **Woman**. *Starts to go but turns back.*

WAPO 4 (*half-whisper to* **Son**)   'E's in the mud. Tryin t' dig a
'ole in the water.

WAPO 7 (*off*)   The shite-bag!

WAPO 4 *goes out.* **Son** *picks up the water bottle and stands it
upright.* **Woman** *flinches as he passes her. He doesnt look at her.
He goes out by the lookout.* **Woman** *goes right.*

WAPO 7 (*off*)   If yer ain get 'im quick –

WAPO 5 (*off*)   Careful!

WAPO 6 (*off*)   'Ain break 'is –

WAPO 3 (*off*), *a thin spiralling scream. The scream stops the* **Woman** *for a moment. Then she goes out right.*

Treg (*off*)   Keep 'is 'ead up.

WAPO 5 (*off*)   Dont jerk – dont drag it – !

The **WAPO***s carry on* **WAPO 3**. *He is drenched in muddy water. They are splashed and their trousers wet up to where they were in the water.* **Son** *follows them. He sees that* **Woman** *has gone. He stops at the lookout and watches the others.*

WAPO 5   Careful – 'is 'ead.

The **WAPO***s lay* **WAPO 3** *on his back.*

WAPO 6   'E's still tryin t' say –

Treg   Let 'im breathe –

WAPO 3*'s head jerks from side to side like the tail of a landed fish.*

WAPO 5 (*drawing back*)   Ain get nothin out a' that – water wash out anythin left.

WAPO 4 (*despair*)   Why dont 'e die – ?

Treg (*holding* **WAPO 3***'s head*)   Tell us. Yer 'ear me?

WAPO 4   Should a' let 'im drown.

Treg *lets go of* **WAPO 3***'s head. It has stopped swaying and judders rapidly.*

Treg   Give 'im some water – (*Looks round for a water bottle.*)

WAPO 5 (*derision*)   'E just swallowed arf 'n ocean!

The **WAPO***s stand back.* **WAPO 3***'s head judders.*

Treg (*notices* **Son**)   Look – 'e's 'id 'is mug again. Thinks 'e's still in charge –

Son   We're 'ere. The worse ain 'appened. We stick it out together or end up dead on our own.

Treg   Ain talk yerself out a' this. We still ain know why she called yer –

The **WAPO***s look round for* **Woman***.*

Son   She's gone.

WAPO 6   Jees.

WAPO 5   Ran while we –

Son   Listen. I know 'oo I am. 'Ain 'er son. She saw me scar? Everyone's got scars round 'ere. We're scars walkin round on legs.

WAPO 7   Later! (*Going left.*) We got 'a stop 'er before she –

WAPO 5   She ain go that way. We'd a' seen 'er.

The **WAPO***s hesitate. Look right.* **WAPO 5** *goes to the gear. Looks under it without hope. Silence.*

WAPO 7   She gone out there, she's dead.

WAPO 6   Jees.

Son   We go in 'n get 'er.

WAPO 6   Ain go in that.

Son   Now before she get away.

WAPO 7   No path.

Son   Now! She bring 'er mates we ain stand a chance. (*Goes right.*) She ain go in if there ain be a way over.

WAPO 6   Jees.

WAPO 5 (*going right*)   Yer do what yer want. I'm gettin the bitch.

WAPO 5 *goes out right.*

Son (*calls to* **WAPO 5**)   Keep by the reeds.

The **WAPO***s move right – hesitate.*

WAPO 6   Bloody dragons in that – 'uman snakes – baby crocodiles –

WAPO 5 (*off*)   'S okay – shallow where the – oaw!

WAPO 8   Chriss! Come back yer bloody lunatic –

WAPO 5 (*off*)   'S alright – slip –

Son *goes out right.*

WAPO 7 (*flat*)   No choice is there.

The **WAPO***s go out right.* **Treg** *is alone. He watches them.*

WAPO 7 (*off*)   Stay on the reeds –

Son (*off*)   Give yerself space –

WAPO 4 (*off*)   Slime muck –

WAPO 5 (*off*)   Over 'ere –

Son (*off*)   No – keep spread –

Treg *goes to the gear. He packs ammo in a backpack. Then tins of food.*

WAPO 6 (*off*)   Never get 'er – if she ain dead already –

WAPO 5 (*off*)   On the ridge –

Treg *goes to* **WAPO 3**. *He doesn't look at him. Takes off his boots.* **WAPO 3***'s final spasm – abrupt.*

WAPO 7 (*off*)   Stinks!

Son (*off*)   Dont bunch –

WAPO 8 (*off*)   Gas! –

WAPO 6 (*off*)   – bodies rottin in the swamp –

Treg *hangs* **WAPO 3***'s boots round his neck. He goes to* **Brother**. **WAPO 4** *comes on and watches him. He lifts one of* **Brother***'s legs, looks at the boot and drops it. He sees* **WAPO 4**.

Treg (**Brother***'s boots*)   Trash.

WAPO 4 (*half-sad*)   What yer doin?

Treg   Yer chose out?

WAPO 4   Yer stole 'is boots.

Treg   They ain come back alive. If they do, they ain last.
(**WAPO 4** *looks across at* **Treg**'s *backpack.*) Waste t' leave 'em
grub. They eat it, be dead before they can shit it. Know what
yer think. Ain rattin on no one. I give 'em a chance. I said
pack. Get out. Ain listen. – Come with me. We make a team.
Got a chance. Dont waste yer life. Time's run out 'ere. Yer
can feel it. Yer can 'ear the emptiness tickin away.

WAPO 4   Yer stole our ammo. We ain survive without it.

Treg   They ain survive anyway.

WAPO 4 (*looks at* **WAPO 3** *but doesn't go close*)   Come back t'
see if 'e was –

WAPO 7 (*off, distant*)   Whass that – why's 'e goin t' the – ?

WAPO 6 (*off, distant*)   Got t' go back –

WAPO 4   It'll always be like this now.

He goes to the gear. Sits on the boxes and looks right.

Son (*off*)   Keep spread out.

WAPO 6 (*off, distant*)   Less go back –

Treg   Listen t' it. Little blobs a' people bobbin about in a
swamp. Yer age, anyone told me I'd end up in this shit I'd 'a
said they need their 'ead tested. 'S all changed. Nothin turned
out like we said. I ain what I thought I'd be.

WAPO 4   Ain changed for me. Always bin like this. Yoo 'ad
it different. When the wind come I seen trees flyin through the
air with people clingin t' the branches 'n the roots. Then the
water. Then the mobs. Then the trucks. Never knew there was
so many people. WAPOs truckin 'em off t' 'uman kennels. All
that saliva. Be a WAPO with a gun, not a 'uman dog – ain

much choice. We only laugh at bad things now. Yoo used up all the good times. Never left some for us.

WAPO 5 (*off, very distant*)   Oi! – I – whass that –

WAPO 6 (*off, very distant*)   Bastard got me! – Drag me under the –

WAPO 7 (*off, very distant*)   Body in the water –

Treg   World's full a' people shouldnt be in it. Wasted on 'em. Animals shittin in each other's graves. Git rid a' 'em. 'Ose 'em out. Whass left might 'ave a chance. Take yoo – tol' yer t' keep watch on 'im 'n 'er. Yer didnt. 'Ad t' come 'n ave a look. None a' this 'd 'a 'appen if yer done what I said. Tired a' clearin up other people's mess.

WAPO 4   If 'e did rat on 'is mates 'e ain deserve t' die like that. Guts is the worst. Least I learnt that. – Yer kill 'im when yer took 'is boots off. (*Sad. Reflective.*) I used t' like toffee-apples.

Treg *shoots* **WAPO 4** *in the back. He topples over.*

Treg (*to* **WAPO 4**)   Say thanks – yer would if yer 'ad any sense.

Treg *picks up* **WAPO 4** *in a fireman's lift. Starts to take him off. Meets* **Ancient Crone** *as she comes on from the right. She is older and more ragged. Still carrying* **WAPO 4**, **Treg** *jerks his weapon round to aim at her. He decides she is not dangerous.*

Ancient Crone (*points at* **WAPO 4**)   Ooo – yoo got one.

Treg   Too young t' leave 'im on the ground.

Treg *carries* **WAPO 4** *out right.* **Crone** *sees* **WAPO 3**. *Goes to him. Peers at him closely.*

Ancient Crone (*fingers to her mouth*)   Ooosh.

Treg *comes back. He has been splashed. He looks at* **Ancient Crone**, *his weapon half-aimed.*

Treg   Nothin left even for 'n 'ag like yoo. What yer doin out there? – Can yer speak?

Ancient Crone Watched yer day 'n night. (*Gestures left.*)
The soldiers always look that way. Ain see me.

Treg Watched?

Ancient Crone (*gestures right*) Watched '*im*. 'E left me years
ago. Ran away. 'Ated me 'cause I love 'im. I followed 'im all
that time. Kep out a' sight. 'E kill me if 'e saw me. Sometimes
'e catch a glimpse. 'E thinks 'e dreamt me – 'e carries the night
round with 'im. (*Little laugh.*) 'E's got eyes as dark as that
knitted wool on 'is face. (*Looks right.*) I know the paths. Me feet
're dry. 'E wont let me show 'im. 'E's lost. Gone. I 'ave t' get a
new one.

Son (*off*) Spread out.

WAPOs, *off, very distant cries.*

Ancient Crone (*goes to* **WAPO 3**) A 'ungry face! Does 'e
want? (*She sits by* **WAPO 3**. *Suckles him at her breast.*) Look 'ow 'e
take the dug! Glug glug glug. Is it better?

Treg Obscene. (*Toying with his gun.*) 'Ag, I should put a bullet
in yer. (*Superstitious. Low.*) Ain do 'im the favour, curse 'im.

He picks up his backpack and goes away by the lookout.

Ancient Crone Shall I tell a story? Yoo sup 'n listen. Long
ago the world was full a' wickedness. A man's time come t'
die. Hush, sup yer milk 'n dont vex yerself with that – it takes
care a' its own. The man went t' be judge. 'E thought a big
book 'd be opened, a great wind turn the pages. No. There
was no book. There was a grain a' dust. A spec. All the world's
sins was written on the spec. 'Is – 'n all there'd ever bin or was
t' be. The spec flies round us in the air. Sometimes it gets in
yer eye 'n then yer weep. (*Off, a few far distant* **WAPO** *cries.*)
Man saw 'is life writ down with the rest. For 'is wickedness he
was sent out in t' space. There 'e was t' go on 'n on for ever.
Out 'n out 'n on 'n on. Out in t' empty space where nothin is.
No one with yer. No one there. Not even nothin. Yer dont
know if what yer see is near or far – there's no difference –
there's nothin there t' tell yer. Not even yer shadow. On 'n on.

It never stops. On 'n on for ever. (*Her eyes stare hollowly.*) Yoo on yer own. On 'n on. Alone. On 'n on. Out 'n out. On 'n out for ever. . . (*Little laugh.*) Ooush! – 'e bit me dug.

She gets up carefully. Looks back to see that **WAPO 3** *sleeps. Creeps to* **Brother**.

Ancient Crone   Another one. P'raps this one's better. (*Lifts the groundsheet from* **Brother***'s face. Draws back in fear.*) No. (*Drops groundsheet back.*) 'E make me old t' look at 'im. The space is on 'is face. (*Holds out her hand to* **WAPO 3**.) Me 'and tremble.

She goes to **WAPO 3**. *Begins to drag him on the groundsheet towards the lookout.*

Ancient Crone   Get away from 'im. Quick. Must go. Come with me. Bumpity, bumpity. Get away. On 'n on. On 'n on. (*Pulling.*) Yer come. Not alone. (*Her voice rises in anxiety.*) On 'n on. On 'n on. On 'n on. (*Flat.*) On 'n on. On 'n on. On 'n on. On 'n on.

She drags **WAPO 3** *out at the lookout.* **Brother** *lies under his groundsheet.*

Four

The first clearing in the fen. Pitch black night.

Woman *is huddled downstage. A backpack on the ground.*

Woman   . . . What'll become a' me? . . . must sleep. . . where can I 'ide from 'im? (*Suddenly.*) Oo's there – ? (*Stands.*) Yer – ! (*Silence.*) Is it the last time we meet? Is this 'ow it 'appens? Ain kill me. Dont take that on yerself. Yer kill yer mother – yer mark for ever. Dont wish that on yer. I thought I kill yer when I give yer up. That marked me. I lived alone even when I was with 'im. Dont kill me. Dont dont go in t' that empty place.

Treg *comes out of the darkness.*

Woman   'Oo – ?

Treg   Ush! Ush! Dont scream! (**Woman** *starts to go. He grabs her arm.*) They'll 'ear! – carry over the water.

Woman (*pulling away*)   The soldiers – !

Treg   No! No soldiers 'ere!

Woman   Soldiers – yer 'ad me son –

Treg   Not now! No soldiers 'ere! Listen. (*Moment's silence.*) Ain 'urt yer. (*Quieter.*) I left 'em –

Woman   Left?

Treg   – ain go back.

Woman   Yer tol' 'im t' shoot me –

Treg   Not now! Everythin's different. I'm like yoo – I 'ave t' get away. We'll go together. Yer know the paths. I'll keep yer safe. (*Taps weapon.*) Got this for any trouble. – Chriss – yer wet. Yer clothes 'll drown yer. I got a groundsheet. Army gear. Yer 'ain eaten. (*Opens his backpack.*) Look – food. Tins. Open one. Make a fire. (*Gropes round.*) Bracken. Kindlin – soon get it goin. In the mornin we'll go away. (*A little flame.*) Thank God yer a woman. Put yer 'ands closer. (*The flame flutters but there is no sound of wind.*) Everythin's change. Y 'ave t' grab it or lose what yer got. (*The flame goes out. Darkness. Silence.*) The wind'll come back.

End of Part One.

Part Two: House

Five

*A two-storey farmhouse or agricultural store on a mountain path.
Behind it only the sky is seen. The house is clad in wooden boards. It is
neglected and part of the front wall is damaged. A tarpaulin sheet covers
the whole of the wall. Window holes and, right, a hole for the door are
cut into it. A path leads down left and up right. The earth before the
house is trodden flat. On it are a kitchen table and chairs made of the
same wood. An old salon chair with carved ornamental frame and arms
upholstered in green velvet or leather. On the table a basin, crockery and
a few other utensils. Against the house wall, right of the doorway, a
wooden storage chest. A few wooden crates. On one a man's jacket, on
another a towel. Left of the house a wooden bench with a view into the
unseen valley.*

Clear, mild midday.

Treg *comes from the path left. He wears a shabby long dark grey
military greatcoat and heavy working boots. On his back a large dark
grey backpack. On a strap over his shoulder an old woollen 'ethnic'
slop-bag – a faded but still colourful weave of red, yellow and green.
His face is older, weatherbeaten and wary but not as rigid as before.*

He looks around. Goes to the door, puts his head inside and calls.

Treg   Anyone 'ome?

*He waits. No reply. He looks in through a window. Goes to the table.
Touches the side of a cup – it is cold. Looks up the path right. Goes out
left.*

Pause. **Grace** *hurries in from the right. She wears a pale mauve frock
with a paler abstract pattern. Socks. Staying close to the house she goes
left and looks off. Then she hurries into the house.*

Pause. **Treg** *and* **Woman** *come on left. She wears a worn black
overcoat and old hiking boots. On her back a large mid-blue backpack.*

Tied to a corner of it a light-brown hemp shopping bag. She uses a walking stick.

Treg (*half-nods to bench. Quiet*)   Sit.

The **Woman** *takes off her backpack and stands it upright on the bench. She sits next to it and rubs her legs.* **Treg** *takes off his backpack. He sits on the bench and puts his backpack by his feet.*

Treg (*nods to door*)   No door. Anyone could walk in.

Woman   Shouldnt we –

Treg   Someone 'll turn up. Well settled in. No kids.

Woman   We could –

Treg   Probably out workin. Cleared a bit a' land. Work that. – Rest yer legs.

Grace *appears in a window.* **Woman** *unlaces both her boots. Then she takes them off and rubs her feet.*

Treg (*quiet*)   Dont look. Bein watch. (**Woman** *stiffens, goes to put on her boots.*) Leave it. (*Aloud.*) Safe. Out the way. View like this. Place t' settle. (*Acts seeing* **Grace**. *Stands.*) 'Ope it's alright usin yer seat.

Grace *goes from the window.* **Woman** *is going to stand.* **Treg** *puts his hand on her shoulder to push her down.* **Grace** *comes through the door.*

Treg   On our way up.

Grace   O.

Treg   Sayin 's a nice view. Called inside.

Grace   My friend'll be 'ere soon. I saw yer from the road. I come down a'ead. (*To* **Woman**.) Yer feet – ?

Woman *goes to put her boots on.*

Treg   Steep. Walked too far.

Grace (*to* **Woman**)   Leave them. (*Little pause.*) Can I get yer
a drink?

Woman   We've got our own.

Grace   There's plenty. We got a stream.

She goes to the table and pours water from a container. She takes it to
Woman*.*

Grace   It's good. No muck in it.

Woman (*drinks*)   Yes. – Thanks. (*She hands the cup to* **Treg***.*)

Treg (*drinks. To* **Grace**)   Kind.

Grace   Yer come far?

Treg   Yes. Keep on the move. Still 'ave t' dodge the WAPOs.
They round up any strays. Yoo 'n yer friend on yer own?

Grace   There's a few more further up. – Dont know what's
keeping 'im.

Woman (*spills water on her coat*)   O sorry –

Grace   It's alright. There's plenty. Yer wet yer – (*She dabs*
Woman*'s coat with the towel.*)

Woman   – waste yer –

Treg   She's tired. I told 'er we could afford one day's rest.
She 'as t' press on.

Grace   When my friend comes we're goin t' eat. (*To*
Woman*.*) Nothing special. Yer welcome t' –

Woman   We mustnt be –

Treg   Yer cant refuse 'n offer like that. If there's any odd
jobs I could do t' pay yer back –

Grace   My friend wouldnt like that. 'E sees to things. (*To*
Woman*.*) Why dont yer come in for a bit? – yer could lie
down.

Woman   I dont want t' –

Treg   While yer wait.

Grace   Be more comfortable there. (*She pushes* **Woman**'s *boots on to her feet.* **Woman** *stands.*)

Woman   Yer very kind.

Grace   We dont get many comin through.

She starts to lead **Woman** *to the doorway.*

Treg   She needs a good night's rest. She drop off yer wont wake 'er till mornin. If yer got a room we could use? – for the night. We'd be off early in the mornin.

Grace (*to* **Woman**)   Take me arm.

She takes **Woman** *into the house.* **Treg** *goes to the tarpaulin. Lifts a corner, looks under it, lets it drop.*

Treg (*calls*)   'Ad I better put the packs inside? (*No answer. He picks up the two backpacks and carries them to the doorway.*) Dont want t' clutter the place up for yer friend.

He goes into the house with the packs. **Son** *comes on. He is thinner. His clothes are pale – jeans, shirt, denim jacket. He carries a spade. For a second he pauses – he had expected to see someone. He goes a little left and glances down the path. Goes to the chest and leans the spade against it. Goes to the table. Pours water in a basin to wash his hands*

Son (*washing. Calls*)   Grace.

Behind him **Treg** *comes through the doorway.*

Treg   'Ello there. We was passin through.

Son *turns to* **Treg**.

Treg   The young lady was kind enough t' –

Son *and* **Treg** *recognise each other.*

Treg   Wait. Wait. Didnt know yer was – . 'S an accident. Didnt know – . Good lor'! – I thought yer was – . (*At a loss.*)

Yer 'er friend! (*Silence. He walks to the salon chair and sits.*) Well. Thass – . 'Ow long is it?

Son (*calls*)   Grace.

Treg   No. Dont. Settle this us-selves. Between us.

Son *goes towards the doorway.*

Treg   Wait. There's somethin else – . (**Son** *stops.*) The girl took me companion in for a lie down . . . God!

Son   Why yer come?

Treg   I tol' yer, 's 'n accident. Didnt know yer –

Son   What yer want?

Treg (*shrugs*)   Suit yerself. (*Tries again.*) 'Ow could I know yer was 'ere? I thought yer was dead. Drown in the swamp.

Silence.

Son   Why yer kill 'im?

Treg   'Oo?

Son *picks up the basin. Goes up to the bench. Throws the water away. He comes back. Wipes his hands on the towel.*

Treg   I tell yer this for the best. Dont dig up the past. Got enough problems with the present. – Yer done alright 'ere – got yerself a nice –

Son   'E was shot.

Treg   'Oo? (*No reply.*) 'Oo was shot?

Son   In the water. Yer shot 'im in the back a' the 'ead.

Treg   Might 'ave. We did them things those days. 'Ad t' survive. I regret it, if it 'elps. (*Quiet.*) If I remembered all the things I carry round on these 'ands I couldnt lift 'em in the morning t' get me clothes on. Doin 'em was the punishment for doin 'em.

Son   Yer shot 'im!

Treg   Shot 'im! Shot 'im! Yer sound like a kid. Yer ain shot no one?

Son   Not me mates.

Treg   That make a difference? (*A half-laugh.*)

Grace *comes from the house.*

Treg   We're ol' pals.

Grace   O?

Treg   Didnt know 'e was 'ere. We was in the WAPOs.

Son   She ain interested.

Grace (*to* **Son**)   Are yer alright? (*No answer. To* **Treg**.) I put 'er t' bed. Went straight off. (*To* **Son**.) Yer friends can stay for a few days if yer like. I can easy –

Son   'E wants t' be off.

Slight pause.

Treg   I'll go 'n see she's . . .

He goes towards the door.

Grace   Yer'll find 'er top a' the stairs.

Treg *goes into the house.*

Grace   Did yer know 'im well?

Son   Goin for a walk.

Grace   Yer 'avent eaten! I thought we could all eat together –

Son   Ain 'ungry.

Grace   Please dont get upset.

Son (*starts to go*)   Just for a walk.

Grace   I'll come with yer.

Son   No.

Grace   Why did this 'ave t' appen?

Son (*stops a moment*)   Stay 'n keep 'n eye on 'im.

He goes out right. **Grace** *watches him. She goes into the house. The space is empty.*

Six

Late dawn. **Treg** *sleeps in a kitchen chair at the table.* **Woman** *comes from the house. Looks at* **Treg**. *Decides not to wake him. Goes to the bench. Sits looking out at the distant view.* **Grace** *comes from the house.*

Grace   Did yer sleep well?

Woman   Very, thanks.

Grace   Yer look rested. – Was 'e there all night?

Woman   'E fell asleep.

Grace   I'll get some breakfast. – Where're yer making for?

Woman   Somewhere t' settle. – I'll know it when I see it.

She goes to **Treg** *and touches him. A second later he is wide awake. Stares at* **Woman**.

Treg   What time is it?

Grace   Still early.

Treg   Everyone up?

Grace   I'm getting some breakfast. (*To* **Woman**.) We didnt eat last night. – Yer'll get a surprise. 'E knows my friend.

She goes into the house.

Woman   'Oo is it? 'Oo d'yer know?

Treg   Someone. Chriss this is 'arf the way t' nowhere, 'n
someone 'as t' turn up 'n ruin it – . Just the place we bin lookin
for. Could get sorted 'ere. Ain get many chances our age.

Woman   Yer cant move in on someone else's –

Treg (*flat*)   I could fix it. Know'ow. Ain be stopped by 'n
accident –

Woman   A young couple dont need –

Treg   Then what yer want? Yer never let up. Always on 'n
on. 'Ad years a' it. We find a place like this 'n it's still no.

Woman   We'll find somewhere.

Treg   What 'appens if we dont? When yer wore out – I 'ave
t' carry yer? I'd like a bit a' decent life while I can still enjoy it.
(*Low. Vehement.*) I'm tired a' on 'n on. We can split up if thass
what yer want! – go on on yer own. I mean it. There's plenty
a' road yer ain bless with yer feet yet.

Woman   Let's not row. We've 'ad t' put up with so much
in – I want somewhere we can be at peace – not a burden t'
other people.

Treg   Goin t' sort out some washin.

He goes into the house. **Woman** *hesitates. She sits at the table. After
a moment she turns to look at the doorway. Decides not to go in. She is
turning back – stops – a moment later becomes rigid. Stands. Knocks
over a metal bowl. Hurries to the house. Stops. Looks round. Hurries
to the tarpaulin. Lifts the far corner by the bench – goes behind it out of
sight. Pause.* **Son** *comes in from the right. He goes to the house.
Hesitates for a moment in the doorway. Decides to go to the table. Sits
in the chair* **Woman** *had sat in.* **Grace** *comes from the house. She
carries food on a tray.*

Grace   Where were you?

Son   Walkin.

Grace   All night? Yer scared me.

Son   Wont 'appen again. I'm okay.

Woman *is moving behind the tarpaulin towards the door.* **Treg**
comes from the house. He carries dirty washing. **Woman** *stops.*
He looks around for her. He comes down to the table. **Woman** *starts*
to move towards the door again.

Treg   Think we could wash a few things as we're 'ere?

Grace   Leave them. I'll do them.

Treg (*to* **Son**)   Yer was up early.

Son   Last night – when we said – it dont matter. It's finished.
(*He bends down to pick up the fallen bowl.*) Bury it. Dont wan' the
past walkin round on two legs.

Woman *reaches the open doorway.* **Son** *stands. He holds the bowl.*

Son (*to* **Grace**)   I'll 'elp yer get the – (*He turns. Sees* **Woman**
standing in the doorway.) 'Ello.

Treg *and* **Grace** *turn to look at* **Woman**

Grace   Yer must've thought breakfast 'd never come.

The tarpaulin unwinds. It falls till it exposes the corner of the house
next to the bench. Then it stops.

Son   Damn! Come off the 'ooks.

He goes to the tarpaulin with **Grace**. *Looks up at the roof.*

Son   Worked loose.

Treg *goes to* **Woman**. *He grips her shoulders. Behind the others'*
backs he forcefully pushes her forwards.

Grace   Can we –

Son   'S nothin. Easy fix it.

Treg *comes to a halt with* **Woman** *as* **Son** *turns. He is confronted*
by her. He holds the bowl. She is blank. **Treg** *still holds her shoulders.*
Grace *gathers the fallen tarpaulin against the side of the house.*

Grace   Least it didnt all come down.

Son (*to* **Woman**)   'Ear yer come far.

He goes to the table. Puts the bowl on it.

Treg   We ain used t' people. (*To* **Grace**.) She's shy.

Son (*to* **Grace**)   I'll do that. Get breakfast.

Son *and* **Grace** *go into the house.* **Woman** *slumps against* **Treg***'s side.*

Treg (*hiss*)   Get up. Get up. – I tol' yer t' get –

He bundles **Woman** *to the table. Half throws and half rams her down into a chair.*

Treg   'E ain recognise yer.

Woman   . . . 'E's my son.

Treg (*vicious*)   'E ain! O chriss not all that again! (*Swings the back of his hand – threatens to hit her across the face.*) 'E ain know yer! 'S a bit a' luck!

Son *comes from the house with a canister. He puts it on the table. Turns back to the house.*

Son (*going. Gestures to tarpaulin*)   Not a problem.

He goes into the house.

Treg   Ain recognise yer – even after last time. We 'ad a bit a' luck!

Woman   . . . 'E's my son.

Treg   Yer cant drag that back! It ain count 'ere!

Woman   Cant look at 'im 'n not – cruel –

Treg   Everythin's cruel! It's cruel draggin us 'arf way round the world! (*Calmer.*) If 'e is yer son 'e ain know! Leave the poor sod in peace. Our luck's change at last. – If 'e was yer son it might stir up things in the back a' 'is mind – make 'im more willin t' let us stay. Play our cards right we could be 'ere for ever.

Woman   . . . (*Shocked.*) Couldnt . . . it's cruel . . . –

Treg   I ain 'is father. I'm bloody sure a' that. One piece a' luck yer cant grab away from me. If yer 'is mother, 'e certainly ain wan' 'a know. (*Calmer again.*) Sit there. Be'ave. Get through it now 'n it'll come easy after. Compare with what we bin through this ain nothin. I stood by yer – now yer do this for me.

Grace *comes from the house with food.*

Grace   We eat out 'ere when we can. Gets dark in the 'ouse. (*Puts food on the table.*) When I think of 'ow we used t' eat – 'n we still complained.

Treg   'S better 'n we're used to! (*To* **Woman**.) The advantage a' settlin down.

Son *comes from the house with food on a board.*

Treg (*to* **Son**)   People up there 'elp yer with the tarpaulin?

Son (*gives plate to* **Woman**)   Use that. Short a' plates. I got the board – (*He puts his food on the board. To* **Treg**.) Ain need 'elp. Put it up by meself.

They eat in silence.

Grace (*to* **Woman**)   Yer ain eatin.

Woman   . . . Ain 'ungry just yet.

Grace   Sorry it's nothin better.

Treg   'S fine. Fine. What we pick up on the road animals wouldnt eat.

Woman *stands.*

Treg   Sit down. (*Through teeth.*) Eat luv. Our friends took the trouble.

Woman (*leaving the table*)   I dont feel –

Treg   It's the walking. (*To* **Woman**.) Yer make yerself sick 'n then –

He picks up a chair. Takes it to **Woman** *and sits her in it.* **Son** *eats. Doesn't look round at* **Woman**.

Treg   Sit there. Yer'll feel better in a – . (*Goes to the table. Sits.*) She ain used t' this sort a' kindness.

Son *stands. Puts food on the* **Woman**'s *plate and takes it to her.*

Son   Try t' eat a bit.

Woman *takes the plate. Her hands shake violently.* **Son** *looks at* **Grace** *and half shrugs. Goes back to his place at the table. Takes no notice of* **Woman**. *Silence as they eat.*

Treg   Now buttons is interesting. D'know if yer ever 'ave any spare? Always droppin off in the road 'n yer can never find 'em when –

The food slides from **Woman**'s *plate and rolls on the floor.*

Grace   O yer poor –

She goes to **Woman**. *Crouches to pick up the food.* **Treg** *eats resolutely.* **Son** *eats and doesn't look round.*

Grace   O dear. I thought yer'd be better after last night.

Woman   Sorry –

Treg *gets up. Helps* **Grace** *to pick up the food.*

Treg   Waste a' people's kindness. . . (*Takes the food he has picked up back to the table. Puts it on his own plate. Eats.* **Son** *glances at him.*) Crime t' waste it.

Woman   . . . 'E's my son . . .

Grace   What is – yer got a son? (*Turns to* **Son**.) I think she's lost 'er son.

Treg   'S nothing. Story she's got 'old of. Mix 'erself up with some other woman. Us meetin yoo – got confuse –

Woman *slumps sideways from the chair. She curls up like a foetus on her side with her face to the ground.*

Woman (*whispers*)   'E's my son.

Treg   'Ear that? She's still at it!

Grace (*lost*)   I dont know what t' do – . (*To* **Son**.) 'Elp me.

Son *eats.*

Treg   Ignore 'er. (*To* **Son**.) She's always doin it. Gets 'erself in t' real trouble. The lads dont like it. World's full a' crazy women think they got the right t' put their claws in t' anyone they fancy. Yer tell me 'oo *is* normal these days!

Grace *tries to lift* **Woman**.

Grace   Give 'er some water –

Treg (*stands*)   Leave 'er t' me. I'll talk t' er. She'll apologise for makin a fool a' 'erself in front a' –

Son *stops eating. Stands. Goes to* **Woman**. *Looks down at her. Steps over her and goes into the house.* **Grace** *stands.*

Grace (*calls*)   What yer doin? (*To* **Treg**.) 'Elp 'er – I must see t' 'im – . Give 'er some water – (*To* **Woman**.) Yer'll be alright –

Treg *is at a loss. He doesn't try to get water.* **Son** *comes from the house. He has the two backpacks.*

Son   Out. Take 'er. Yoo 'n 'er. Five minutes. (*Starts to leave right. Sees the washing. Grabs it. Starts to stuff it into a backpack. Through his teeth.*) Lyin 'ore!

Grace   Dont – dont – stop it –

Son *goes out right.* **Grace** *holds* **Woman**, *rocks her and weeps.*

Grace   O dear. O dear. O dear. O dear.

Son *comes back.*

Son   Out! Take yer 'ore – ! (*He goes to* **Woman**. *Pulls her away from* **Grace** *and twists her to face the backpacks.*) Take yer trash! Get out! (*Starts to go. Sees pieces of scattered washing. Picks them up. Throws them at the backpacks.*) Take it! Ain wan' yer rags for souvenirs! (*To* **Grace**.) They ain gone when I'm back – (*His voice falters.*) I'll go!

Son *goes out right.* **Treg** *picks up a crust from the table. Nibbles.*

Treg   I'd be upset if a mad woman turn up 'n make accusations a' me.

Grace   I must see t' 'im. (*Going.*) Can yer take care a' er?

Treg   Calm 'im down. I'll look after this.

Grace (*to* **Woman**)   It's not yer fault. (*Hesitates. Comes back to* **Woman**. *Cradles her.*) Wait in yer room till I come back –

Woman   I must go away.

Grace   No – . (*Decides not to go after* **Son**.) I'll see t' 'im later . . . 'E gets upset. The fighting. There were terrible things.

Woman   I must go.

Grace   No. We'll sort it out. We'll find what's best. (*Looks right.*)

Treg (*eating*)   I'll fix it.

Silence. **Treg** *chews.*

Woman   I saw all the young men down there. I never thought one a' 'em was 'im. I knew 'im the moment I saw 'im. I got a right t' say 'e's my son.

Grace   Yer must be wrong – surely? If 'e was yer – (*Tries again.*) if yer knew 'im, 'e'd known yoo.

Woman   'Ow could 'e? 'E was a tot when I lost 'im.

Grace   Then 'ow could yer know 'im – after all that time?

Woman   'E's the spit of 'is brother.

Treg   Got 'n answer t' everythin.

Woman   'Is brother grew up with me. I saw 'im every day. I couldnt make a mistake. They 'ad the same eyes.

Treg   Mad . . .

Grace (*resigned*)   I cant say. – Yer calmer now. Yer' ll be alright if I leave yer – t' go t' 'im –

Woman   Dont leave me. 'E's angry.

Treg   I ain. It's a mess – but it's done. I'll think a' somethin. – (*Eats.*) It's all just fuss.

Grace   Yes – we're bringin it on ourselves. It doesnt matter 'oo we are, we got a right t' live in peace 'n take care a' each other. We 'avent committed a crime.

Treg   Everyone's past is a crime.

Grace   . . . Somethin 'appen. It's why 'e gets upset. Yer all in it. I dont understand what it is. Yer live with someone 'n dont know 'oo they are. What 'm I supposed t' do? – If yer 'is mother . . . (*She touches* **Woman***'s arm.*)

Woman   Yes.

The two women stare at each other. **Woman** *puts an arm round* **Grace***'s shoulders. They go into the house.* **Treg** *chews and watches them go. Then he goes to the fallen tarpaulin. Still eating from the plate in his hand he looks up at the fastenings. He goes back to the table. Puts the empty plate on it. Brushes his hands together to remove any crumbs. Picks up the two backpacks and puts them inside the doorway. Goes out right.*

Seven

Very early the next day. **Son** *comes from the right with a metal ladder. He sets it up against the side of the house by the fallen tarpaulin. He goes to the chest. Takes out a tool box. Goes back to the ladder. Puts the toolbox at its foot. Climbs the ladder and checks the fastenings at the top.* **Woman** *comes from the house. She stops. Stays by the door. Watches* **Son***. He turns to come down the ladder. Sees* **Woman***. Climbs down to the tool box. Searches in it.*

Woman Wont be in yer way. Dont ask yer t' forgive me. Before I left I wanted t' say sorry – for things yer cant know about. I never forgot yer.

Son *goes up the ladder.* **Woman** *goes into the house.* **Son** *comes down the ladder. Looks in the toolbox. Goes up the ladder again.* **Woman** *comes from the house. She holds her backpack by the straps.*

Woman Yer'll 'ave t' make yer own arrangements with 'im. Tell 'im not t' follow me. (*She puts her backpack against the side of the house. Goes to the foot of the ladder. Silence.*) Now I found yer – let me do one little bit a' service before I go. (*She looks around. Goes to the table. Puts left-over food on a plate and pushes it a little in* **Son***'s direction. No response.*) Yesterday I could've 'ad a meal with yer. I didnt know it was the last.

Son *drops his hammer. A thud.* **Woman** *hurries to it and picks it up. Holds it up to him. He fiddles with the fastenings.*

Woman If yer still want t' kill me yer got yer 'ammer. I wouldnt shrug.

Son *comes down the ladder. Snatches the hammer and throws it aside. Goes to the backpack. Picks it up and starts to go towards* **Woman**. *Stops – for a moment he is surprised at the backpack's heaviness. Goes to* **Woman**. *Hoists the backpack on to her back. Jerks the straps into place. He goes back to the ladder. Moves it further along the wall and climbs it.*

Woman *goes out left.* **Son** *comes down the ladder. He doesn't look left.* **Grace** *comes from the house.*

Grace Where was yer last night?

Son (*nods at table*) 'E slep there?

Grace Where was yer? Two nights now. It dont 'elp.

Son 'E 'as t' go. Ain share the place. Us two or no one. Yoo decide. Cant be otherwise.

Grace I cant turn 'er out. She's bin ill. What does it matter if she calls yer 'er – ?

Son   Son! Son! Yer think I care about that crap? I feel sorry for the poor cow – someone as lonely as she is. It's 'im. 'Is sort's what I come 'ere t' get away from. I come back this mornin t' fix this so I left yer the 'ouse in a good state before I went away. I cant go on like this. I cant do it.

Grace   Yer want me to do somethin I know's wrong? 'Ow can I live with that? – in a 'ouse thass bin repaired! It'd be better t' let the wind in!

Son   Is that it then?

He stops – **Treg** *is coming from the door.*

Son (*under his breath*)   Chriss – yeh yeh 'ere it comes.

Treg   Mornin. (*Looks at ladder.*) Yer start early. We've all forgot about yesterday. I'll make 'er drop all that. – Let me give yer a 'and. (*Goes to the fallen tarpaulin.*) This ain – 's 'ardly worth puttin up –

Son   I dont need 'elp – I already –

Treg (*puts his arm through a tear in the tarpaulin*)   Four 'ands is better'n two. Look – fallin t' bits. (*Picks up hammer. Gives it to* **Son**.) Yer drop this. (*Calls through door.*) Luv! – (*To* **Son**.) We ain force ourselves on yer. 'Ave a look round up the top. Find a place t' do up. Be neighbours. Give yer a bit a' company. (*Goes to door. Calls.*) Luv? – (*To* **Grace**.) See if she's alright.

He goes into the house.

Grace   'E's offerin – why cant yer co-operate with 'im?

Son *turns away from her. Leans face-to against the treads of the ladder. The hammer hangs from his hand.*

Son   Thass 'ow it always is. I told 'im t' go. 'E's still 'ere. 'E moves in up there. Down 'ere every day. Pokin in 'n out – till 'e moves in 'permanent 'n I'm push out. I'm repairin this for 'im. Yer cant see it. Yer give everythin away. I cant stop yer. What do I 'ave t' do? 'Ammer someone's 'ead in?

Grace   Yer shouldnt say such things. What can I do? If 'e
wants t' live up there I cant stop 'im!

Son   'E will – 'e'll take over.

Treg *looks out through an upper window.*

Treg   She ain 'ere. (*To* **Son**.) Yer seen 'er?

*He doesn't wait for an answer. Disappears. Comes through the door
way.*

Treg   'Er pack's gone.

Grace   We must stop 'er – she was talkin – she said she
could – . . .

She goes into the house.

Treg   Chriss – she 'ad arf our gear in that pack!

Son *starts to slowly climb the ladder.*

Grace (*in the house*)   Take some water! If we 'ad proper
medical things! There's nothin – nothin –

Treg   Yer dont think she'd . . .

Grace *comes from the house with a blanket. She pours water into a
carrier.*

Grace (*to* **Treg**)   She told me she didnt want t' live. – Take
some rope – !

Treg   Rope?

Grace   To climb down the – if we 'ave to –

Treg   Chriss! – all this because yer too bloody criminal t' say
yer 'er son –

Grace   The rope –

Treg   Where – ?

Grace   The chest –

Treg *goes to the chest.*

Treg   'Arf our gear! Took years t' collect!

He takes rope from chest.

Grace (*to* **Son**)   'Elp us! (*Goes right. Stops. To* **Son**.) – She could be dead by now!

Son *ignores her. He runs his hand slowly and methodically along the fastenings at the roof.*

Treg (*rope*)   'S that enough? Where're we – ?

Grace (*going*)   I know the place – 's bin used before –

Treg *and* **Grace** *go out right.* **Son** *comes very slowly down the ladder. Goes to the table. Sits. Doesnt look left or right – stares down at the food* **Woman** *put on the plate. Doesn't eat. His jaw is set. He gets up and walks out left. Pause.* **Minty** *comes in from the right. He is a young settler from higher up the path. He wears working clothes. His hands and boots are soiled. He is bent and carries a used door on his back. The hinges are still screwed to the side. He leans the door against the house and goes to the doorway.*

Minty (*calls*)   'Ello. (*No reply. Mildly ironic.*) Deliverin.

He waits a few seconds. Then very roughly tries the door to see if it fits. Satisfied. He leans the door against the side of the house and goes to the table. Looks at the food **Woman** *put on the plate. Whistles briefly and checks by looking back at the house. Takes a work cloth from his pocket and wraps the food in it. Puts it back in his pocket. Sees something, left. Goes out right. Pause.* **Son** *comes on left. He carries* **Woman**'s *backpack by its straps. He sets it down. Is going to climb the ladder. Changes his mind and goes to the table. Sits.* **Woman** *comes on. She stops. Stares at him.*

Son (*points right*)   Up there. Lookin for yer.

Woman *goes to the backpack. Lifts it.*

Son   'Eavy. Should put some a' it in 'is.

Woman (*starts to put it on her back. Mumbles*)   Used t' it.

Son *stands. Goes to* **Woman**. *Opens the top of her backpack. Takes out some things and half-throws, half-drops them, on the ground. Goes back to his chair. Sits.* **Woman** *hesitates. She picks up the scattered things and puts them on the top of the chest. Goes back to the backpack.*

Woman   If I was some mad woman yer'd take care a' me. Do it for a stranger, not for me because I'm yer mother. Yer got a right t' 'ate me. When I lost yer it 'urt – still 'urts – same 'urt – never goes away – yer must feel some a' the –

Son (*flat*)   Dont. Yer got yer life. I got mine. Nothin t' say.

Woman   I ain got my life. When yer was on the roof – I went 'n stood in yer shadow – I touched it – then I thought I can go away – kill meself where 'e ain find me – ain 'ave t' see it –

Son   Dont say any more. (*Gets up. Moves towards the ladder.*) No need. Ain cry. They come back 'n see.

Woman (*struggling to put on her backpack. To herself*)   Cant –

Son   There's nothin.

Woman (*fumbling*)   – manage t' – t' get –

Son *goes to* **Woman**.

Son (*heaves the backpack on her back*)   Lift yer –

He turns. The backpack drops. He walks away dragging it by a strap behind him on the ground. **Woman** *goes to him.*

Woman   Gi' me. I'll – I can manage –

Son *cries.*

Woman   Dont. Dont. Gi' me. I'll go.

She tries to take the backpack. He clings to it. Pushing. He clings to her. Cries.

Woman   Come – come – 's alright – alright – I'll go –

Son (*crying, clinging to her*)   Go. Go. Go away.

Woman (*crying*)   It's alright. (*He half-falls, is half-taken, to the table. A chair.*) It's alright – alright now – yer cried for me –

Son (*crying, howling*)   Chriss. Chriss. Chriss. Chriss.

Woman   'S alright. Better. Better. Thass why I'm 'ere –

Son *tries to calm himself. Gets up. Tries to walk away. Falls on his knees facing away from* **Woman**. *Doubles over. Cries.*

Son   'Urts. 'Urts.

He falls forwards face down on the ground. **Woman** *goes to him. Crouches and clings at his back.*

Woman   I know. (*Dry tears.*) 'S alright. All. 'S all. Be 'appy. (*She falls prostrate on his back.*) Be 'appy. My son.

Son *turns round. They lie face to face on the ground. Holding each other. Crying. Rocking.*

Son   Go. Go. Go away from me.

Woman   Yes. All. Be 'appy. All I wanted. My son.

They cry and rock from side to side together on the ground.

Son   Want – .

Grace *comes in with the blanket.*

Grace   Let go of – ! Get off – get off – ! (**Son** *and* **Woman** *rock.* **Grace** *pummels him. Flails him with the blanket.*) Get off! (*Dashes to the table. Snatches a metal jug. Goes to* **Son**. *Strikes him.*) Get off – ! Get – !

Woman (*to* **Son**)   It's alright. Alright.

Son *stands. A huge gasping sigh shakes him. He staggers away from* **Woman**. *Stops. Hunched. Sways. Turned in on himself.* **Woman** *stands. Her arms half reach out for* **Son**.

Son   Me – me – Chriss me clothes're burnin me – (*He tries to pull his shirt away from his body.*) burnin – . (*Lost. Looks.*) The 'ouse . . . table . . .

He goes to a chair. Sits upright but shoulders hunched.

Grace (*to* **Son**)   I thought yer −

Son (*turns to* **Grace** *as if he wondered who she was*)   What?

Grace (*to* **Woman**)   I thought 'e was −

Son (*stranger's voice*)   It's alright. It's done. She's a poor woman. She's me mother.

Woman (*bewildered*)   . . . Shall I go away . . .? (*Turns uncertainly towards her backpack.*)

Son (*stranger's voice*)   No. Stay. Stay.

Woman   . . . 'e cried . . .

Son (*sits upright. Calm. Stranger's voice*)   Stay. She is 'oo she is. Cant go. Too late. (*Looks round.*) I dont know what'll 'appen.

Grace (*to* **Woman**)   Why were yer − ?

Woman *straightens herself.*

Woman   Lost me breath − . 'E loves me. 'E knew all along.

Grace (*to* **Woman**)   Are you sure? It's so many years.

Son   Thass 'er 'ouse too. Cant chuck 'er out. A mother's 'ouse.

Treg *comes in from the right. He carries the rope.*

Treg (*to* **Woman**)   Bin lookin. We thought yer was . . .

Grace   'E knows 'oo 'e is. They're t'gether.

Treg (*to* **Son**)   Yer know 'er?

Woman   'E follow me on the road − didnt say a word − took me pack cause it was 'eavy even before 'e'd said I'm 'is mother. What a good son − !

Treg   Well! . . .That it? − It's settled? Yer cant change yer mind again. (*Notices the rope in his hand.*) Difference a day makes. (*Goes to the chest to put the rope away.*) Ain say I ain pleased.

Son (*doesn't point*)   What's that?

Treg   Rope?

Silence.

Treg (*realises*)   Ah. (*Puts the rope in the chest. Goes to the door to inspect it.*) Did they bring the right one? Put me initials on it. (*To* **Woman**.) Store up there. Ain big but good gear. Stuff they pulled out the 'ouses. Went up yesterday 'n 'ad a choose. Did somethin useful after all the wranglin.

Son   Will it fit?

Treg   Easy adjust it. If yer ain like it they got more yer can choose. I think I got the best.

Grace   Why're we talkin about a door? We should be celebratin!

Treg (*to* **Son**)   Let's be clear before we celebrate. From now on we work on the basis she's yer mother, that it? It'll mean big changes. (*Hesitates.*) Yer all seem so sure. Be 'appier if yer 'ad some doubts. That'd be more 'uman.

Woman   I got all I ever wanted. Never 'ad any doubt. I knew the first time I found yer. (*Takes his hand.*) Yer looked at me just like yer brother. Yer 'ad one pair a' eyes between yer.

Treg (*to* **Grace**)   Yer 'appy with this?

Grace   We 'ave t' celebrate!

Woman   Everythin's a celebration now.

Treg (*to* **Woman**)   Take yer time. 'Ave t' get used to a lot a' things. Livin in a 'ouse, for a start. (*To* **Grace**.) Cant 'ave 'n 'ole in the wall 'n call it a door. (*To* **Woman**.) We'll go up 'n recce the store. They got all sorts. 'Ave t' provide for four now. (*To* **Son**.) Dont worry, ain make no improvements yer ain approve of.

Grace   We'll cook a big meal.

Treg *takes* **Woman**'s *backpack into the house.*

Woman (*to* **Son**)   Yer dont mind 'im 'n 'is doors?

Son   No.

Woman (*kisses him on the side of his face. Runs her hands up and down his arm*)   I got a right t' stroke this now. (*Looks at* **Grace** *and* **Son**. *Turns to the chest.*) Take 'em in before 'e notice.

She picks up the things taken from her backpack. Goes towards the house.

Son   'Ave I got a brother?

Woman *goes into the house.* **Grace** *goes to* **Son**.

Son (*draws away*)   They'll see.

Grace   Yer 'appy now?

Son   Need time t' . . . –

Grace   Come inside while we cook.

Son   In a minute.

Grace   Dont like t' leave yer out 'ere.

Son   Ain leave me. Thass over. 'S all settled.

Grace *goes into the house.* **Son** *goes to the ladder. He lies prone against it facing the rungs. His head is turned towards the house. Inside the house a snatch of laughter from* **Woman** *and* **Grace**. **Son** *turns his head to face left.*

Eight

Early next morning. The ladder is still against the side of the house. **Treg** *stands at the foot.* **Minty** *is at the top. He is tapping with a hammer to test the wood.*

Minty   Wood's rotten.

Treg   Tol' 'im. 'E said it's the fastenin.

Minty *pulls off a piece of rotted wood. Drops it on the ground.*

Minty   'Ole place bin neglected. – Where is everyone?

Treg   Overslep. Busy day yesterday.

Minty   Yoo stoppin 'ere?

Treg   Yeh.

Minty (*climbing down the ladder*)   Dont see a lot a' 'em. They work their bit a' land. Keep theirself t' theirself. (*Reaches the ground.*) Needs 'ole new plankin.

Treg   Got any?

Minty   Might 'ave.

Treg   Yer got a lot a' potential up there. Needs developin.

Minty   Yeh – suppose. Yer put the work in – then y' 'ave t' move on again.

Treg   Make the best a' it while it's yourn.

Minty   Suppose.

Son *comes from the house.*

Minty   Mornin.

Son   'Lo.

Treg   'Avin a poke round the roof. Show 'im. Wood's gone.

Minty (*shows* **Son** *the piece of rotted wood. Flakes it*)   Rotten.

Treg   They got new plankin.

Son   Yeh. Ta. I'll see t' it.

Woman *comes from the house.*

Minty   Mornin.

Woman   'Ello.

Minty (*doesn't offer his hand*)   Minty – (*Points right.*) up there.

Treg   They can let us 'ave the new roofin.

Minty (*indicates* **Son** *and* **Woman**)   Yer know each other?

Woman   'E's my son.

Minty   O. (*Slight pause.*) Ain said yer was comin.

Treg   Separated years. The fightin.

Minty   Yeh. Mess everyone up. Jimmy – (*Points right.*) up there – abandon 'is dog. 'Ad t' leave it be'ind. Turn up eight years later. Scratch 'is door one mornin. Waggin 'is tail 'n pantin 's if it bin runnin non-stop ever since Jimmy left it. Funny 'ow a dog knew. 'Ung around a week then keel over. Wore itself out.

Silence. **Treg** *nods to* **Minty** *to signal 'tact'.*

Minty (*to* **Woman**. *Grins*)   Nice meetin yer. . . Yeh, dog called Arnold.

Treg *and* **Minty** *go out right. Pause.*

Woman (*gestures to house*)   Is – ?

Son   Still asleep.

Little pause.

Woman   I thought it was on the other side.

Son   The other . . .?

Woman   Yer scar. On the other side. (**Son** *stares. Silence.*) Does it give yer signs? (**Son** *stares.*) Some scars throb when it's goin t' rain.

Son   The other side?

Woman   O it's not the scar that told me 'oo yer was.

Pause. **Son** *moves a chair at the table for* **Woman**. *They sit. He looks at her.*

Woman   Yesterday was lovely. (*Pause.*) Can I wash it? (*No response.*) Yer scar.

Son (*embarrassed*)   It doesnt 'ave t' be –

Woman   No a' course, I know. – Just my fancy. I use t' wash it in me sleep. Pour water on it 'n it was wash away. (*She makes an awkward sound like a broken grin.*) Was there special times when yer thought a' me?

Son   I didnt think a' yer. I 'ad a mother.

Woman (*shocked*)   Yer thought she was yer – ?

Silence.

Son   She was like a dead woman 'oo wouldnt go away. 'Ow did yer lose me?

Woman   She never tol' yer – ?

She stands.

Son   Tell me.

Woman (*irritated*)   If yer keep askin questions – ! (*Calmer. She moves to a chair further from him.*) Yer was a tiny –. Less 'n a normal baby. The want – the poverty – was terrible. I give yer t' er.

Son   Give! – t' 'er? She was dead. She was worse 'n dead: *she wouldnt go away.* Yer give a livin – I was tiny, yeh? – baby t' a dead –

Woman   In those days –

Son   – the poverty was terrible! So yer make it worse – give me away!

Woman   Not give –

Son   Yer said –

Woman   She found –

Son   Yer said give!

Woman   She found –

Son (*stands. Frozen*)   Dont matter. 'S long ago. (*Walks away.*)
It never 'appen! Bin wash out by a drop a' water! (*He goes to the
bench. Sits with his back to her. Looks into space.*) Tell me.

Woman   No right t' sit at yer table . . . 'Ow can yer
understand? I put yer on the ground 'n went away.

Son   I could a' died.

Woman   I pull yer wrap tight round yer so – . In those days
someone 'ad t' die. Did yer know yer can put nails in water?
Yer can. I learnt that when I left yer. She'd followed me. Took
yer when I went. I come back – I couldnt leave yer t' die.
Found yer with 'er. I didnt know it then but I was glad –

Son   Glad – !

Woman   Be quiet! Listen when yer mother speaks!
Sometimes yer forced t' be glad. (*Silence.*) Yer can put nails in
water – but they 'urt more when yer take 'em out ! – Little
babies cling. Their 'ands cling like nails. When I left yer on the
ground yer turned t' cling t' it. Then she come. 'Er stink 'eld
'er together – not 'er bones. When I put yer in 'er 'ands I put
yer in yer coffin. Thass when I was glad. Yer'd die wrap in 'er
rags. They give yer more comfort 'n they give 'er in a 'undred
years. Yer die in a bit a' warmth. Thass 'ow we lived then.

Son   Yeh, yeh. Yeh if yer like. I can understand that. But
why do it again? Why bring another kid in t' the world?

Woman (*confused*)   There werent no other –

Son   My brother! Yer said I 'ad a brother!

Woman   Yer brother – ?

Son   Then why did yer – ?

Woman   'E was with us when – . I 'ad the two a' yer –

Son   The two a' us? The two a' us was there? (*Silence.*) Yer
took 'im –

Woman   I couldnt keep two. Y 'ave t' use yer reason even
when it drive yer mad. I 'ad t' tell one a' yer no. It was right –
good. Cant yer understand? I 'ad t' live t' take care a' one a'
yer. I suffered for yer both –

Son *stands.*

Woman   But yer lived! We all lived. I did what was best.

Son *goes to the doorway.*

Son (*calls*)   Grace. (*Listens at the door. Leaves. – Explains.*) She
'eard.

Slight pause. **Grace** *comes from the door.*

Son (*to* **Grace**)   Yer like that door?

Grace   It's nice. Why didnt we think a' it?

Son   Yer think it's suitable?

Grace   It fills the gap.

Son *goes to the foot of the ladder. Picks up pieces of rotten wood.
Takes them aside and drops them.*

Grace (*to* **Son**)   Why did yer let me sleep? – (*To* **Woman**.) 'n
leave yer t' find where everythin is.

Woman   We 'ad a talk. There's a lot yer 'ave t' tell me. 'Ow
yer come 'ere – 'ow yer –

Son   Where's me brother? Why ain 'e with yoo?

Woman   We parted.

Son   'Ow?

Woman   When yer men found me. (*To* **Grace**.) 'E nearly –
'as 'e tol' yer or does 'e 'ave 'is secrets? – kill me. I didnt want
t' live. I wanted 'im t' 'ave 'is way. But I couldnt let 'im do the
worse thing a son can do. (*To* **Son**.) Couldnt burden yer with
that. When I saw yer face the sufferin was over. I wanted t' lie
down at yer feet 'n be at peace. But I 'ad t' save yer from
yerself. I ran away. Yesterday I ran away t' die. Yer came 'n
brought me back – t' live with me son 'n me new daughter in

me new 'ome. No more secrets. Cant live with 'em. They're like insects buzzin in yer brain.

Treg, **Minty** and **Stewart** *come in from the right.* **Stewart** *is middle-aged, thick-set and sturdy. He is in charge. He has frightened eyes.* **Minty** *carries a trestle and* **Treg** *a small packet.*

Treg (*to* **Son**)   Brought Stewart t' ave a look. (*To* **Woman**.) Yer okay? – Stewart's from up the road. (*To* **Stewart**. *Indicates roof.*) Yer see the problem.

Minty (*picks up pieces of rotten wood to show to* **Stewart**. *Flakes a piece*)   Rotten. (*Puts the wood on the table.*)

Treg   The 'ole edge.

Stewart *perambulates round the foot of the ladder. Looks up at the roof.*

Treg (*to* **Woman**)   Stewart's in charge a' the store.

Stewart (*sucks air through his teeth*)   Hhssss – big job.

Treg   But yer got the plankin for it?

Stewart (*stares at the roof in silence for a moment*)   Ain safe. (*Scratches behind his ear.*) Make a 'ole in the reserves. (*To* **Son**.) Yer know the set-up. Everyone chip in. Yer take out, yer put back. Else the cupboard'd soon be bare. Nothin left lyin out in the fields. Thass all bin brought in long ago. (*Shakes head.*) Cant leave it, thass for sure. Dont want it fallin on yer 'eads.

Minty   Should never bin left t' go that far.

Stewart (*nods at house*)   Am I right yer got some iron beds in there?

Son   'Ere when we come. Ain out yer store.

Stewart   Thass true. – Didnt mean – . Tryin t' find 'n acceptable solution.

Grace (*to* **Son**)   We must 'ave something.

Son (*door*)   'Oo pick that?

Treg   Me – I tol' yer.

Son   Got a crack.

Treg   Easy fix it. 'S best one for 'ere.

He moves the door to the opening. **Minty** *helps him.*

Son   'Ave t' keep openin 'n shut it.

Stewart   What?

Son   When yer go in 'n out.

Stewart   Well – yeh – yer do with doors.

Grace   Yer mother needs a door.

Treg (*to* **Minty**)   'Old it while I put the blocks under.

Stewart   Minty give yer a 'and t' fix it. The roof 's a bigger proposition. – (*Salon chair.*) Thass a nice piece yer got.

Grace   It's our only comfortable chair.

Stewart *goes to help* **Treg** *and* **Minty**.

Grace (*to* **Son**)   We cant leave the roof.

Minty (*whisper*)   Y'ave t'open 'n shut it when yer go in 'n out.

Stewart   Shush.

Minty (*giggle. Whisper*)   In 'n out.

Treg, **Minty** *and* **Stewart** *start to fix the door in place.* **Treg** *fetches the toolbox from the ladder. Opens the parcel of fittings.*

Son (*picks up a piece of rotting wood from the table*)   'Oo put that on the table?

He knocks woodlice on the floor. Throws the wood aside.

Son (*scraping out the woodlice with his sole*)   Whass my brother's name?

Woman   Name? (*Slightly surprised.*) 'E never 'ad one.

Son   But 'e –

Woman   No need. I call 'im son.

Son   Son.

Woman   There was just the two a' us. We wouldnt use a name.

Son   Crawlin – . (*Brushes a woodlouse from the table. Treads on it.*) Was 'e good?

Woman   It was always dark. Fog. Yer can still be a 'uman bein t' each other even when . . . I'd a' like t' give 'im things. Make things better for 'im.

Son   Why'd 'e leave?

Woman   I dont know.

Son   Must've 'ad a reason.

Stewart (*to* **Minty**)   Needs a bit off the top.

Treg   Frame warped. Old 'ouses.

They rest the door on the trestle. **Minty** *planes a strip from the top – a rhythmic rasping.*

Woman   Woke up one morning. Seems like yesterday. 'E was packin. (*Touches her face.*) 'Ow could 'e do it to me after the years I'd . . . (*Falls silent.*)

Son   'Oo broke the cup?

Grace   What?

Son   Crack. (*Points at cup.*) Not there before.

Grace   A little –

Son   I know it's little. Cracks grow. Yer use the cup it'll grow. Might as well chuck it in the – . 'Oo crack it?

Woman   I dont think it was –

Son   I never said it was. I just said it's crack 'n no one –

Grace   Accident. 'Oo-ever did it didnt know they –

Son   Yer crack a cup yer know. The world ain a china shop.
If we 'ad rows a' cups on 'ooks – someone should say – (*Brushes
the side of his hand across the table.*) bad wood, bloody lice – they
knew it'd be see – bound to – so why ain they – ? (*Not shouting
but relentless.*) I dont mind the crack – accidents 'appen –

Stewart (*to* **Minty**)   Steady. Not too much.

Son   – they could a' say –

Woman   P'raps I did it. I try t' be –

Son   'I try t' be'! – whass the good a' that? –

Grace   Dont speak t' yer mother like that. Treat 'er with
respect.

She puts her arm round **Woman**'*s shoulders.* **Minty** *stops work to
watch.* **Treg** *gestures to him to go on working.*

Son   – it's wrong wrong wrong – it's put there 'n we cant –
yer cant put it back – cant take a crack out a cup once it's –
cant 'wash it out' with a splash a' water – cant wait till it gets –

Grace (*reaches for cup*)   I'll put it in the –

Son (*picks up the cup*)   Leave it! – dont want it took – I'm just
sayin – it's crack – yer use it 'n the crack'll grow – go down the
side – thass all – it's just a cup so why should someone? – they
ain care – ain own up they – it's just a crack so – (*Mirthless
laugh.*) ha! –

Grace   Dont, dont – please – what'll people think when
yer –

Son   I ain upset – I'm sayin – thass all – sayin – yer think I
care about a cup? – be mad t' care about a cup – ain mad –
I'm sayin the crack could spread – run down the table – spread
'n crack the floor – crack the 'ouse 'n no one – it's just a crack
so no one – run 'n run 'n no one – go through the ground –
the mountain we're stood on for chrissake – on 'n on – 'n no
one – it's just a crack so no one – we sit 'ere 'n could be sittin
in the crack – be dead 'n livin in the crack – be buried in it 'n

no one – it's just a crack – I'm sayin – yer dont understand –
dont try t' understand –

Grace   Stop it, stop it. Please.

Treg (*to* **Minty**)   That should do it –

Minty *stops planing.*

Stewart   'Ave a see.

Minty *and* **Treg** *raise the door in the door frame.*

Stewart (*quietly to* **Treg** *and* **Minty**)   We all 'ave our troubles.
Clears the air. Brings yer closer together after.

Silence.

Son   Even a dog's call Arnold. 'Try t' be.' – A cup is crack.
I could 'a crack it. I dont know. I try t' say – we sit 'ere – sit –
thass all – (*Shows the cup to* **Grace**.) – crack – run down the side –
tryin t' get away from – get off the cup – 'n get the – crack the
sky – crack the world – it ain real what I say, I know a cup
cant – but if yer saw the cup like that – its way – then yer'd – !
(*To* **Treg**, **Minty** *and* **Stewart**.) I dont want the door.

Treg   Nearly finish.

Son   Dont want it. Ain 'ave it in me 'ouse.

Treg   Let 'im show yer 'ow –

Minty   Go careful till it's – (*Demonstrating opening and shutting.*)
In 'n out. (*The door scrapes on the bottom.*)

Son   I dont want it. Take it.

Treg   I chose it special for the –

Stewart   'Ang on, 'ang on. This requires some thought. Our
friend 'ere dont want the door. Is that because I said the chair?

Son   I dont want it.

Stewart   Yer cant take 'n not give. That's stealin from yer
comrades.

Son   Just take it.

Minty   'E could 'a said before I took the top off. Fit 'is wonky frame. Useless somewhere else.

Son   I never told yer t' –

Treg   Yer can choose another door. They got more.

Son (*turns back to the table. Cup*)   It's crack.

Stewart (*to* **Grace**)   Didnt mean t' trespass on –

Grace   Not a trespass. Leave the door. I'll come up t' thank everyone. (*To* **Minty**.) Minty's been a real 'elp –

Stewart   I appreciate that.

Son   Take it away.

Grace   Dont be silly – I want the –

Son   Yer dont want it.

Silence.

(*Weary*)   The crack dont want the door – thass for sure.

Stewart   Didnt come down this mornin t' cause 'n upset. It's a small community. We respect each other's way a' seein things.

Son *goes to the door. Opens it. It comes off the top hinge and sags. He goes into the house.*

Woman   I upset him when I said about the past. But 'e asked – 'n it's 'ow we lived . . .

Treg   'E'll take the door when 'e's got over 'is paddy. 'S 'ad a difficult time.

Minty (*low*)   We aint.

Grace (*tired*)   Please leave it. 'E accepts what things are when 'e sees what's right.

Treg (*goes to the table*)   I'll talk 'im round. 'Umiliate 'im if 'e 'as t' go up 'n ask for it back. (*Picks up the cup. Stares. Mystified.*) . . . Yer got spare cups up there?

Son *comes from the house. Steps round the sagging door and stands in the doorway.*

Son   I dont know when I was born. 'Oo I am. Where I bin all me life. I'm a 'uman bein. Whass that? No one knows any more. (*He lifts the door half free – supports it near the top with one hand. The bottom grates.*) Good stuff. Ain want it damage.

The door falls with a crash to the ground. **Treg** *sits at the table. Puts the cup in front of him.*

Stewart   Yer want the planks for yer roof?

Son   Dont know. 'Ave t' think.

Stewart (*to* **Grace**, *low*)   Yer know where t' find us. (*To* **Minty**.) Pick it up.

Minty   'E twist the 'inges.

Stewart   Pick it up.

Minty *and* **Stewart** *put the trestle on the door. They carry it out as if it were a stretcher.* **Son** *goes to the table. He picks up the cup – doesn't stare at it, his glance glides over it as he puts it down further away from* **Treg**.

Son   Crack's grown – the noise.

Treg   'S right takin care a' things. Everythin's precious now.

Son (*sits*)   A cup is cracked. If there was someone 'oo understood. 'Oo listened. If I 'ad a brother. If 'e 'ad a name. I could think. Talk. (*Quiet.*) What's a cup? – it's crack – crack – crack – crack – crack – crack – . (*His voice has trailed away.*) 'Oo broke it? (*Slides his hand across the table.*) Woodlice. Rotten wood. Get up in the mornin. Eat – (*Mounting rage.*) who broke it? – no one! – no one saw – no one 'eard it crack – crack – a snake comes out the crack that – (*Gestures off.*) crack that – all that – out there – pick the cup up 'n chuck it – crack it – crack the sky!

Smash the – . Ah good! 'e's mad so we dont 'ave t' worry what 'e – ! *'Oo crack the cup?*

Treg   I crack it.

Grace   I crack it.

Woman *gestures to them to be silent.*

Son (*sits in despair*)   They ain even want t' tell the truth!

Grace *breaks the cup.*

Grace   I broke it! Now yer know! – Yer got no right t' –

Son (*points*)   Ain broke. Yer cant. Ain got the violence in yer – yer too good. Look. All the pieces left – (*Points to* **Woman**.) eyes starin at 'er!

Woman *goes to* **Son**. *She stands behind his chair. She slides her arms round his shoulders.* **Grace** *watches.* **Treg** *stares at his hands.*

Woman   I wish yer'd bin with us. I'd a' give yer brother t' yer as a friend. We'd be three. 'E'd've 'ad a name then. I knew yer when I 'eard yer speak. Before I'd only 'eard yer cryin as a kid. When I 'eard yer voice I 'eard the cryin in it. I used t' 'ear birds. Animals at night. I pushed through crowds – 'im in me arms – t' market once or twice – t' purchase things. When yer talked about the cup I 'eard yer singin like a kid. New songs. Songs I 'never 'eard before. I understand yer. Once I thought I was a dolls' house. Empty – 'ollow, 'ollow – but I was full a' kids. So many kids. All a' 'em. Now I 'ave a son again.

Son   I'm afraid t' be sick in the 'ead. I want t' be a 'uman being. Just that. In all this shit 'n rubble.

Treg *twiddles with his hands. Glances back at the doorway.*

Son   I 'ave t' find 'im.

Woman   Oo?

Son   Me brother.

Woman (*smiles*)   Yer cant. 'E's gone.

Son   I 'ave t' find 'im.

Woman (*calm, almost sing-song*)   Yer cant. I found yoo. Thass enough.

Son   I 'ave t' find 'im. Whatever 'appens after – whatever I do – if I shout – get angry – 'ave rages – all that means nothing. Dont notice it. I 'ave t' find 'im.

Woman   No – yer mustnt say that – yer cant –

Son   I cant live if I dont.

Woman   Yer cant. Yer cant. 'E's gone. Yer found me – yer followed me on the road 'n brought me back. Now we're 'appy together –

Son   I cant live like this after whass 'appened 'ere today. I 'ave t' find 'im.

He stands and moves away from **Woman**.

Woman   Yer cant. 'Is place – it ain nowhere now – it's gone –

Son   Is she afraid 'e'll tell me why 'e ran away from 'er?

Woman   I dont *know* why! – If I knew I'd tell yer – !

Son   Yer'd think she'd kill 'im!

Treg (*stands*)   That's enough! – She killed 'im? What? – only one! In all that killin there was then? If 'e was like yoo I ain blame 'er.

Grace   Please! –

Son (*to* **Grace**)   I'll go in the morning.

Grace   Where could yer begin? It's years since 'e –

Son   Go back where I was. It's easy –

Grace   'E wont be there –

Son   I'll begin there.

Grace   Yer'll never find 'im!

Son   They found me!

Grace   I cant bear any more. (*To* **Treg**.) Dont let 'im go.

Son   I'd 'ave t' go even if I didnt want to. Yesterday I didnt know 'e existed. Now I dont want t' live without 'im. 'E's whass bin missin all me life. When I find 'im things'll change. It'll solve everythin. 'E's me only chance. 'E'll tell me why my life's bin wasted. How I should live. – Why did I stick this place so long? Shabby, shoddy, shoddy – . I 'ave t'go for 'is sake. 'E's like a ghost 'ere. I'll bring 'im back t' live. I'll take such care a 'im 'e'll never go away. Thank God I got a brother.

Woman   What 'ave I done?

They are silent and still.

Treg   Little bastard wants murderin upsettin decent people for nothin.

Nine

The fens. A vast smooth open space sloping away upwards. Towards the back **Village Woman** *sits on a kitchen chair. Her clothes are dark except for her head scarf: red with white spots. She does not move. Behind to her left, the shape of a window. A half-length curtain pulled aside to cover part of it. From time to time a gentle wind stirs the bottom. There is nothing else.*

Pitch black night.

WAPO 3 *sits downstage.* **Son** *comes on right. He wears the clothes he wore at the house but they have faded to a lighter grey. He is tired but intense.*

WAPO 3   'Ave yer brought me water?

Son   I thought yer was dead –

WAPO 3   'Ave yer brought it?

Son   Where's me brother?

WAPO 3   Water.

Son (*calls to* **Village Woman**)   Where's me brother?

WAPO 3   She ain 'ear.

Son (*starts to go to her*)   Is this me brother's place?

WAPO 3   No. Yer cant cross –

Son   Why not?

WAPO 3   It's where they buried the dead killed in the fightin
'n then in the cities 'n the camps. 'S their place as far as yer
see. A mass – mass – I forget the word. (*Pulls* **Son** *down to his
side. Remembers.*) Grave. In the grave there's a village. In the
village there's a woman. Give me some water 'n someone'll
come. (**Son** *gives him water from a WAPO-bottle. Drinks.*) More!
Me stomach's leakin.

Son   Not till I find me brother!

WAPO 3   Look – someone comin – I told yer.

Son   Where?

WAPO 3   There – 'is fingers crackin the 'orizon – grippin
the edge – draggin 'is-self up.

The curtain moves. **Silhouette Soldier** *stands in* **Village
Woman***'s room. He is completely in black: work tunic, boots, gloves
and a balaclava hiding his head and face.* **Village Woman** *doesn't
react.*

Son (*stands. Calls*)   I've come for me brother!

WAPO 3   'Ush! Let it sleep.

Silhouette Soldier (*to* **Village Woman**)   Where's me
brother?

No answer.

Son (*to* **WAPO 3**)   Why ain 'e make 'er say? 'E's a soldier!
(*Calls to* **Silhouette Soldier**.) Stamp on 'er! Kick the words
out 'er gob!

WAPO 3   Wait! Yer'll see.

Silhouette Soldier   Yer 'id 'im in the village!

Son (*to* **WAPO 3**)   Look at 'er! Silence all over 'er face!
(*Calls.*) Kick 'er jaw in! Make 'er splutter it out with 'er teeth!

WAPO 3   'E's got a better way.

Silhouette Soldier   Give me yer kid.

Son   The mother's got a kid?

Silhouette Soldier   Give it.

Off, the distant voices of the **WAPO**s *in the fen.*

WAPOs (*off*)   Kid! Kid! Kid! Use 'er kid! Make 'er say!

Silhouette Soldier *takes a baby from* **Village Woman**'s *lap.
It is a white featureless bundle. He holds it up.*

Silhouette Soldier   Babies 'urt more 'n we do. They cant
speak – the 'urt curdles inside. All the 'urts cram in that little
space so they 'urry t' grow big quick.

WAPOs (*off*)   Whass 'e doin? Got the kid. Ain see. 'Old it up!

Son (*to* **WAPO 3**)   Does she tell 'im? (*Calls.*) Where's me
brother?

Silhouette Soldier   Spare the kid. Spare yerself. Yer got
me brother lock? I open the lock 'n e'll run out! We'll all run
out! Leave yer 'n the kid! We'll all be free!

WAPOs (*off*)   'Ang it! 'Ang it! 'Ang it! 'Ang it!

Silhouette Soldier *pulls a hawser from the ground – it comes up
like a snake out of a hole.*

Silhouette Soldier   Our rope! The rope we use. It know
'ow t' 'ang.

WAPOs (*off*)   Rope! Rope! Rope! Show 'er the rope!

Silhouette Soldier   Tell me.

He puts the baby on the ground.

Son   Wass 'e do now?

WAPOs (*off*)   'Ang it! 'Ang it! 'Ang it!

Silhouette Soldier *ties a large noose in the hawser. He shows it to* **Village Woman**.

Silhouette Soldier   The noose is tied. Where's me brother?

WAPOs (*off*)   Brother! Brother! Brother! Brother!

Silhouette Soldier *puts his arm through the large noose.*

Silhouette Soldier   'Urts! Arm 'urts! Aint touch – still 'urts! (*His fingers writhe.*) Fingers show the arm 'urts! (*Picks up baby.*) Shall I? Put baby? In the noose?

WAPOs (*off*)   Noose! Noose! Noose! 'E's noosin the baby!'

Silhouette Soldier (*holding the noose in one hand and baby in the other*)   Last time a' askin! The world go in the noose when the baby 'ang!

WAPOs (*off*)   Noose it! Noose it! Noose it! Noose it!

Silhouette Soldier *puts baby in the noose.*

WAPOs (*off. Scream*)   Ywow!

The baby falls through the noose

Silhouette Soldier   Too big! Drop out the noose!

WAPOs (*off*)   Drop! Drop! Baby done a pratfall out the noose!

Silhouette Soldier   Straight down on the ground! Tryin t' get in! Too soon! Ain be buried yet! Ain earn the right!

He makes the noose smaller.

WAPOs (*off*)   Tighter! Tighter! 'Ang it! 'Ang it!

Silhouette Soldier   We go again? Where's me brother?

Silhouette Soldier *tosses the baby through the noose. It falls to the ground.*

WAPOs (*off*)   Fell! Fell! Fell! Cant 'ang a baby!

Silhouette Soldier   Where's me brother? Ave t' know. (*Points to the horizon.*) Come all way from there t' 'ere. Tell me! (*Waves the hawser.*) Too big t' bite the little neck!

He drops the hawser. It coils back in its hole. He pulls a rope from the ground. Shows rope to **Village Woman**.

Silhouette Soldier   Look! Not so thick. Better for the task in 'and. Thin! Twang! Twang! 'Ang t' music!

WAPOs (*off. Music-hall chorus*)   Twang! Twang! Twang 'n 'ang!

Silhouette Soldier (*tying a noose in the rope*)   Knot it! This 'll do it! Bite its 'ead off!

Son   Will the rope work? Does she tell 'im now?

WAPO 3   'Ush. 'Ush.

WAPOs (*off*)   'Ang it! Twang it! 'Ang it! Twang it!

Silhouette Soldier *puts baby in the noose.*

Silhouette Soldier   Do it careful. Get the weight. Get the balance. Get the angle.

The baby falls through the noose.

WAPOs (*off*)   Fell! Fell! Fell! Fell!

Silhouette Soldier   Arm ain made a' wood. Aches 'oldin up the rope. Stop it now. Where's me brother?

WAPOs (*off*)   Tell! Tell! Tell! Tell!

Silhouette Soldier (*to* **Village Woman**)   Yer wake the dead. Dont want that. (*Shouts through the window.*) When the dead look at yer yer naked.

WAPOs (*off. Obscene roar*)   Wooooooo!

Silhouette Soldier *drops the rope on the ground. It lies where it falls. He takes a string from his pocket.*

Silhouette Soldier   'Ave t' use me string!

WAPOs (*off*)   String! String! String! String it up!

Silhouette Soldier (*ties noose*)   Tie it neat. Easy slide. The ol' stale sweat make it run. (*He shows the string noose at the window.*) The string'll do it!

WAPOs (*off. Cheer*)   String! String! String! String it up!

Silhouette Soldier (*turns back to* **Village Woman**)   Give me me brother! Baby ain fall out the string. It wriggle – make it tighter. I jerk it – make it worse. Where's me brother?

Silhouette Soldier *puts the baby in the noose. It holds.*

Silhouette Soldier   Baby in the noose!

WAPOs (*off*)   In the noose! In the noose! In the noose!

Son (*calls*)   Give me me brother!

WAPO 3 (*to* **Son**)   Wait. Not yet.

Silhouette Soldier   I cheated. Put me finger in the string. See? Finger 'old it off the windpipe – string cant bite it. Finger feel the pulse: ploppityploppityploppity. Knockin on winder! Knockin on sky t' open it up! Where's me brother?

WAPOs (*off*)   Show! Show! Show! Show!

The **Silhouette Soldier** *holds the baby in the noose out of the window.*

WAPOs (*off, a cheer*)   Finger out! Finger out! Finger out! Get yer finger out!

Silhouette Soldier (*calling to* **WAPO**s)   Me arm aches. A mountain cant bear this pain. Only a 'uman arm can bear it. (*Turns back to the room.*) Listen! – the dead 're movin. Yer woke 'em up!

The dead stir and murmur. The sound of earth moving in waves.

WAPOs (*off. Fear*)   Urgh! Urgh! Urgh! Urgh!

WAPO 3   Listen. It comes now.

Under the murmuring another sound – the sonorous sustained rattling of bones.

The dead are rattlin their bones t' soothe the sufferin baby.

Son   It dont matter . . .

Silhouette Soldier   Where's me brother? I bin through the village! All the 'ouses! Me feet wore the streets bare! All the locks! Turn the keys! The locks bled! Old rust sprung out! Ain touched since the locksmith made 'em! Where's me brother?

Son   I dont want me brother!

Silhouette Soldier   Where yer 'id 'im? Tell me! Tell me! Tell me!

WAPOs (*off*)   'Ang it! 'Ang it! 'Ang it! 'Ang it!

Silhouette Soldier   Me finger's dyin. Got frostbite in the fire!

Son   Dont 'ang it!

Silhouette Soldier   Tell me!

Village Woman (*icy*)   No.

Silhouette Soldier   The 'angin starts!

WAPOs (*off. Mock hanging sounds*)   Eeeek! Oook! Weeek! Ker-reek! Plop!

Silhouette Soldier   They're off!

He takes his finger from between the baby's neck and the string. He sucks his finger and shows the hanging baby in the window.

WAPOs (*off*)   'Igher! 'Igher! 'Igher! 'Ain see! Turn it this way!

Silhouette Soldier *jerks the curtain down.*

WAPOs, *off, cheer.*

Silhouette Soldier
O baby piss 'n cry
Wipe the window
Wash the sky

He wipes the imaginary glass with his elbow. Sweeps his free hand over the sky.

Son   Dont want 'im! Dont want me brother!

Silhouette Soldier (*jerks baby on string*)   Stab! Stab! Stab! Stab!

WAPOs (*off*)   Mob! Mob! Mob! Mob! Mob!

Son (*to* **WAPO 3**)   Make 'im stop! Tell 'im! Ain want me brother!

Silhouette Soldier (*looks round. Holds the hanged baby on the string*)   Dont want – ? 'Oo said dont want? Dont matter?

Son   Dont 'ang the baby!

Silhouette Soldier   'E must want 'is brother. 'E drag it out a' me – the effort t' get 'is brother – drag half me body out a' me! – now 'e dont want 'im! Hhhuh! (*Falls down.*)

Dead (*crying from the ground*)   The baby's dead. The dead weep for their own.

The sound of the dead dies away. **Silhouette Soldier** *twists on the ground, trying to stand.*

Silhouette Soldier (*gasping*)   No wind. Gone.

He stands up with the baby. It is completely black and closer to the human shape – the ball of the head, the stumps of the arms. The longer stumps of the legs burnt together. A charred child from Hiroshima. It dangles on a string from the end of **Silhouette Soldier**'s *weapon. He comes down to* **Son***.*

Silhouette Soldier   I kill 'em in the ground – I was given the order – train t' kill – all them – layers 'n layers – 'n the ones under that – all them was practice – t' be ready t' kill when yer tell me t' get yer brother – 'n yer say it aint matter!

Son   If yer kill one less –

Silhouette Soldier   One less? 'Ow yer find one less in that! (*Points to the mass grave.*) Yer think God count the dead on 'is fingers? Kill one less? Save the kid? Save this! Save that! Save the world! So yer can say it ''aint matter'! Yer want the truth? This thing on the string 'd grow up t' kill yer brother! 'Oo stops it? I stop it so yer can tell me not t' stop it! I'll tell yer the truth! (*Points to the mass grave.*) All them I kill – all the layers – in all the wars – the big ones – the dirty little scraps – since they learnt the art a' throwin stones at each other's 'eads – me breath accuses me a' murder each time it comes out me mouth! – I'm the purpose a' the world! – 'n it aint enough! I ain kill enough! Never enough! Dont matter? That kid dont say dont kill me it ain nice – it say dont kill me I want t' live! Dont save the world save me! I'm more naked than the dead! I destroy the innocent! I suffer each time I kill. That still ain the truth – the truth's worse than that. Yer the truth. (*To the baby.*) Tell 'im! – The truth dont dribble down its chin when it tells it – it drops out its mouth like ash! (*He drops the baby.*) I do yer killin for yer. That's the truth. Yer ain afraid a' killin. Yer want t' kill. Yer afraid a' me. Yer afraid a' me glamour. I dare. I kill. Yer afraid a' the dark glamour in me soul. (*Starts to go. Turns back and points to baby.*) They give me this as a curse. I made it me mascot.

Silhouette Soldier *goes away.* **Village Woman** *stoops to pick up the baby from the floor. It is now white rags.*

Village Woman (*nursing the rags*)   Poor little bundle a' rags. The edge where he rip yer 's frayed 'n ravelled. Never repair it.

Nothin t' 'old the stitches. Poor little bundle. Fold yer – wrap yer round yerself. Keep out the wind. O it's shockin t' see where 'e's tore yer. I couldnt stop 'im. If I give 'im 'is answer it wouldnt stop 'im. 'E'd've asked more. Raged 'n trampled. Always more questions. Never 'n end t' it. Try t' sleep. I couldnt save yer from 'im but I can watch over yer while yer sleep. Poor little bundle. Thass all yer are, pieces a' rag. One day children grow up. Get big 'n strong. Go out in the world. I cant save yer from that. Cant save yer from wars or starving in cities or madmen with guns. There's no end t' it. An' the worst is still t' come. I cant save yer from yerself. Yer tear me 'eart out. Yer poor little bundle a' rags. Shall I tell yer a story? Yer dig the grave a' the world. Thass the story.

Village Woman *nurses the child and goes out up right.*

WAPO 3   I watch the ground crumble. Dont want t' go in there with them. Let me be yer brother.

Son (*water bottle*)   Drink yer water.

WAPO 3 (*drinks. Wipes hand on mouth. Licks finger*)   Emptied it. We'll get more where we go, wont we?

Son   Cant take yer. Yer go down there.

WAPO 3 *tilts the bottle. Sucks out the dregs. Spits them into* **Son**'s *face.* **Son** *goes out right.* **WAPO 3** *stumbles towards the grave.*

Ten

The clearing before the house. Later.

The clearing is barer. The tarpaulin has gone. Part of the wall is repaired. The door is in place.

Treg *watches* **Stewart** *and* **Minty** *pick up the salon chair and put it on a handcart.*

Stewart   Careful. Dont want it damage. (*To* **Treg**.) Sure about this? Dont want any bad feelin.

Treg   She cant keep yer 'anging on no longer.

Stewart   Right then. 'Ad me eye on it for years. – Yer comin up?

Treg   Later.

Stewart   We can wait – in case.

Treg   Nothin'll go wrong. Yer'll be alright.

Stewart   Right then. (*Nods to* **Minty**.) We're off.

Minty *starts to push the handcart out right.*

Minty   Run out a' puff 'arf way up – 'ave a sit in the chair.

Stewart   Yoo watch where yer go.

Minty *and* **Stewart** *go out right.* **Treg** *watches for a moment. Then he calls through the door.*

Treg   'S gone.

He goes to the table. Rearranges the chairs. He sits. **Grace** *comes from the house. She goes slowly left. Glances off. Goes to the bench and sits facing the clearing.*

Treg   They open the kiln this mornin. First time. Come up with me.

Grace   No.

Treg   Take yer mind off things. (*No response.*)

Grace   She's down there all the time now. I followed 'er yesterday. She was standin as still as the trees. Never took 'er eyes off the road. The place where 'e fetched 'er back. Uncanny. I left. I couldnt speak t' 'er.

Treg   'E wont come back. 'S all under water now. Anyone survive the WAPOs get 'em – or the roughs. Take things as they are. Dont spend yer life knockin a dent in a brick wall with yer 'ead. Brick walls always win.

Grace (*pause*)   I worry.

Treg   She's tough. (*He goes and sits with her on the bench.*) Is it the chair? We're better off with the door. 'E left the place in a shambles. Ain blame 'im –

Grace   'E always looks after the important things –

Treg   *Did.* I know thass 'arsh. I say it for yer own good. Whatever 'e got up to down there in the end – it wouldnt a' bin pleasant. God knows what was inside 'is 'ead. I'm no saint, I bin around. But 'e done things that ain 'uman. When I saw 'im with yoo I was shock. I wanted t' warn yer – which'd bin right, look what 'appened! – only she wouldnt 'ave it. I 'ad t' drop 'ints – tell yer not t' trust yer life t' 'im. Then 'e 'opped off 'n left yer in this mess. The lads up there're no better 'n they should be that age. There's no choice, is there? What there is ain appetisin. Yer pretty. Yer are! Young. One 'a them try the ol' hanky-panky – a little community like this, it'd tear itself apart over yoo.

Grace (*shocked*)   O I dont think –

Treg   Thass why I insisted on the door. Show 'em it ain open 'ouse!

Grace *gets up. Goes to the table. Sits.*

Treg   It ain just worry. Yer scared. (*She jerks her head to look at him.*) Yeh I knew I was right. Dont be. (*Strokes the place where she was sitting.*) I tol' yer – I'm 'ere for yer. Yer can turn t' me any 'our a' the day or night. I know there's a differ in the ages. The idiots can laugh! – but I got all sorts a' experience yer can use. From now on I ain takin me eyes off yer.

Woman *comes in from the left. She walks towards the door. Stops – turns to look at* **Grace** *and then at* **Treg**.

Treg   Tellin 'er about the kiln. First bricks out today. Lads're excited. Be a ceremony.

Woman *goes on. Stops again.*

Woman   Chair.

Treg   It was out a' place 'ere. People think we give ourselves airs.

Woman   Why dont yer leave 'er alone?

Treg   Someone's got t' look after 'er. Yer no 'elp.

Woman   It wasnt yer chair t' give away.

Treg   'E ain comin back.

Woman *starts to go towards the house.*

Treg   Yer see! – Yer waste yer time down there – then come back 'n take it out on us. (**Woman** *stops.*) 'S all yer do now: watch. Watch the road. Watch 'er. Watch me. I can 'ear yer watchin! It's like livin with a ghost.

Grace   Dont let's –

Woman   Yer dont want 'im back.

Treg   Be mad if I did! 'E was always trouble. The only decent thing 'e ever did is take 'is-self off. Yer'll never see it that way – but it's a fact. 'E's gone but we still ain rid a' 'im! Why 'ave I 'ad t' spend all me life with people like yoo? Chriss, if I still knew 'ow, I'd cry. (*To* **Grace**.) Sorry yer got t' listen t' this but it 'as t' be said. – (*To* **Woman**.) Is it wrong t' talk t' 'er? Wrong t' talk t' a 'uman bein? – instead a' sharing the silence with a ghost? Is it wrong t' talk t' a woman, for chriss sake? Whass wrong with a bit a' 'appiness? – God knows yer ain easy t' live with. I try. I do me best. If yer did the same we could start again. Forget the rows. Get on like it was. It's what I really want – when it comes down to it. It'd be best for all a' us.

Woman   Yer be late for yer ceremony.

Silence.

Treg   Yeh well – ask for 'elp 'n yer deserve what yer get! Wont make a habit a' it. *E's dead!*

Woman   'E'll come back.

She starts to go towards the house.

Treg   Least I ain complain about crack crockery. (**Woman** *stops*.) I ain goin on like this.

Grace   'Ow does this 'elp?

Treg   D'yer want me t' go? I only stay cause a' 'er. Ain leave 'er with someone 'oo ain notice she exists!

Grace   Please stop –

Treg   Shall I tell yer why I picked yer up? In them days things was so bad yer never knew if yer'd see the next mornin. Thugs. Maniacs. Mobs. I thought good: a woman. When yer in trouble a woman's 'andy. Yer got something t' negotiate with. If me life was threaten, I'd a' 'anded yer over 'n bin off 'n never look back. 'S not the best way t' carry on, is it? – sometimes there ain no choice. Y 'ave t' cope 'n 'ope for the best. Yer did alright out a' it – I kept yer alive. When things got a bit better I still stuck by yer. What gratitude did I get? Always on the move lookin for somethin with me in tow t' carry the luggage. 'Alf the time yer never knew I was there. (*To* **Grace**.) If I went now I dont think she'd notice. (*He goes closer to* **Grace**.) Yer age yer still ain know what yer want out a' life. Yer confused – but yer got time. I know what I want.

Treg *waits a moment to let it sink in. Then goes out right.*

Woman   The air's so clear today. I could've counted the pebbles. The road was empty – that shows 'e'll come. It takes time t' do what 'e went to do. 'E cant come till it's finish. I wait – I 'ear a stranger talkin t' me. It's me own voice tellin me what I'll say when he comes. I sound like a stranger because I'll be different when 'e comes – 'appier than I've ever bin before.

Grace   I'm not sure 'e'll come.

Woman (*smiles*)   There has t' be a day when a mother smacks 'er daughter 'cross the face for the first time. – 'E wouldnt leave yer. If 'e comes back without 'is brother e'll need t' be nursed. 'E's not like us. 'E's not always in this world. Sometimes 'e ought t' be invisible. There's someone else inside 'im. Even when 'e's unhappy 'e's still 'appy – as if bein unhappy gave 'im a terrible 'appiness deep inside 'im. I didnt understand these things till now. I think all the time down there. The two a' yer must live a proper life. Not with a bundle on yer back. Everythin in its right place. – Where did the chair come from? I'm very thoughtless. All the time I've bin 'ere I never asked.

Grace   The woman where my mother worked –

Woman   Is yer mother – ?

Grace   She's dead. The woman gave it to 'er. That was before the 'ouse was burnt down. I used t' sit my dolls on it in a row 'n teach them lessons I made up. I never bin t' school. When we met we brought the chair with us because we –

Woman   Of course I knew why 'e went with me. Yer think 'e'd 'a realised that. Men can be so blind. – Were yer upset when I came 'ere?

Grace   O no! . . . I used t' lie in our bed 'n 'ear yer working. I 'eard the pots, then yer feet. Yer 'ear everythin in the silence up 'ere. I didnt see me mother killed – I 'eard it. When yoo came I didnt 'ear it any more. She was in a room. I 'eard the door bangin. She was tryin t' get out. Fightin against the door. They didnt interfere with 'er. They didnt 'ave the time. She wouldnt tell them what they wanted t' know. Bangin. I was in the roof with me dolls. Afterwards I crep' down 'n looked through the key'ole. Nothin. Then the door moved. She was fallin against it – slowly because 'er dress was caught on the – . She was dead but she open the door for me. I 'eard the bangin for years. It went when I 'eard the sound a' yer feet. – If 'e doesnt come, dont leave me.

Woman   'E will –

Grace   But if –

Woman (*she puts her arms round* **Grace**)   Men need everythin. If we give a little it's enough. Give 'em more they destroy their selves. They die before us – so if yer love 'em yer mourn 'em while they're still alive. Yer understand? (*She touches* **Grace**'s

head.) I wont leave yer. – (*Nods at the house.*) 'E's right about my
son – 'e didnt repair the house, didnt even fit a door . . .

Son *has come in. His skin and clothes are pale with dust. His head is
crudely bandaged. He is exhausted and limps slightly from tiredness
and strain. He has sat down at the table.* **Grace** *sees him – stiffens.*

Son   Is this the place?

Woman *sees him. She rushes to him, pushing a chair aside.*

Woman   Yer 'ere. Yer 'ere. (*She embraces him. Kisses his face.
Kisses his hands.*) I knew. I knew. Yer'd come t' me. Yer 'ere! –
O yer poor – the state a' yer – ! Yer come. Yer come. I tol'
'em! No one believed! Yer come back. – What've yer – ? (*To*
Grace.) 'Is 'ead! – 'is 'ead – it's – !

Grace   Are yer alright? D'yer know where yer are?

Woman   A' course 'e's alright! – it's 'is 'ead – just 'is 'ead!
'Oo bandage the – ? . . . Can yer speak? – 'Oo bandage yer –
(*Steps away from* **Son**. *To* **Grace**.) Look – look – see if someone's
on the road – quick! –

Grace *starts to go left.*

Son (*vaguely puts out a hand to* **Grace**)   . . . Not go.

Grace *hesitates.*

Woman   Look! Look! 'Urry! I cant leave 'im – !

Grace *glances off left – no one. The women look at each other for a
split second.*

Woman   Someone bandage it . . . (*To* **Son**.) Yer must be
alright. O God – if 'e's come back 'n 'is 'ead's damage – 'is
mind . . . I've lost everythin! I said dont go! Tol' yer dont go!

Son   Climbed a long way. (*Bows his head down on the table.*)
Tired.

Woman (*sees the back of his head*)   O God. Look. The blood 's –
dirt in the – . (*To* **Grace**.) Get some water!

Grace (*goes to* **Son**)   D'yer know where yer – ?

Woman   Water! Must wash 'is – !

Grace   Do yer know me?

Woman   Later! Later! Ask 'im later! Get the water! – I must wash it or –

Grace *goes towards the house.* **Son** *vaguely puts out a hand to stop her. She doesn't see this. Goes into the house.*

Woman   Did yer meet 'im? Was 'e – ? (*Ecstatic.*) If I can 'ave two sons! – (*Shock.*) O God did yer fight? (*Goes left. Looks off. Turns back. Calls to* **Grace**.) 'Urry! (*Goes to* **Son**.) Yer alright now. Yer safe with me. – 'Ow did yer 'ead get – ?

Son *has lowered his head to the table again.* **Grace** *comes from the house with a bowl of water. She puts the bowl on the table. Starts to undo the bandage.*

Woman (*afraid to touch the wound*)   Careful . . . careful – dont make it –

Grace *undoes the bandage. Puts it on the table. Dips the cloth in the water. Squeezes it. Presses it to his head.*

Son (*vaguely*)   No –

Grace *hesitates a moment.*

Woman   Go on, go on – yer must wash the dirt –

Grace *dips the cloth in the water. Squeezes it. Wipes the wound.*

Son   No. (*Weakly pushes her away. She persists. He stands. Wanders from the table.*) No – dont want –

Woman (*to* **Grace**)   Yer must wash it – or it'll get worse –

Grace (*goes to* **Son**)   It 'as t' be –

Woman (*angry, tearful*)   My fault! I got upset! – upset 'im! Stupid –

Son *wanders a little, vaguely gestures as if pushing people away.*

Son   No –

Grace (*goes to him with the wet cloth. Tries to bend his head. Dabs with the cloth*)   Let me.

Son (*vaguely pushing*)   No – no –

Woman (*to* **Grace**)   Go inside.

Grace   I cant leave 'im –

Woman   In the house. (**Grace** *stops.*) – Leave us alone. 'E needs attention.

Grace *hesitates. She puts the cloth into* **Woman**'*s hand. She goes into the house.* **Woman** *puts the cloth in the bowl.*

Woman   Where've yer bin? (**Son** *turns in her direction.*) The sulks wont 'elp. Come 'n sit down. Yer cant stand there for ever. I was so worried. Let me look at yer properly. (**Son** *goes to her.*) All that time. Yer not a kid anymore. Old enough t' know better. (*She draws him down on to her lap. He leans sideways against her.*) Good boy. I shall 'ave t' look at that cut. (*He begins to strain away.*) Later. When yer ready. (*He settles.*) Where was yer?

Son   Dont know.

Woman   'Oo 'it yer 'ead?

Son   Dont know.

Woman   Tell me. I'll make it better then.

Son   Dont know. Bin tired a long time. Tired all me life. Sometime I cant see. Me sight goes.

Woman (*fear returning*)   If yer ruin yer 'ead – lost yer sight –

Son   No. Not blind. It goes for a while. Comes back. Per'aps I fell. 'Avent eaten for a long time.

Woman   Sleep. Yer'll wake up better. Yer 'ome at last. I never 'oped t' see yer again. It's painful t' 'ope. I lived with it for years. Almost died a' it. When I met yer again I didnt 'ave t' 'ope. I *knew* one day I'd 'old yer in me lap. Yer asleep now, as good as. (*Reaches for the bowl. Draws it closer. Picks up the cloth. Dabs at his head.*) There. (*Dabbing.*) Wash the dirt away.

Son   Dont touch the scar.

Woman   No wont touch the scar.

Son   Dont touch the scar.

Woman   Where the blood run –

Son   Dont touch the scar.

Woman   No just wash the blood where –

Son *stands. Walks away.*

Son   Yer touch the scar.

Woman   No – I –

Son   Yer did! Liar! (*Touches scar.*) Wet! I tol' yer dont touch the scar 'n yer did!

Woman   The water must've run in the –

Son   Liar! Liar! I said no – 'n yer did it!

Woman   I only wanted t' stop the –

Son   Liar!

Woman   It doesnt matter! Let me dry it –

Son   Keep off!

Woman   No no, please –

Son   Keep away!

Woman   Yer not upset – I didnt mean t' – ! (*Throws him the towel. Pleads.*) Yer dry it! Please!

Grace *comes from the house.*

Grace   What's the matter?

Son (*buries his head in the towel*)   O God I told yer – dont touch the – I said –

Woman (*to* **Grace**)   Go inside! 'E's not upset! It's all normal 'ere! Go away!

Grace (*to* **Son**)   What is it!

Woman   Dont meddle! Yer upset 'im!

Son   She dont do what I – all along she knew she – knew she'd touch me –

Grace   Yer touch 'is scar?

Woman   I've a right t' touch 'is scar! Go away! – yer no use 'ere – yer was spyin on us from the 'ouse!

Son (*throws towel off*)   Cant see. Cant see. (*Looks round.*) O God it's gone again. I cant see.

Woman (*to* **Grace**)   I tol' yer! – look what yer done! – yer make 'im worse – ! Go away! Go away!

Son   Cant see. (*Gropes towards the table. Knocks a chair over.*) Is this the place? I went t' find me brother. Not there. (*Bumps into* **Grace**.) Are yer me brother? (*Touches her. Turns away. Calls feebly.*) Are yer here? – I wanted 'im so bad. I couldnt find 'im. I failed. I'm blind. Never find 'im, never see 'im now.

Silence

Woman   There's no brother. I said there was so yer'd think I 'ad a reason for leavin yer. (*Flat.*) I just left. – I'd lie t' 'elp yer. Tell yer I ain yer mother. But what I said's the truth. There's no brother.

Son   Will me sight come back? The blindness is different this time. Darker. Not like before. Am I blind now – all me life?

Grace   Let me wash it.

Son   Wash it? – yer cant wash sight back in t' eyes that've see what I've seen –

Woman (*to* **Grace**)   Go away! Yer confuse 'im!

Grace (*ignores* **Woman**)   Wash yer 'ead.

Son (*confused*) Why yer worry about little – stupid little – t' be blind? – there's worse things 'n that –

Grace I dont know what t' do. (*To* **Son**.) – 'Elp me. Let me do something.

Woman *walks away.*

Woman Appeal t' 'is better nature? – Yer got a lot t' learn about men. (*To* **Son**.) Tantrums ain 'elp. D'yer wan' t' be blind? – 'Oo that spite?

Son *gropes to the table. He finds the bowl. Holds it out to* **Woman**.

Son Is the water red where yer wash me blood out? (*No answer. He throws the water at* **Woman**.) Now it's in yer face.

Woman Yes yes. 'N when yer cripple yer'll expect me t' nurse yer. Why are yer always violent? – Because I 'ad t' leave yer once? Werent at yer beck 'n call? Did I 'urt yer so much? I'm sorry. Does it make yer feel better t' 'ate me? Yer cant 'ate me. If yer could yer'd 'ave a chance t' be at peace. (*To* **Grace**.) The towel. (**Grace** *tries to dry her. She snatches the towel away. Dabs at herself.*) I thought yer'd come back with yer brother. At least teach 'im t' be grateful. Yes yer got a brother. Another wound I 'ave t' bear! Yer couldnt even do that. Do I have t' teach yer 'ow t' find someone? – I found yoo *twice*!

Son 'Ow'd I find a brother without a name?

Woman 'E didnt need one! We were so close!

Son Then why'd 'e leave yer? (*Split silence.*) Least I got a brother again! I congratulate 'im if 'e ain bin born! Ain 'ave t' suck 'is life out a' 'er tits! (*To* **Woman**.) Go up the store 'n ask if they got brothers! If it was yer store it'd be a morgue! O God if I cant see! – one thin' bein blind I never 'ave t' see 'er lyin face again!

Woman Nothing 'll 'elp yer. Lies or the truth. I did one thing – years ago – 'n I 'ave t' answer for it ever since. No I ain be blamed for what I couldnt 'elp –

Son   Listen t' er! She's boastin 'ow good she is!

Woman   I'm tired a' feelin sorry for yer – an' for 'im! Yer as bad as 'e is! I'm glad yer never found 'im! (**Son** *yelps in pain.*) All yer could teach 'im is 'ow t' waste 'is life 'n other people's. Yer sorry yer didnt kill me when yer 'ad the chance!

Son (*reels away*)   My brother's 'ere. I know 'im. 'Ere. Feel 'im in my – 'e ain let go a' my – ain let me – look – e's there! – 'im! – (*Pulls his sleeve back to bare his arm.*) Look – look – 'is arm – come out a' my – (*Points with one hand at the other arm.*) Look – 'im – 'im – (*Tries with one hand to pull the arm back.*) Wont – wont give – pull – pull – pull – t' – (*The stiff arm punches the air towards* **Woman** – *piston.*) Punch! – punch! – punch! – yelp! – yelp! – yelp! – yelp! –

Woman *stays rigid. Bolt upright in her chair. Doesnt try to get away.*

Woman   Dont! Dont! Dont do that!

Son (*flings the other arm wide in a gesture of amazement to show the punching arm*)   Look – aoh! – aoh! – aoh! (*To* **Woman**.) My brother's anger! (*Stops. Shaking.*) I did it for 'im! . . . feel me veins . . . trembling like wires . . .

Woman (*stands and goes to the door*)   Other women've stood over their dead kids 'n rocked the cradle. They wished they'd been born barren. Only men are barren. Only a man can die in another man's body.

She goes into the house. **Grace** *starts to follow her. Stops. Turns to* **Son**.

Son   Did yer see? Me arm . . . I was a puppet . . .

He makes ineffectual half-movements with his arm and looks overhead as if for a puppeteer. **Grace** *picks the bowl up from the floor. She is holding it as* **Woman** *comes from the house with a bowl of water.*

Woman   Wash it –

Grace   'E'll say 'e's sorry when 'e –

Woman   – before 'e 'arms 'is-self any more.

Grace *puts her bowl on the table. Takes the bowl from* **Woman**. **Woman** *goes into the house.*

Son   Is she there?

Grace   Gone inside. I 'ave t' wash the cut. I'll do it when yer quieter –

Son   Do it now.

Grace *goes to him. Takes his hand. Leads him to the table.*

Grace   Chair. (**Son** *sits in the chair. She washes the wound.*) Not deep. Dirt made it look worse. It couldnt damage yer sight.

Son   Before it was grey. Shadows movin in it. When she touched me it went black. Perhaps it's not me eyes – something in me mind. ''Oo broke the cup.' 'Open 'n shut the door.' Why do I say those stupid things? Accusin? Blamin? Why'm I angry? Why'm I blind? Why does my body make a fool a' me? Punch-punch-punch . . . O God the terrible things I've seen in my life. (*Touches her.*) I scare yer.

Grace   Not now. (*Washing.*) Can yer see?

Son *moves his hand in front of his eyes. Says nothing.* **Woman** *comes from the house. She wears a long black coat. She doesn't look at the others. Goes right.*

Grace   Where yer goin?

Woman (*stops as if she is going to turn round but doesn't*)   Walk.

Grace (*cut*)   Not as deep as we thought.

Woman *goes out right.*

Grace (*calls*)   Dont be long. (*To* **Son**.) I dont know what we'll do. She cant live without yer. – When yer was shoutin just now I sat inside 'n waited. I thought I'll go out when it's over. I could've waited for yer all the time yer was away. The 'ouse seemed full a' light – 'n yer was in the dark. Where did yer go?

Son   Dont know. I went on all fours for a long time. I 'eard voices across the water. I came t' a place – the people were

skeletons with skin – their faces were bones but they moved –
their expressions changed. They wrote something down. I dont
know where. I dont know what it was. It doesnt matter. It'll
never go away. – Take me t' the bench.

Grace *takes* **Son** *to the bench.*

Son   Is this – ?

Grace   Yes.

Son *sits facing away.* **Treg** *comes in from the right. He carries a
parcel wrapped in a small blanket.*

Treg   Knew yer was back – 'eard the shoutin. (*To* **Grace**.)
If 'e's stayin e'll make yer life a torment. (*Blanket.*) Brought yer
a present. – Yer trouble son, yer think too much about right
'n wrong t' do any good. The lads up there ain know 'alf a' it –
at least they try. They just need someone in charge. I saw 'em
chippin away in the rubble. I said bricks. They said no kiln.
I said build one. They said no bricks. I said use a' ole in the
ground. They said no clay. I said look. We looked 'n found it.
(*He unwraps the parcel – a brick.*) The first firin. Feel it. (*He gives*
Grace *the brick.*) Wrapped it in the blanket t' keep it warm.
Yer can use it as a door stop. (*To* **Son**.) Respect things – work
'ard – 'n yer luck'll change. When yer 'elp yerself, yer 'elp
everyone. That way yer get a decent life even in this rat 'ole of
a world . (*He waits for an answer.*) That brick makes more sense
'n all yer rantin 'n ravin. I'll tell yer the truth. The WAPOs
'ad a padre. 'E tol' us mankind's redeem by someone 'oo did
our sufferin for us. Then we went out 'n made some more
poor buggers suffer. Yer want it said big? – Mankind's redeem
by a brick. – I pass yer mother on the road. She's gone.

Grace   Gone? – But she'll come back.

Treg   No.

Grace   She must – ! Did she say she –

Treg   We never spoke. No need. I could tell.

Grace (*to* **Son**)   We must stop 'er –

Treg   Yer wont change 'er mind.

Grace (*starting to go right. Stops*)   She didnt take 'er things!

Treg   Wouldnt take anything from 'ere. Yer the past.

Son *bends forward on the bench.* **Grace** *hurries back to him.*

Treg   Whass the matter with 'im?

Grace   'E cant see.

Treg   Ah! – the latest. – I'm movin out anyway. Ain stay where 'e is. Take me things.

He goes into the house.

Grace (*hesitating between going to* **Woman** *and helping* **Son**)   . . . Shall I fetch 'er back?

Son   She wont come. She knows when t' go. She always did.

Grace   It's dangerous there – the edge. I'll take yer t' –

Son *straightens up.*

Son   Let me sit. Me sight'll come back.

Treg *comes from the house. He carries his backpack by the straps. The top hangs loose.*

Treg   She packed for me.

Grace   What'll 'appen t' 'er?

Treg   She'll end up with a piece a' clapboard 'n a sack – if thass what she wants.

He starts to go right. **Son** *straightens up.*

Son   Tell 'im 'e's wrong. (**Treg** *stops.*) I 'ave 'n ache carved in me body. I want t' be 'uman. Thass why I fight. Meself 'n everyone else. If I didnt there'd never be peace anywhere.

He stands. Turns to face the table. Goes towards it. **Grace** *comes towards him. He reaches the fallen chair. She stops and watches.*

He picks up the chair and stands it upright. **Treg** *goes out right. The brick is on the bench.*

Eleven

A space. It is empty except for a wooden kitchen chair in the middle.

Woman *comes on left. She wears the long black coat. She sees the chair but shows no interest in it.*

Woman   I passed a little 'eap a' bones in the road. They'd bin chewed. I didnt look at the sky. I looked down so I didnt dash me shoe against them.

She takes off her coat. Under it she wears a dress something like a shift. She drapes her coat over the front of the chair so that it hangs to the ground and covers the chair. The arms hang down the back. She takes matches from a pocket of the coat. She strikes a match and sets light to the coat. She begins with the tail flaps. She strikes more matches and lights the upper parts – the waist, chest and shoulders. The coat smoulders. Little flames spurt and consume the cloth. She walks away and watches it burn.

I 'eard children a'ead on the road. I come round the corner. It was a stream fallin down the rocks. They'll 'ave children. I'll never 'ear 'em or see 'em. The children'll 'ave children. 'N the children children. I'll never 'ear 'em. Never see 'em. Never know 'em. None a' us will. They'll feel the pain I feel now. I must be 'appy so they feel that too.

She goes to the coat. She lights more matches. She sets fire to the rest of it. The fire spreads. She watches and tends it till the whole coat burns. She turns and walks away. She doesn't look at the coat.

One day me bones'll lie in a little 'eap in the road. They were chewed in me body while I was still alive.

She goes out. The coat seethes. Lumps of cloth fall and splutter on the ground. Little flames creep and here and there flare up. Smoke rises and drifts and jumps in sudden little spurts and then drifts away. The coat shrinks. Burnt cloth clings to the charred frame.

The coat smoulders for a long time.

The Balancing Act

The Balancing Act was first staged by Big Brum at Holte School, Birmingham, on 13 October 2003. The cast was as follows:

Viv	Katie Baxter
Nelson	Richard Holmes
Foreman	Bobby Colvill
DSS Officer	Joanne Underwood
One-legged Thief	Bobby Colvill
Foreman's Wife	Katie Baxter

Directed by Chris Cooper
Designed by Ceri Townsend
Stage Manager Ian Lewis

Scene Five was added by the author after the first production. The role of Old Woman was played by Joanne Underwood in the play when it was re-toured by Big Brum in 2006.

Characters

Viv
Nelson
Foreman
DSS Officer
One-legged Thief
Old Woman
Foreman's Wife

Setting

City
Now

Room in derelict house
Room in derelict house
DSS office
Street
Street
Room in Foreman's house

One

A bare room on the first floor of an abandoned house. A door on the right of the rear wall. No window. The room is empty except for **Viv** *and a crumpled blanket. She sits with her back to the wall. The blanket is beside her. She is still. She stares expressionlessly at a spot on the floor across the room. After a while she stretches her arm straight out in front of her and makes a practical calming gesture with her hand. She lowers her arm. Silence. A knock on the door. She does not react.*

Nelson (*off*)   It's me. (*Pause. He taps on the door.*) You asleep?

Viv *gets up. Staying close to the wall she creeps carefully to the door. Her eyes are still on the spot on the floor. She reaches the door. The key is in the lock. She unlocks the door.* **Nelson** *comes in. He carries a full plastic shopping bag.* **Viv** *closes the door behind him and relocks it.*

Nelson   You alright?

Nelson *comes further into the room.* **Viv** *gestures him to the blanket. He stares at* **Viv** *but does not move. Suddenly he holds out the carrier.*

Nelson   'Ungry?

Viv (*blanket*)   There.

Nelson *goes to the blanket. He unpacks food from the carrier. Crisps, rolls, cheese, salad, milk, soft drinks – all food that can be consumed without cooking. Whenever* **Nelson** *is looking at* **Viv** *she does not look at the spot. When he looks away from her she stares or glances at it.*

Nelson   Got yer crisps. Not yer favourites. They was out. (*Pause.*) Get stuck in. Dont try t' tell me yer ain 'ungry.

Viv   In a minute. (*Pause. Offers.*) You eat.

Nelson   'Ad a meal indoors. (*Pause.*) Was yer asleep?

Viv   No.

Nelson   What yer bin doin?

Viv   I'm alright.

Nelson   'Ow long's this goin on? (*No answer.*) 'Ow long yer keep it up?

Viv   I never arst yer t' fetch for me. I'll manage.

Nelson   Yer wont. (*Pause.*) What's it for? What's the point?

Viv   Yer spent a lot.

Nelson *opens a can. Gives it to her. She drinks. He sits.*

Nelson   Want a radio?

Viv (*chokes on the drink*)   No no.

Nelson   Yer 'ad a row at 'ome? Yer mum says yer always rowin.

Viv   Yer bin t' – ! I told yer not to!

Nelson   'S alright. I ain said. I just ask if she knew where yer was. For all she know yer could've bin done in.

Viv   Fat lot she'd care.

Nelson   She look at me as if *I'd* done yer in: actin the innocent, come round askin t' put up a blind. She go t' the police they'll search local – come 'ere. (*Watches* **Viv** *drink.*) Is it someone else?

Viv   No.

Nelson   Yer bin threatened?

Viv   No.

Nelson   If yer bin threatened yer should go t' the police. They'll sort it out.

Viv   They wouldnt understand.

Nelson   Yer bin up t' somethin yer shouldnt?

Viv   No.

Nelson   Then why yer 'ere?

Viv   Cant tell yer.

Nelson   Why not?

Viv   Yer wouldnt understand.

Nelson   I dont 'ave t' understand. I just need t' know. (*Ironic.*) 'No one understand me' – that it?

Viv   Not answerin no more questions.

Silence.

Nelson   I'll go t' the police.

Viv (*half-confident*)   Yer wont.

Nelson   Anythin 'appens the police'll know I bin 'ere. I'm involved. I got a right t' know what I'm mix up in.

Viv   I never ask yer t' get involved.

Nelson   Course I'm involved! Derelict block a' flats. On yer tod every night – I 'ave t' leave yer 'cause a' me job. Any weirdo could burst in. Beat yer up. I'm just suppose t' get on with me life? I'm scared. I dont know what's 'appenin t' yer.

Silence.

Viv   Yer wouldnt understand.

Nelson   If yer say that again . . .!

Viv   I dont understand meself!

Nelson   Yer ill – ?

Viv   No no no! – Yer see! I tol' yer yer wouldnt understand! It's none a' that! Threaten – rows at 'ome – in trouble – if that's all it was I could tell yer!

Nelson   The more yer say the more I dont know where I am! Tell me everythin. Yer got to now.

Viv   Yer wouldnt understand!

Nelson   Yer say that once more – ! (*Controls himself.*) Eat.

He sorts out food. Behind his back **Viv** *stretches out her arm to the spot and makes the calming gesture.* **Nelson** *sees this.*

Nelson   What's that for? (*No answer.*) What's it suppose t' mean?

Silence.

Viv   Why they left the key in the door?

Nelson   Who?

Viv   The people when they left.

Nelson   They left it 'cause they aint need it. The flats're empty. They're goin t' be pull down.

Viv   Said yer wouldnt understand.

Nelson *puts his head in his hands. She makes up her mind. She points at the spot.*

Viv   It's there.

Nelson (*looks*)   Dont see anythin.

Viv   That's the point.

Nelson *stands to look at the spot.*

Viv (*panics. Flattens herself against the wall*)   No no dont dont! Go away! (*She makes gestures frantically at the spot.*) It's terrible – 'n yer cant see the danger! 'Ow can I 'elp yer? Go away!

Nelson   Shut up! Listen! Yer got t' tell me everythin! I cant leave yer in this state!

He grabs her arm. Holds her still. She breaks away. Flattens herself against the wall.

Viv   No no! Yer make it worse! No one can 'elp me now!

Nelson   Stop it!

He shakes her. Her teeth rattle.

Tell me! Let me 'elp yer!

Viv (*crying. Throwing the food to the door*)   Take yer muck! Dont need it! Ain' eat! No point! (*To herself.*) Why did I say? 'E went on 'n on! (*Calms herself.*) 'S alright. (*To* **Nelson**.) I came 'ere t' get away from – came for a bit a' quiet peace. Now yer come pesterin. I know yer dont mean it. Go 'ome. I'll come back soon. I was bein silly.

Nelson   Why yer do that with yer 'and?

Viv   T' quieten the – if anythin disturbs the air – I 'ave t' stop the shock waves.

Nelson   Viv.

Viv   If I could make yer understand. We could take it in turns t' watch. I could go out. Walk in the street. Change me clothes. I know it's silly t' still want all that. If I could share it with someone.

Nelson   I'll share it.

Viv   Whatever it is?

Nelson   Yeh.

Viv   Yer mustnt tell no one.

Nelson   Start at the beginnin.

Viv   Cant remember that far back. Lived with it for years. Always bin in the back a' me mind. I pretended it wasnt. In the end I couldnt look at anythin without thinkin of it. Every time I met someone I look in their face t' see if they know. No one did. Yer said I got nice eyes. No I just stare. When I found the key in the empty 'ouse I was relieved. I knew it'd come at last.

Nelson (*reassuring*)   Yeh? –

Viv   The world's unbalanced. All the changes. Everythin's too fast. Buildin's too tall. Too much traffic. Accidents. Crowds too big. Messages flyin through the air. It's never quiet. Even at night. Wars. Bombs. Rockets. It's all unbalanced.

Nelson   An' that spot?

Viv   I 'ave dreams t' explain it. A huge ship's on the flat sea stretches for ever. The ship goes through the water 'n crunches it like bones. The passengers dont 'ear it. They're dancin t' the orchestra. High up in the sky there's a grain of sand. It falls on the ship. The ship sinks. Straight off. Goes straight t' the bottom. The people go on movin – the water pushes them. They think they're still dancin. They dont know they're dead.

Nelson   So the spot?

Viv   Keeps the world in balance. If it was trod on the balance'd go. The world'd spin. Fast. Everythin spin off in t' space. People'd be pull out a' their 'ouses. Then they'd be pull apart. They'd go tearin through the air tryin t' catch their own 'ands. They wouldnt scream – their tongues'd be pull out. The sound comes from the wind. (*She spills the packet of crisps on the floor.*) They'd go like that. Dead 'n silent like the crisps.

Nelson   That spot keeps the – ?

Viv   It could even be under the floor.

Nelson   'N if I tread on it – ?

Viv   Even a grain a' sand could do it.

Silence.

Nelson   Everythin moves – people – cars – trains – planes – accidents – wars: yeh. So the balance changes all the time.

Viv   Chaos.

Nelson (*points*)   So why –

Viv   The spot 'ad t' be somewhere. In the past the whole world was balanced. Now it's just that spot.

Nelson (*patient*)   No – I asked yer why the –

Viv   Suppose yer 'angin from a cliff – twistin 'n turnin. There's one spot that's still: the spot under yer 'ands where yer 'old on t' the cliff. That's the spot that keeps yer up there. I 'ad a fright after I found the key. I didnt know which bit was the spot. I crawled round the whole floor – like a minefield. In the end that was the only spot left – so that was it. The people 'oo lived 'ere didnt know. Must've bin under a cupboard. Now people walk by outside 'n dont know.

Nelson   These 'ouses 're goin t' be pull down –

Viv (*stares at him darkly*)   Yer dont know that. P'raps I ain the only one t' know the truth. What if the planners know? That's why they empty the 'ouses. They ain pull em down.

Nelson   If they know why dont they say?

Viv   No one'd believe 'em. No one'd believe me 'cept you. Me mum'd 'ave me certified. Drugged stupid all me life. The only way it could be proved a' be t' tread on it – then it'd be too late. It all fits. That's why I'm a prisoner in this room.

Nelson   What yer do *if* they pull the 'ouses down?

Viv   Lie on it – 'old it against me 's if it was a kid inside me. Be like coverin the whole world. What else could I do? I'd 'ave t' stop the sufferin. Yer dont know what it'd be like. I've known for years. I bin alone all me life.

Nelson *walks up and down against the wall. He stops. Looks at* **Viv**.

Nelson   Yer're potty. (*Pause.*) Stark starin potty. Bonkers. Off yer trolly. Round the twist.

Viv (*to herself*)   What've I done . . .?

Nelson   Ain goin t' tread on the spot. *Jump* on it. Kick the floorboards in. (*Counts.*) One.

Viv   Yer mustnt! The 'ole world'll suffer! All a' it! All the pain come t'gether at once – like a flash! – it couldnt last any longer – it'd be too much.

Nelson   Two.

Viv *runs to the blanket. Hides under it. Struggles violently as if she's fighting with animals. Gasps. Howls.*

Nelson   Three. I'll count t' six.

Viv (*looks from under the blanket*)   Monster! Cruel! Old people – children – sufferin! Cruel! Cruel!!

Nelson   Four.

Viv (*stands – throws open the blanket*)   Come t' me! Quick! Come! Come! Children! Children! (*Holds the blanket out.*) I'll 'old yer in the blanket! Shelter yer! Come t' me! Come t' me! (*Cradles the blanket.*) All a' yer! All a' yer!

Nelson   Five.

Viv (*suddenly calm, sits*)   If it 'as t' end, let it. If it dont, I got the wrong spot – 's all. P'raps it'll be in the mad'ouse where they send me. I'll find it. Wont let 'em destroy the world. 'Ave yer said six yet? I didnt 'ear. So clever. So easy. Yer like the people dancin on the ship. Passin in the street. Yer dont know where yer are. What yer're doin. (*Puts the blanket aside. Half gestures to wall.*) I sit 'ere in chains. Yer dont see 'em. If they was metal yer could take 'em off. They're stronger than that. Stronger than you. They're the truth. In me 'ead. I carry me chains for other people. All their sufferin's waitin in this room. I give 'em a little more time before they 'ave t' bear it. Did yer say six? All you do is prove yer can count.

Nelson *gathers the food and puts it in the carrier. He picks up the scattered crisps and puts them back into the packet.* **Viv** *watches expressionlessly. He carefully puts the bag of crisps on the spot.* **Viv**'s *hands shoot out in the calming gesture.*

Nelson   Yer get away with this lark 'cause I feed yer. Ain no more. Somethin 'as t' knock sense in t' yer. (*Crisps.*) If yer want t' eat yer'll 'ave t' take it from there. (*He goes to the door and stops.*) Ain comin no more Viv. Yer'll 'ave t' come t' me.

He goes out. He bangs the door. **Viv** *stands, draped in the blanket. Leans forward, holding out both hands to the spot. Then she shrinks back – sidles along the wall to the door. She is completely exhausted. She reaches the door. Locks it. Starts to sidle back along the wall. Strokes the blanket as if it were her chains.*

Viv   Chains.

She reaches her place. Sits. Drags the blanket round her. Her head is free. She doesn't look at the spot but sideways along the wall away from the door, as if she could see to the world outside.

Viv   . . . clank . . .

Two

The room. The crisp packet is where it was. **Viv** *is alone. She sits huddled under the blanket. She has made a hole in it. Her eye stares through the hole at the spot. She moves her head. The blanket swivels like a periscope to survey the room. Then it swivels back to focus on the spot.*

Silence.

Nelson (*off – he doesn't knock*)   Viv. (*No response.*) Viv open the door. I know yer're there. They're knockin the street down Viv.

Silence. **Nelson** *rattles the door.* **Viv***'s arm comes through another hole she has made in the blanket. She makes the calming gesture towards the spot.*

Nelson   I brought yer some crisps. Ain yer favourites. Sorry – they're out again. 'S three days. 'Ow yer think I feel knowin yer starvin? Open the door Viv.

Viv *uncovers her head. She stands slowly, still holding the blanket round her. She is terrified her movements will set off vibrations. She edges along the wall with her back to it. She makes for the door but stares at the spot – forcing her eyes to stop blinking. Her blanket catches on a nail. She freezes in panic. She tugs at the blanket as carefully as a bomb-disposal expert removing a fuse.*

Nelson (*off*)   I'm off. No point in stayin if yer aint co-operate. (*Further off.*) The workmen'll drag yer out.

Viv *tugs at the blanket. It comes loose with a jerk. She collapses in terror against the wall. She stares at the spot. She slowly recovers. She edges closer to the door.*

Nelson (*very close*)   Viv. Dont take my word for it. The foreman'll tell yer. I asked 'im t' come up. They got a great iron ball on a chain. Weighs tons. Swing it t' knock the wall down. Give yer a 'eadache Viv.

Viv *reaches the door. Silently she takes the key from the lock.*

Nelson   Yer need proper 'elp Viv. We'll see a doctor. If yer're right but they dont believe yer – so what? Believe what yer like so long's it makes yer 'appy eh?

Viv *takes off the blanket. She folds it neatly and carefully places it on the floor.*

Nelson   Viv this is the foreman.

Foreman (*off, to* **Nelson**)   She in there? 'Ello young lady. Can you 'elp me dear? Dont know whether this lad's havin me on. Is 'e your boyfriend? If you've had a fallin-out there's no reason to be'ave like the princess in the tower. I can see he's contrite up to 'is eyeballs.

Nelson   Tell 'er yer're demolishin the place.

Foreman   Dont be impatient. Ladies 'ave to be handled with finesse.

As **Nelson** *and the* **Foreman** *talk* **Viv** *carefully lifts up some floorboards – she has already loosened them. She climbs into the gap out of sight and pulls the floorboards back into place over her head.*

Nelson   It's an emergency!

Foreman   All the more reason to stay calm. Women are obstinate. (*Calls.*) We're demolishin the street dear. Everythin's comin down. They'll put up some really nice residential properties instead. Sort of place that 'as window boxes. Now open this door and stop interruptin the march of progress. If

you keep the lads waitin they'll want overtime. The company
sues when there's obstruction. When you see their bill you'll
think it's the end of the world. (*To* **Nelson**.) You picked a
handful with this one. My lady wife argues for hours over how
many crisps there are in a packet and she always gets it wrong.

Nelson   For Chris' sake Viv!

Foreman   One of my dogs was called Viv. At the end she
wouldnt eat. You could study arithmetic on her ribs.

Nelson   Viv!

Foreman   Right – lets be 'avin yer.

A crash as the **Foreman** *shoulders the door. It sags into the room.*
The **Foreman** *steps in.* **Nelson** *follows.*

Foreman (*looks round, treads on the loose floorboards*)   Some of
these places've bin fallin down since the day they were put up.
She's give you the slip young man. If you ask me she needs her
bottom spanked.

The **Foreman** *goes out.* **Nelson** *stares at the crisp packet. Then at*
the folded blanket. Then at the crisp packet again. He walks towards
it. Hesitates. Gingerly picks it up. Goes to the blanket. Picks it up.
Presses it against his chest. Goes towards the door. Suddenly turns,
dashes to the spot. Jumps on it and dashes out.

Nelson (*yells as he goes*)   'Elp!

Three

DSS office. Two chairs. A woman **DSS Officer** *and* **Nelson**.
Officer *has two bulky files.* **Nelson** *has the blanket and crisp*
packet. He is frozen in immobility.

DSS Officer (*studying a file*)   Sit down.

Nelson *sits.*

DSS Officer   I'm sorry to have kept you waiting. I almost cancelled your appointment. We are busy. The feckless and inadequate are particularly numerous today. The fine weather must have got them out of bed. I expect you amused yourself. There are comics in the reception area. I presume from your blanket and self-pitying expression that you are a street dosser. The counter staff have issued you with a voucher for a drink and a healthy sandwich. We do not provide crisps.

Nelson *hides the crisps under the blanket.*

DSS Officer   They have also issued you with a form for travelling expenses. It is designed for easy comprehension. Should you have difficulty in comprehending it the counter staff will assist. I advise you not to apply to the West Indian lady with the earrings. (*Looks up at* **Nelson**. *Smiles.*) Well what have we been up to?

Silence. **DSS Officer** *looks at her watch.*

DSS Officer   Our conversation is confidential and unrecorded.

She takes out a pen. Silence.

The young lady had been visiting the derelict house for six weeks before its demolition. We know this from squatters in illegal occupation of the building opposite. Anti-social elements but on this occasion I am minded to believe them – no doubt the malice one finds in these rundown estates inspired them to tell the truth for once. The young lady completely immured herself in the room for the final week. During that week you visited her – how many times would that be?

Silence.

Four. Your visits to the neighbourhood supermarket were recorded on CCTV. Matching receipts with your times of visits we know that – for instance on the last occasion – (*She reads from the file.*) you purchased goods to the value of eight pounds ninety-nine pence. Crisps and other life-threatening consumables. You were feeding the girl. The conclusion is not so much elementary as unavoidable (you will notice the literary reference to Sherlock Holmes). Why?

Silence.

A young girl is dead. She enjoyed good health. She did not take drugs. A few debts but nothing serious. A supportive mother particularly devoted to her daughter's welfare. Tell me why such a girl with everything to live for –

Her mobile rings. She answers it.

(*To mobile.*) No you're not interrupting me. I'm having a one-sided conversation with a monk who has taken a vow of silence. (*Listens briefly.*) No – no – no – no – no. (*She switches off the mobile.*) Nelson – may I address you familiarly? – I am here to –

Her mobile rings. She answers it.

(*Immediately, to mobile.*) No – no – no – no – no.

She switches off her mobile.

Over the gateway of hell is written: 'All hope abandon you who enter here.' The literary reference is to Dante. He might have been quoting from the entrance to his local DSS office. If you knew the misery that enters this building each day you would not sit here clutching your blanket. Broken marriages. Beaten wives. Abused children. Damaged teenagers. Delinquent vandals. Deranged pensioners. Silly women in debt for frivolities they dont even unpack. A fair proportion of the world's misery passes before me. But this – (*Taps file.*) is different. A novelty has turned up in my workload. I should like to understand.

Silence. The mobile rings. **DSS Officer** *ignores it. It rings on.*

DSS Officer (*explains*)   A client. She rings up twenty times a day to threaten to commit suicide. Promises, promises. It's the only way she can get anyone to listen to her. (*Answers the mobile. Immediately.*) Leave a note dear. It'll be cheaper than the phone bill. (*Immediately switches off the mobile.*) What was it you were not saying when we were interrupted?

Silence.

It's that West Indian woman on the reception counter isnt it? The one with the noisy earrings. What did she say about me? You heard her earrings? She wears them to annoy me. I can bear people with music in their fingertips but not in their ear lobes. If the earrings get any bigger they'll catch in a door handle and her head'll be yanked off. (*Drifts into a private reverie.*) If it's a revolving door the head will bounce about like a ball in a game of skittles played by lunatics. Mm . . . (*To* **Nelson**.) Our misfortunes come not only from the riffraff of the public highway. They penetrate to the heart of the department.

Silence.

Dont you like me? Is it something I said? I try to help but you people will not co-operate. You've worked this out with your mates. Have a laugh. Wind her up. Get her on to the earrings. She wears them at staff meetings. When the department head speaks she's so still you'd think she's dead – bored to death by what he's saying, like the rest of us. When I speak she nods in ecstatic agreement with all I say even before I've said it – nods her head like a lunatic wearing a straw hat that's on fire. She can play 'Jingle Bells'. On her earrings. Fiendish. One day they'll be mistaken for the fire alarm. The innocent will be trampled under foot in the stampede. Then I shall strike. I keep a personal file on her. (*Taps another file.*) I shall produce it when my hour comes. – Two can play at your game. I shall be silent.

DSS Officer *and* **Nelson** *sit in silence.*

DSS Officer   . . . I can hear her earrings . . . and we're five storeys up . . . (*The papers fall from the file and spread over the floor.*) Ignore them. What do we have cleaners for?

Silence.

I hate you. It's a pleasure to tell you. Dont bother to report me
to the authorities. No one would believe a man who carries his
bedding through the streets. Actually I hate everyone who
comes through that door. Battered, beaten, abused, burgled –
I hate all of you for your helplessness. You let yourselves be
victims. This city is a giant jigsaw where none of the pieces fit.
The world spins out of control. The chaos. Confusion. I'm
dizzy. If you ask me – which seems improbable – the world
will end any day. Probably just before my long weekend
break. – To the matter in hand! It's clear that you killed the
young woman. No doubt you fed her poisoned crisps (no I do
not want a crisp). The police fell for your ridiculous tale of a
spot where the world kept its balance. The police are not what
they were. Once you could rely on them to prosecute everyone,
even the innocent – *especially* the innocent. Think of the effect
that had on the guilty. Well according to the law you are
innocent. But what are you morally? You abandoned the girl
for days at a time – and every night because you had to work
and money comes before loyalty. You tried to starve her into
submission – the squatters saw you leave with a *full* carrier of
groceries. Did you go to her mother to help? The Samaritans?
The police? Did you come to me? You dont trust me? Then
did you go into the street and ask strangers for help? Lay in
the roadway to stop the traffic? Did you go out on the roof
and shout 'Help this girl'? Isnt that what roofs are for? – O
and a few other things such as keeping the rain off and
providing a night-time roost for pigeons – but arent they really
for you to go out on to shout the truth to the city? You sit in
silence. It doesnt matter now. You were silent *then* – and a girl
is dead. Why were you silent? Because you know nothing. Do
nothing. Are nothing. The law has let you go – but what I say
will ruin your life. My good deed for the day. Your conscience
will never be free of torments. They will pursue you day and
night like the hounds of hell let loose on a greyhound
racetrack. Leave my office.

Nelson *goes.* **DSS Officer** *gathers up the scattered papers.*

DSS Officer (*shouts after* **Nelson**)   When you pass through reception I hope the earrings deafen you!

She goes out with the files.

Four

Street. Empty. **Nelson** *comes on. He is draped in the blanket. He holds out his hand to beg from passers-by. Nothing. The day ends. He goes to the wall and sits down. He wraps the blanket closer round him. He takes out the crisp packet. He takes out a crisp. He stares at it in silence.*

Nelson   Sorry Viv. No one gives. 'Avent eaten all day. Got t' eat one a' yer crisps. No more, Viv. One. Promise.

He goes to put the crisp in his mouth. A police siren.

Bloody 'ell Viv! – it was only one.

He puts the crisp back in the packet. **One-legged Thief** *runs in on a crutch. He wears a top hat.*

One-legged Thief   Quick! 'Ide me! I'm innocent! Yer can tell from me respectable headgear.

He gives **Nelson** *his crutch, takes his blanket and hides under it.* **Nelson** *sits holding the crutch upright.* **One-legged Thief** *looks out from under the blanket. Puts his top hat on* **Nelson**'s *head.*

One-legged Thief   'Ave a borrow a' that. (*Examines the effect.*) Suits yer.

One-legged Thief *goes back under the blanket. Sound of a police car roaring up. Stops.*

Police (*off. Shouts from car*)   Evenin sir. You havent seen a one-legged thief with a top hat and a crutch run by by any chance?

Nelson   Yes officer. (*Points with the crutch.*) 'E went that way.

Police (*off*)   Thank you sir. The force is grateful for your co-operation.

Nelson (*raises top hat*)   Not at all.

Police (*off*)   We'll catch him never fear. Good night sir.

The police car roars away.

One-legged Thief (*under the blanket*)   'E gone?

Nelson   Yes.

One-legged Thief *comes from under the blanket.*

One-legged Thief   An old woman come up t' me in the street. Accused me of snatchin 'er 'andbag. Bold as brass. (*He points with a handbag.*) On the corner in broad daylight.

Nelson   'Oo's 'andbag's that?

One-legged Thief   Me mother's. She give it t' me t' 'old when she went in t' a shop. We were separated. I was twelve at the time. Bin lookin for 'er ever since. I shant give up. I'm a man of resolution. (*He looks into the handbag.*) Pension book.

Nelson (*takes the pension book*)   Was yer mother on the pension?

One-legged Thief   No. It's a mystery. Give us a crisp.

Nelson   They ain mine.

One-legged Thief   'Oo's is they then?

Nelson   Me girl's.

One-legged Thief   Ask 'er if I can 'ave one.

Nelson   Cant.

One-legged Thief   Why not?

Nelson   She's dead.

One-legged Thief   That'd make it difficult. I'll join 'er if I dont eat. Give us a crisp.

The police car roars up. **One-legged Thief** *throws the handbag at* **Nelson**. *Hides under the blanket.* **Nelson** *sits with the handbag in one hand, the crutch in the other and the top hat on his head. The police car stops.*

Police (*off. Shouting from police car*)   Evenin sir. The one-legged thief with the crutch and top hat hasnt run back this way by any chance?

Nelson (*spreads his arms in an expansive gesture of ignorance*)   Sorry.

Police (*off*)   A slippery customer sir. Never mind. The force will find him. Sorry to have troubled you, sir. Goodnight.

The police car roars away. **One-legged Thief** *comes from under the blanket.*

One-legged Thief   Pity me. I'm an orphan. Give us a crisp.

Nelson   Yer said yer was lookin for yer mother.

One-legged Thief   An' she was lookin for 'er 'andbag. As she ain found it yet she'll be dead a' grief. Give us a crisp.

Nelson   No.

One-legged Thief   What flavour is they? – I'm taking part in a consumer survey for the food industry.

Nelson   Liver 'n bacon.

One-legged Thief   They 'er favourites?

Nelson   She didnt like bacon.

One-legged Thief   Why yer buy 'em?

Nelson   All they 'ad.

One-legged Thief   She died a' disappointment.

Nelson   She lives in my 'eart.

One-legged Thief   She must find the accommodation cramped.

Nelson *bursts into tears.*

One-legged Thief   Give us a crisp.

Nelson   No.

One-legged Thief   Yer must learn t' let go lad. She's dead. Clingin t' a bag a' crisps wont bring 'er back. Especially liver 'n bacon. I'll eat 'em for yer 'n yer'll be free.

Nelson   I miss 'er.

One-legged Thief   Yer got a noble soul. Sorry I was rude about yer 'eart. (*Takes the crisps and eats them as he talks.*) Dont cry son it puts me off me grub.

Nelson   I did 'er a great wrong.

One-legged Thief   Buyin liver 'n bacon? They ain *that* bad.

Nelson   I wanted t' force 'er t' come t' 'er senses.

One-legged Thief   That's always a mistake of colossal proportions. What 'appened?

Nelson   She died.

One-legged Thief   I'm not surprised.

Nelson   I lead a life a' penance.

One-legged Thief   That wont 'elp 'er.

Nelson   Every day I rue me mistake.

One-legged Thief   That's just makin another one.

Nelson   I'm a criminal.

One-legged Thief   We all are – dont boast. (*He bends his head back. Funnels the crumbs in the packet into his mouth.*) Allow me t' introduce meself: 'Bernard the One-legged Dancer'. I put me 'at on the pavement. A top 'at, you observe. Wouldnt use less. It intimidates the punters. I dance. I could afford t' retire t' the Costa del Sol. Unfortunately there's a drawback. There always is. I dont like the sun. I could teach yer the dance. Yer could go t' the Costa del Sol.

Nelson   I got two legs.

One-legged Thief   Typical! People always look on the dark side a' things.

He takes his crutch and puts his hat on the ground. He dances 'The Dance of the One-Legged Thief'. At the climax he finds his missing leg. It is bare.

Nelson (*surprised. Points at the leg*)   Look!

One-legged Thief (*looks*)   Good 'eavens! 'Ow did that get there? (*He takes a few awkward experimental steps.*) I'm dizzy! Off me balance! The world's spinnin round! (*He falls to the ground.*) Well I suppose in time yer get used t' 'avin two. It's very inconvenient. Yer ain got another packet a' crisps t' 'elp me get over the shock a' findin I got two legs?

Nelson   No.

One-legged Thief   Yer need a friend my friend. I'll give yer a piece of advice. Look after number one. Pee on the rest. Eat the crisps 'n give 'em the packet. (*Gives* **Nelson** *the empty packet.*) Drop that in a bin. I 'ate litter. Now I'll tell yer somethin else. Somethin yer ought t' know. The secret a' life. Ready? If the one-legged dancer dance long enough he finds 'is other leg. (*Taps his nose with his finger.*) Think about it! (*Looks in handbag. Finds coins.*) Run down t' the corner shop 'n buy us a packet a' crisps. The exhibition dance done me in. I'd go but the old woman might still be loiterin with intent. (*He gives* **Nelson** *coins.*) Cream cheese 'n chives.

Nelson *starts to go.*

One-legged Thief   I'll watch yer blanket. The old woman 'd put 'er thievers on it.

Nelson *puts the blanket on the ground. Goes out.*

One-legged Thief (*shouts after* **Nelson**)   Provençal olives 'n aubergine'd do in an emergency. (*He picks up the blanket. Examines it. Finds the holes.*) A starvin moth on a diet wouldnt touch that.

One-legged Thief *drops the blanket. Puts on his top hat. Picks up the handbag. Disposes of his second leg. Goes out on his crutch. Police siren. The police car roars by.* **Nelson** *comes on with a bag of crisps.*

Nelson   Liver 'n bacon. All they 'ad.

The police car roars up. Stops.

Police (*off. Shouts from police car*)   Some good news sir. We got the one-legged thief with the top 'at. Did a dance 'n fell over 'is crutch – broke 'is neck. Keep well sir. G'night!

The police car roars away. **Nelson** *stares before him in bewilderment. Then he turns in the direction taken by* **One-legged Thief**.

Nelson (*roars*)   Liver 'n bacon! (*Long pause. Roars.*) All they 'ad!

He picks up the blanket and goes.

Five

Another street. Empty. A gust of wind. It blows a blanket on – it comes to rest on the ground. **Nelson** *comes in from the opposite direction. He is wrapped in* **Viv**'s *blanket and has the packet of crisps. He stops in front of the other blanket. The two blankets are identical.*

Nelson   Good lor'!

He examines the other blanket. He finds a packet of crisps identical to his own.

Old Woman (*off*)   My son!

Nelson *hurriedly drops the packet of crisps.*

Nelson   Was just lookin! 'Onest. Werent goin t' pinch yer –

Old Woman *comes on. She wears a battered straw hat. She carries a cloth bag with wooden handles. It is bulging and breaking at the seams.*

Old Woman   My son! Embrace me!

Nelson   Pardon?

Old Woman   Give us a 'ug! Its bin so long!

Nelson   I'm sorry – yer got the wrong –

Old Woman   Twenty years! Where yer bin? Upsettin me! Yer deserve a good 'idin! That'll 'ave t' wait. First give us a 'ug!

Nelson   I ain yer son!

Old Woman   Poor lamb dont recognise 'is own mother. Well I ain wearin the same dress. Still yer recognise the blanket. Yours – mine: identical alike! Proves yer me son!

Nelson   There's thousands a' that sort a' blanket.

Old Woman (*demonstrating*)   Not with the same 'oles!

Nelson   Everythin's got 'oles these days. What's more: the blanket ain mine.

Old Woman   'Oo's is it then?

Nelson   Viv's.

Old Woman   Viv? No I never 'ad no daughters – yer me son.

Nelson   Yer ain me mother – she's –

Old Woman   'E disowns me! 'E's ashamed a' me cause I ain got proper shoes 'n fancy pearls! Twenty years ago I stood yer on the pavement outside the shop. Told yer t' wait. I was longer 'n I thought. I went in for a packet a' crisps. They only sold chandeliers. I couldnt tell 'cause the lights blinded me. When I come out yer was gone. I couldnt take yer in 'cause all the shops barred yer. Yer was a notorious shoplifter even from yer time in the pram. The pram 'ad a false bottom.

Nelson   That dont surprise me.

Old Woman   Ah – now yer remember.

Nelson   I ain yer son. I met 'im. 'E lost a leg.

Old Woman   First yer lose yer mother then yer lose yer leg!

Nelson   'E found it again!

Old Woman   I can see that! – Now yer found yer mother!
Give us a 'ug!

Nelson   No!

Old Woman   I was asleep on me place at the bus stop.
Along comes this wind 'n strip me blanket off! I jumps up –
give chase along the street – what do I see? Me son stood in 'is
blanket – with my blanket come t' rest at 'is feet! It's the wind
a' destiny son!

Nelson   I'm not yer son!

Old Woman   'N ill wind! 'Ow'd yer support yerself without
me –

Nelson   Yer son took up dancin.

Old Woman   Dancin! Show us!

Nelson (*declining*)   Sorry – I dont –

Old Woman   'E refuses 'is mother after all these years!
Even if I werent yer mother yer could do a few paltry steps t'
bring some 'appiness in 'n ol' lady's last years. God knows
there ain bin much a' that so far!

Nelson   It's just that I'm not –

Old Woman   No no dont bother! I'm a bereaved mother
'oo waited twenty years for this moment 'n now she's t' be
denied.

Nelson *dances a few steps,*

Old Woman (*sits on her blanket*)   Tell me when yer ready 'n
I'll concentrate.

Nelson   That's it.

Old Woman   That? I thought that was the warm up.

Nelson   I 'avent got the top 'at. It makes a difference.

Old Woman   I suppose yer lost it.

Nelson   'N I ain got the knack a' dancin on one leg.

Old Woman   I brought a complicated son in t' the world. I'll eat me crisps t' get over me disappointment. It's not every mother 'as t' suddenly suffer ante-natal depression twenty-seven years after she give birth!

She opens her crisps and eats. **Nelson** *watches her.*

Old Woman   Liver 'n bacon. Story a' me life. 'Ave t' take what they got.

Nelson   . . . Yer couldnt spare a . . . ?

Old Woman   What's that in yer 'and?

Nelson   Ain mine.

Old Woman   'Oo's is they then?

Nelson   Bought 'em for yer son.

Old Woman   I see I brought a maniac in t' the world.

Nelson   Yer should show a bit of respect for yer son. 'E's dead.

Old Woman   Dont take this personal Josephine. But yer a very confused person.

Nelson   I'm not Josephine.

Old Woman   If yer lose yer mother young 's natural yer forget yer name Josephine. I set me 'eart on a daughter. After you come I was pass me child-bearin years. You're named after the daughter I never 'ad.

Nelson   I'm not yer son 'n I'm not called Josephine.

Old Woman   Well what are yer called Josephine?

Nelson   Nelson.

Old Woman   Least yer got the right 'istorical epoch. Son or no son I must turn in. The day dont linger on for family reunions.

Nelson   Where yer live?

Old Woman (*points*)   At the bus stop.

Nelson (*looks*)   There ain no bus stop.

Old Woman   They took it away.

Nelson   When?

Old Woman   Years ago.

Nelson   Why?

Old Woman   They closed the service. No passengers. These days they rush round in cars. I've never taken to 'em.

Nelson   So?

Old Woman   I sit 'n wait where the bus stop was. Bus might come. Not everythin does what authority tells it. Some thin's 'ave minds a' their own.

Nelson   If it comes where'll it take yer?

Old Woman   Dont know.

Nelson   Where yer wan' it t' take yer?

Old Woman   Dont know. If I knew that I'd wait at the bus stop that'd take me there. Yer ain very thoughtful at times Josephine. It'll go somewhere transcendental. Eternity, I wouldnt be surprised. (*Bag.*) I'm all packed ready. Wont cost me nothin. I got me pensioner's free pass. (*Peers at* **Nelson***.*) Them tears Josephine? I see sufferin in that face.

Nelson   The world's in a bad way.

Old Woman   It's worse 'n bad: it ain exist. 'Old them. (*She gives him the crisps. Puts her palms together.*) Om. Om. – Dont try 'n lift one. I got second sight when me eyes're shut. An' I counted 'em. Dont take long – each time yer buy a packet there's less

in. If I 'eard right, just now yer said yer was dead. Me son
turns up after sixteen years 'n the only accomplishment 'e's got
t' boast of is 'e's dead. Dont boast Josephine my boy. We're all
dead. Om. The world dont exist – yer dont exist – me – the
street – the blankets – even the crisps dont exist, which ain the
only reason they taste a' nothin. We are but playthin's in the
'ands a' destiny. Reflections in the swiftly flowin waters a'
time. I got that off the back of a matchbox. I found it very
illuminatin. It struck a chord. Give us me crisps. Yer might be
tempted t' eat 'em t' get over the shock a' 'uman non-existence.
(*Takes back the crisp packet.*) Some winter nights when I lie on
the cold pavement – the wind in these streets 's got no
consideration – it bites yer ankles somethin cruel – I'm 'alf
tempted t' chuck it in 'n go 'n kip in the park – but then the
bus 'd come 'n I'd miss it. Them nights it's a comfort t' know
I'm in the 'ands a' destiny.

Nelson *tries to put an arm round her shoulder.*

Old Woman   Too late t' get round me – the crisps is gone.
Om. (*She breathes into the empty packet. Screws the top airtight.*) Best
get t' me place before someone else snatches it. Once that
starts they'll all come. (*Grumbles.*) Do 'ave these nightmares –
great crowd a' layabouts waitin at me bus stop 'n I cant find
me place in the queue.

Old Woman *bangs the inflated crisp packet: pop! Throws it aside.
Automatically* **Nelson** *reaches for it.*

Old Woman   Leave it. It dont exist.

She wraps herself in her blanket and starts to leave.

(*Over her shoulder to* **Nelson**.) Yer can come Josephine. Room
for you.

Old Woman *goes out.*

Nelson   Viv – yer're not there Viv – I pretend yer are 'cause
I cant be without yer. I ought t' eat yer crisps 'n forget yer.
When yer died it was bad – now it's worse. If yer could 'ear I'd

promise I wont give up till people understand yer – I wont Viv
– I –

A bus approaches from the distance. **Nelson** *stands and stares.*

Nelson   A bus . . . bus . . . (*Half shouts to* **Old Woman**.) It's
got L-plates up – the driver's took the wrong turnin. My God
she's put 'er arm out t' – she's steppin in the road t' – (*Shouts.*)
dont – dont – let it go – 'e dont know what 'e's doin –

Nelson *scuttles to the side. Ducks under his blanket. The bus roars
up. Brakes slammed on. Tyres screech. A huge crash. A wall knocked
down. Vicious short sharp reversal. And the bus roars away.* **Nelson**
*comes from under his blanket. Half-mesmerised he walks slowly
towards the crash. Goes out. The sound of bricks and debris falling.*
Nelson *comes back. He clutches* **Old Woman***'s blanket. It is
drenched in blood.*

Nelson (*awe*)   . . . 'E went right over 'er 'n buried 'er under
the bricks. 'E must be on a job-trainin scheme. (*Silence. He looks
down at the bloody blanket. Looks up and shouts.*) Yer dont exist now
yer bloody stupid cow! (*Looks down at the blanket. Silence. Suddenly
shouts at the blanket.*) I'm not called Josephine!

Nelson *goes out with* **Old Woman***'s blanket.*

Six

Foreman*'s living room. A table and two chairs. In the corner
a patch of dust and fluff.*

Foreman's Wife *comes in. She brings two table napkins and two
place mats. She sets them on the table. For a moment she looks across
at the dust. She goes out. Pause. She comes back with cutlery. She goes
to the dust. She crosses her arms and stares at it. She nods her head as
she reaches a decision. She goes to the table. She sets the cutlery. She
goes out.* **Foreman** *comes in. He wears his work overall and a bow
tie – red with white spots. He carries a parcel. He sets it down in the
corner.*

Foreman (*calls*)   Home my dear.

He sits. He starts to take off his shoes. **Wife** *comes in. She brings salt and pepper shakers. She sets them on the table.*

Foreman   Nice day beloved? Did you –

Wife (*calm*)   My mother's coming.

Wife *goes out.* **Foreman** *takes off his shoes.* **Wife** *comes in with slippers and a carafe of water. She drops the slippers on the floor beside him. She puts the carafe on the table. She looks at the table to see what is missing. Minimally repositions the salt. Goes out.*

Foreman   That's nice dear.

Wife (*off*)   What is?

Foreman   Your mother coming. (*To himself.*) Olé!

Wife *comes on with a bottle of tomato sauce. She sets it on the table.*

Foreman   Will she stay long?

Wife (*calm*)   Who?

Foreman   Your mother.

Wife   Five minutes.

Foreman   O?

Wife *examines the table for anything missing. She goes out.*

Foreman (*calls*)   Why she do that dear?

Wife (*off*)   What?

Foreman (*calls*)   Stay five minutes.

Wife *comes in with a butter dish and two tumblers. She sets them on the table. She does a fancy arrangement of the napkins in the tumblers.*

Foreman   Seems a waste of the ticket money.

Wife (*still calm*)   My mother is not used to living in a pigsty. She could never understand why I married you. O good I said when you proposed. Eventually. (What this house needs is pink napkins.) As far as work goes he's not a high-riser I said –

Foreman   I knocked down a tower today dear. Fifteen storeys.

Wife   – but at least he'll provide me with a pigsty. You've kept your word.

Wife *goes out.* **Foreman** *inspects the cutlery. He cleans a knife on the tablecloth.* **Wife** *comes back. She brings a bread board. She sets it on the table.*

Foreman   Were you trying to tell me something dear?

Wife   Not at all. I havent a care in the world.

Foreman   That's alright then dear. The blade of that knife has dried egg on it. We have to watch our hygiene –

Wife (*loses her calm*)   O!

Foreman   It's the sort of thing germs go for – dried egg –

Wife   O!!

Wife *snatches the knife. She goes out.* **Foreman** *examines the other cutlery. He starts to polish a spoon on his elbow. He hears* **Wife** *coming. He hurriedly puts the spoon back on the table.* **Wife** *comes in. She has a large bread knife. She slams it on the table. She goes out.* **Foreman** *examines the bread knife. Polishes it on the tablecloth.*

Wife (*off. Angry*)   Hope that's clean enough!

Foreman (*calls*)   As you ask dear, it's got a spot of . . . (*Changes his mind.*)

Wife *comes in. She has a very large meat knife. She slams it on the table. It knocks over the pepper. She sets it upright. She goes out.* **Foreman** *examines the meat knife. It is spotless. He holds a tumbler against the light. Finds a fleck.*

Foreman   Ah! (*Is going to call, changes his mind.*)

Wife *comes on. She wears an anti-germ mask.*

Wife (*calm*)   You called.

Foreman   No dear.

Wife *goes out.* **Foreman** *twiddles his thumbs.*

Foreman (*stops twiddling his thumbs, calls*)   Er –

Wife *comes in.*

Wife   You called.

Foreman   No. Not as such. (*Reflects. Vague gesture.*) Erm.

Wife   What?

Foreman   You'll have to take it off.

Wife   What?

Foreman *makes a vague gesture.*

Wife   Stop waving your arms like a drunken octopus searching for the keys to its front door.

Foreman   Was I dear? Sorry. (*He puts his arms behind his back.*)

Wife   And stop wiggling your thumbs.

Foreman (*puts his hands in his lap*)   Before you eat.

Wife   Pardon?

Foreman   You cant eat with it on. *Olé!*

Wife   Stop saying that.

Wife *goes out.* **Foreman** *hastily polishes the tumbler on the tablecloth.* **Wife** *comes back. She carries a dustpan and brush.*

Foreman   Is this war?

Wife   No. Victory. Mine.

Foreman   Over my dead body!

Wife   If necessary.

Foreman (*stands in front of the dust patch*)   Put those things down!

Wife   I'm not houseproud. (*She quickly adjusts a fork.*) If I was I wouldnt have married you. There are limits. Three years that dust has accumulated. You dont tell me why dust must accumulate in my dinette. I try to understand. Is he taking up indoor gardening? Other women dont have to put up with dust. I asked round the estate. Now Mother's coming. Explain.

Foreman   My lips are sealed. Never never never never will I open them except at meal times.

Wife   Then you'll have to explain to my mother.

Foreman   In that case I'll tell you. You wont believe me.

Wife   Probably not.

Foreman   The world's in a bad state.

Wife   The world is in a bad state. That's no reason why my dinette should be in one.

Foreman (*clears his throat*)   The world's in a bad state. It has become unbalanced. Armies. Deforestation. New diseases. Pollution.Youth. Gangs. Crime. Knives with blood on them – and dried egg. Anarchy creeps in everywhere. There is one spot that holds – just – the world together. Not even a hair must fall on it. If it did the world would spin like – like – (*Lost for a word.*) a drunken octopus searching for the keys to its front door. People would fly through their roofs and windows. Fly from their armchairs as if they were ejector seats. The mob from the estate would hurtle through your dinette and vanish into space. They wouldnt even stop to wipe their feet. *Olé!*

Wife   Stop saying that!

Foreman *undoes his parcel. In it there is a ceremonial barrier: a white rope supported on four stainless steel legs. He arranges it round the dust.*

Foreman I picked this up cheap in a closing-down sale at a monastery. Your mother will appreciate the ceremonial touch.

Wife Why *my* dinette?

Foreman At least that's obvious.

Wife Not to me.

Foreman I'm a demolition expert. Demolition pays for the roof over our heads and the food on our plates. By the way what are we having for tea?

Wife Why *my* dinette?

Foreman Three years ago a young man came to me in distress. He told me what I've now told you. He had it from his young lady. She came to a sudden end. I went to her funeral. It was posh. They served canapés – what are we having for tea?

Wife Why *my* dinette?

Foreman The young lady was broadly right – but wrong on detail. The spot was not in that room. We demolished it and the world's still here – more or less. On the way home from her funeral I reflected – as one does – on the mortality of things. I realised that destiny –

Wife What?

Foreman (*explains*) – oh a sort of unelected watch committee – had placed the guardianship of the spot in the hands of the man most equipped to notice the slightest change in it: the demolition expert. *Olé!* – I am the chosen one! (*He makes a slight adjustment to the barrier.*) Even your mother will see that.

Wife Step aside.

Foreman No.

Wife There'll be no tea.

Foreman My sympathy for the suffering masses has no limits – they dont deserve it. But I live by my own standards.

I dislike dirt. I'm a fanatic of cleanliness. I'm particular about cutlery. (*Picks up a spoon.*) This spoon has strawberry jam on it – which I do not eat.

Wife   O!

Foreman   But I put up with the inconvenience (*Points at the dust.*) to defend the world. And now I am to have no tea. Perhaps you could provide a few biscuits. Chocolate if possible – chocolate biscuits are the last bastion of civilisation.

Wife   Stand aside.

Foreman   I knew the moment of truth would come. I pondered it at night while you thought I was snoring.

Wife   You were.

Foreman   Not as such. It was part of my plan. I could not appear openly as guardian of the world. I might be called to open bazaars. I must appear to be an ordinary working man. So I snored. (*He starts to put on his shoes.*) The one distinction I allowed myself – as the human race's defender – was a bow tie. The lads at work took the micky. Another burden. At night I lay awake pretending to snore and struggling with destiny like – (*Lost.*) a drunken octopus looking for the keys to its front door, to coin a phrase. I – (*The shoelace breaks.*) You see! – anarchy everywhere. Now the time has come to show why I was chosen for my mission! My apotheosis! One day you will see my name written in letters of fire across the sky! Stand back! *Olé!*

Foreman *snatches cutlery from the table. He performs a tremendous flamenco. For music he shouts and for castanets uses cutlery. At the climax he stamps round the dust heap. Finishes.*

Foreman   *Olé!* I took up Spanish dancing to disguise my role of defender of the world.

Wife   So you can dance. It was awful but the world's still here.

Foreman   Precisely.

Wife   I miss the point.

Foreman   You saw how near I went to the spot. Repeatedly! Within a fraction of the dust! Not one grain rose in the air. That is the control of a man whose life is devoted to the niceties of destroying things. Anyone else would have sent the world to perdition with their first – (*Stamps.*)

Wife   Stop! Mr Pringle downstairs will complain about the noise.

Foreman   Yes yes people go about their petty business with their petty squabbles and whinges. No one knows how close they are to disaster. Or the respect they owe me for my efforts. I dont like Spanish music. I dont even like the Spanish. They cant pronounce their aitches. (*Demonstrates.*) Thwah! Thwah! – as if they're blowing their noses through their mouths.

He puts the cutlery back on the table. He keeps the butter knife to emphasise his words.

From now on your life will be hard. I tried to keep the secret from you. A careless step in this room would end the world. Knowing that will be an even greater burden than your mother or my snoring.

Wife   I refuse to give way to a terrorist threatening me with my own butter knife.

Foreman   Destiny has knocked on the door!

Wife   Well it can come back when I'm not busy!

She advances with the dustpan and brush. **Foreman** *stabs her with the butter knife.*

Foreman   *Olé!*

Wife   You little devil!

She attacks **Foreman** *with the dustpan and brush. He examines the butter knife.*

Foreman   The butter knife is bent – and I'm a demolition expert!

Wife *collapses over a chair.* **Foreman** *goes to the table. He puts down the butter knife. Picks up the bread knife. Sees the meat knife. Puts down the bread knife. Picks up the meat knife. Picks up the bread knife. Weighs a knife in each hand.*

Foreman   Choices, choices!

He decides on the meat knife. He puts down the bread knife. He stabs **Wife** *with the meat knife.*

Wife   Ouch! (*Dies.*)

Foreman   Well I've saved the world. For the moment at least. Who can be certain of anything when you can be attacked with a dustpan and brush in your own home! Still, she did provide the murder weapon – which was thoughtful. (*To* **Wife**.) Thank you. I warned you that from now on your life would be hard. Mercifully it was short.

A knock at the door.

Foreman   That's either destiny knocking on the door or Mr Pringle from downstairs complaining about the noise. The place had better be tidied up. Destiny wouldnt mind the presence of a corpse – destiny always expects the worst. It would make it feel at home. But the Pringles of this world add it to their complaints. Where to put the body? The council doesnt think of these things when they design their houses. The rooms are too small to accommodate the aftermath of a domestic shenanigans. (*Floorboard creaks.*) Olé! – my flamenco has loosened the floorboards. (*To* **Wife**.) An unexpected bonus from expensive dancing lessons.

Foreman *puts* **Wife** *under the floorboards. A knock on the door.*

Foreman (*calls*)   Coming! – Ashes to ashes, dust to dust – so you may need the dustpan.

He drops the dustpan and brush on **Wife**. *Replaces the floorboards. Goes to the table. Inspects it. Wipes the blood on the meat knife onto the tablecloth.*

Foreman   The tablecloth will have to go to the laundry. The caller might stay for a meal. I can hardly offer him a knife dripping with blood. He might be a vegetarian.

Foreman *presses the floorboards down with his shoe. Opens the door.* **Nelson** *is outside. He is wrapped in the* **Old Woman***'s blanket – the blood has darkened a little but is vivid. He has the bag of crisps. He is exhausted. He falls into the room. Sprawls flat on the floor.*

Nelson   Yer wont remember me.

Foreman   I remember you very well. I hoped we'd meet up. I wanted to ask you a question. Why are you called Nelson?

Nelson   Me mother was called Trafalgar.

Foreman   That's one mystery solved.

Nelson   I'm sorry t' disturb you.

Foreman   Not at all. I was afraid I might be bereft of company in the future. It's been an eventful day. I knocked down a tower – fifteen storeys – bent a butter knife – and rearranged my domestic affairs.

Nelson   It was me 'oo –

Foreman   Yes yes the young lady's departure upset you. You didnt touch the canapés. I hope you've eaten since. It's been three years. You look peeky. Can I offer you a bite?

Nelson   I come t' you because –

Foreman   It's no trouble. The meal's ready. We cook for two. My wife isnt eating.

Nelson   I come t' tell yer –

Foreman *goes out.* **Nelson** *stares at the rope barrier.* **Foreman** *comes back. He carries a blackened frying pan.*

Foreman   Burnt. Ruined. The world's falling apart. I can offer you chocolate biscuits.

Nelson   I come t' tell yer that Viv –

Foreman   The young lady in the house –

Nelson   – wasnt like the inquest said. She was unbalanced – well, potty – she thought – this'll seem weird t' you – there was a spot in the room she 'ad t' guard or the world'd end –

Foreman   She died with the house falling about her ears. She must have thought that was confirmation. A happy way to go. Not everyone's so lucky.

Nelson   If I could make one person understand there'd still be 'ope. 'S why I come t' you – a normal workin man'll understand. (*He brings out newspapers. They are stained with dried blood. Spreads them like a giant map on the floor.*) These newspapers're a map a' the world. Look. Wars in every continent. Air polluted. Soil ruined. Sea contaminated. Read it! Fires. Floods. Crime. Cities vandalised. People sick 'cause they're too fat. The poor starvin 'cause they cant buy food. We sell guns t' child soldiers t' kill each other. What we use the papers for? – Fish 'n chips or doss on in the streets –

Foreman (*shows butter knife*)   This butter knife is one of six. I'll never find a replacement. The set's ruined.

Nelson   It werent the sufferin that driv' 'er mad. It was people 'oo turn their backs 'n dont listen – so nothin's done. Nothin's changed. She couldnt change it on 'er own. So she made a little space – in 'er 'ead – in a corner a' that room – where she could take care a' the 'ole world. Look after it. Keep it safe. She werent stupid – 'er 'eart was too big. That's what driv' 'er mad.

Wife *comes up from under the floor. She carries the dustpan and brush.*

Nelson   Look!

Foreman   Pay no attention. She's come back to cause trouble. She did enough of that when she was alive.

Nelson   Is she unwell?

Foreman   Not as such. She's dead.

Wife *squirms along the floor on her stomach. She goes towards the dust, making sweeping gestures with the brush.*

Nelson   She's makin for that thing! – she's alive!

Foreman   She must be. Whoever heard of a ghost comin back to do the housework?

Nelson   We must get a doctor!

Foreman   Certainly not!

Nelson (*calls*)   Doctor!

Foreman   Dont shout! Mr Pringle will have his ear stuck to the ceiling. All this comin and goin – we'll never hear the last of it!

Nelson (*going to the door*)   Doctor! Doctor!

Foreman *hits* **Nelson** *over the head with the frying pan. The blackened food scatters.* **Nelson** *collapses unconscious.*

Foreman   Now look what you've done! This time the meal's completely ruined. I was hoping to scrape the charcoal off a sausage and a potato. (*Picks up the food.*) There arent even any biscuits. Not even plain ones. I looked.

Wife (*squirming forward and making sweeping gestures*)   When I go I'm not leaving dust in my dinette . . . if it's the last thing I do . . .

Foreman   It probably will be.

He heaves **Nelson** *on to a chair. He ties him into it with the blanket. He gags him with a table napkin.* **Wife** *reaches the dust. She raises the brush in an heroic gesture.* **Foreman** *gets to her just in time. He takes the dustpan and brush.*

Foreman   That's twice today I've saved the world. I deserve an entry in the *Guinness Book of Records*. (*He drags* **Wife** *to the* *table.*) You could pop up at any moment. Put you where I can keep an eye on you.

He sits **Wife** *in the chair opposite* **Nelson**. *She still wears the anti-germ mask.*

Foreman   You must be dead – you're silent: in your case an infallible symptom. (*To* **Nelson**.) I dont know if you eat burnt food? (*He puts the plate of burnt food in front of* **Nelson**.) Feel free.

Nelson *comes to and splutters.*

Foreman   What I didnt have time to tell you is that your young lady led you astray – not in the way you hoped. (*Points.*) *That* is the world-spot. Who'd have thought that this humble home – dust brings out my lyrical side, as it does in some authors – holds the world in balance.

He makes a small adjustment to the rope barrier. **Nelson** *splutters and shakes his head.*

The day's long. I demolished a tower – fifteen storeys. Performed a brilliant solo fandango – I'll triumph in the Olympics when they introduce ballroom dancing – buried my wife twice – once under the floorboards and once at the dining table without even opening the gate leg – tied up a rebellious youth – and bent a butter knife. What's the pattern in that? Sometimes the meaning of the universe is beyond the grasp even of a demolition expert. Now I've no chair to sit on. I sacrifice my comfort to those who show no gratitude. I perch on the edge of a table as if I were clinging to a clifftop by my fingertips. In a moment I could lose my balance and fall off. I havent had tea and someone's eaten all the biscuits. I begin to be weary of this world. Has the time come to end it? I'm too weary to decide. (*Tosses a coin.*) Tails – the world must go. The last act of the demolition expert. It's not all bad – the universe will be spared this youth's muffled oratory and be rid of Mr Pringle. It'll be much improved. Maestro music!

Foreman *performs a terrific fandango round the room. He stamps on the table top – not a plate or knife or fork or glass or sausage is* *touched. He leaps to the floor – ratchets on his heels to the rope barrier – raises his foot over the dust –*

Foreman   *Olé!*

A knock on the door. His foot hangs in the air.

Destiny! (*He lowers his foot.*) Destiny never gives up hope. It's the second time it's called today. I'm not sure I'll open the door. It may have come to complain about my dancing. (*He collects the dustpan and brush. Gives them to* **Wife**.) Hold them dear. We dont want visitors tripping over them and breaking their necks. One body is enough in a small room. (*Rearranges the dustpan and brush.*) Try not to look as if you passed on in your sleep. (*Tidies the table.*) Make an effort to show you were active to the end. Lived life to the full and all that.

A knock on the door. **Foreman** *goes to open it. He sees a pot plant. Tests the soil with his finger.*

Foreman   Dry! Typical. (*Waters the pot plant with water from the carafe. Puts the carafe on the table and the pot plant on* **Wife**.) In lieu of a wreath.

He goes to the door. He is about to open it. He notices his hand.

A dirty fingernail! I cant open the door to Mr Pringle with a dirty fingernail. He'd accuse me of lowering the tone of the neighbourhood. (*To* **Wife**.) Where do we keep our manicure set dear? She's dead – any excuse not to answer. (*Goes to the table. Picks up the meat knife. Cleans his fingernail with the point.*) The things one can do with a knife. (*Examines his fingernail.*) Mr Pringle's halo couldnt shine brighter. (*Contemplates the table.*) Not even a biscuit.

He goes to the door. He opens it. Outside is **DSS Officer**.

DSS Officer   I am Mr Pringle.

Foreman   You cant be!

DSS Officer   Why not? It's a respectable name. A high court judge was named Pringle. And a manufacturer of crisps.

Foreman   *Mr* Pringle?

DSS Officer   So you intend to be sexist about it. Early on it became clear that if I was to gain the promotion I was entitled to by the distress I caused the clients – the aim is to deter them from returning – I would have to become *Mr* Pringle.

Foreman   Dont your colleagues notice anything?

DSS Officer   They are civil servants. They notice nothing. For formal occasions I *do* wear a moustache.

She puts a Hitler moustache on her upper lip. It is red.

Foreman (*gestures*)   Um – er –

DSS Officer   Refrain from waving your arms like a drunken octopus searching for the key to its front door. You are pointing at the colour. I dont wish to appear conspicuous. Do I recognise that blanket? One of that sort belonged to an obnoxious youth called Wellington. He smelt of crisps – pork scratchings, unless that was his after-shave.

Foreman   Please dont mention food.

DSS Officer   Is it he? He insulted me with silence. He's still at it. He also murdered his girlfriend. I see from the state of his blanket that he's still at that too. (*Notices* **Wife**.) Is that lady dead? – or was she born with that unfortunate complexion?

Foreman   Dead – I hope.

DSS Officer   So he's still at it. One a day. He's insatiable. (*Points.*) There is the bent butter knife. The attack was frenzied. Who was the unfortunate victim?

Foreman   My wife.

DSS Officer   He preceded the murder with a particularly boring tirade about the state of the world. Here we see the results of a youthful infatuation with politics. I shall give evidence at his trial. They wont dare to cross-examine me. He saw life as a pilgrimage in a blanket. Now he will see it's a hermitage in a cell.

Foreman   Really?

DSS Officer   Is he not the perpetrator of the notorious Bent Butter Knife Murder? It would be best to remove the rest of the cutlery. (*Does so.*) He will be sent down for life. The Pest Control Officer will destroy his blanket. He will protest – the Governor will lock him up in solitary confinement. He will have a lifetime to practise his silence. I did not come up to complain of the noise. I came to congratulate you on your dancing. That virile stamping was a fandango I think?

Foreman (*modesty*)   I did make the effort.

DSS Officer   A welcome change to the chimes of earrings. (*She rattles a fork in a glass.*) I restrain my pleasure: may your wife rest in peace.

Foreman   Well the rest is silence.

DSS Officer (*ecstasy*)   Ah! (*Trills.*) A literary reference?

Foreman   Beg pardon?

DSS Officer   The last words spoken by our dear dying Hamlet. You've studied literature, of course?

Foreman   Not as such. It come with the bow tie.

DSS Officer   When you opened the door I knew destiny had sent me to your side. When I was a slip of a girl I dreamt of marrying a demolition engineer in a bow tie. They are few. That is why I remained a spinster all these years. Now you have made a literary reference. That was another of my girlhood dreams: the demolition engineer in the bow tie must whisper to me in literary references. And we meet on the day your wife has created a vacancy in your domestic arrangements. The hand of destiny!

Foreman   *Olé!*

DSS Officer   Ah! Ecstasy! – you speak Spanish! The last of my longings! The literary demolition engineer in the bow tie must speak Spanish! As I am *Mr* Pringle it falls to me to propose. I shall need to know your first name.

Foreman (*shiftily*)   I'm known as Walter.

DSS Officer (*suspicion*)   Known as?

Foreman   I was christened Walterloo.

Nelson *makes a sound of despair.*

DSS Officer   Walterloo will you – . (*Her mobile rings. She answers it.*) Yes – yes – yes – yes – yes. (*She switches off her mobile.*) A client. She's threatened to kill herself for years. She's finally taken the tablets. The croak was authentic. Walterloo – will you marry me?

Foreman   You keen on housework?

DSS Officer   Certainly not! I'm a bureaucrat.

Foreman   Can you dance?

DSS Officer   In your arms I can do anything!

Foreman   *Olé!*

DSS Officer (*takes crisps from under* **Nelson***'s blanket*)   Your wedding present!

They dance a frantic tango-cum-tarantella-cum-fandango-cum-fandola-cum-flamenco. **DSS Officer** *is transformed. Her mobile rings. She throws it away and they dance on. At the climax* **DSS Officer** *hammer-heels backwards – crashes through the rope barrier – and sits on the dust. An enormous bang. The dustpan and brush fly across the room.* **Wife** *and* **Nelson** *fall from the chairs. The table collapses.* **DSS Officer** *tangles in the rope.* **Foreman** *tries to get under the floorboards. He doesn't make it. The walls fall in and cover them all. And the sky falls on top of that. The end of the world.*

Tune

or

'The Glazier's Gauntlets'

A play for young people of nine years and older

Tune was first staged by Big Brum at Pegasus Infant and Junior School, Birmingham, on 22 February 2007. The cast was as follows:

Sally	Liz Brown
Verny	Richard Holmes
Robert	Danny O'Grady
Girl	Liz Brown

Directed by Chris Cooper
Designed by Ceri Townsend

Characters

Sally
Vernon, *Sally's partner*
Robert, *Sally's son*
Girl

Setting

City
Here
Now

A room. The back wall appears to be solid but is made of malleable material such as cloth. Behind it is another wall which exactly resembles the first wall but is solid. A kitchen table and chair, both wood.

Later, *a city street.*

One

Sally *is letting* **Vernon** *in. He wears a brown suede coat with large side-pockets and a white wool collar.*

Sally Didnt expect you this evening.

Vernon Taking you out for a ride in the car.

Sally Just in from work. Bit tired. It's nice of you.

Vernon Fresh air do you good. We could drop in a pub after.

Sally No, I –

Vernon Or a restaurant. Nice. The sort you like.

Sally I dont want to seem ungrateful.

Vernon Never.

Sally I'd have to dress up.

Vernon Tell you what I'll get us a takeaway.

Sally You're very considerate. I brought stuff in.

Vernon What's the matter?

Sally Bit tired from –

Vernon Where's Robert?

Sally One of those days at work.

Vernon It's more than that.

Sally He's locked himself in his room.

Vernon How long's it been going on? (*No answer.*) It's always him.

Sally Four days. I hoped when I got in today . . .

Vernon Why? He say why?

Sally No.

Vernon Trouble at school? No – you'd've heard.

Sally   He wont talk.

Vernon (*starts to go to* **Robert***'s room*)   I'll have a word with him.

Sally   No no better not.

Vernon   Kids that age never happy less they're making everyone else miserable. Ignore him. He'll come out when he's hungry.

Sally   He can be very stubborn.

Vernon   It's me.

Sally   He hasnt said.

Vernon   I thought it was best if we took it slowly. Give him time to get used to seeing me round the house. Hasnt worked. Best I moved in now. He'll have to lump it.

Sally   No I dont want to upset him.

Vernon   But it's alright if he upsets you?

Sally   We dont know it's us.

Vernon (*calls*)   Robert!

When the adults speak to **Robert** *they do not speak directly to the back wall but only raise their voices.*

Sally   Please dont.

Vernon (*calls*)   You're upsetting your mother.

Sally   You'll only make things –

Vernon (*calls*)   Old enough to know better your age. (*No response.*)

Sally   He wont answer.

Vernon (*calls*)   Got the car outside. Take you bowling. You like that. (*Slight pause.*) Robert? – You beat me I'll give you a fiver. (*Silence.*) Right. I'm taking your mother out to dinner.

Sally   Please dont antagonise him.

Vernon   We're not letting a boy run our life. He cant run his own. Four days ! It's time you gave me the front door key.

Sally   No need. I'm always here when you −

Vernon   Get it cut tomorrow. Not having you shut up with him if he's being rebellious −

Sally   O I wouldnt say he −

Vernon   I would. Anything happen the police social blame me for not interfering. He could do anything.

Sally   He wouldnt do anything to −

Vernon   How d'you know? You didnt know he'd lock you out of a room in your own house for four days.

Sally   It's his room − so he −

Vernon   Get it cut tomorrow. Keep the bill. I know how to handle him. He's a good lad. (*Starts to steer her out.*) We're going.

Sally (*resists*)   But I'm −

Vernon   No need to dress up. Just fetch a coat.

Sally *goes out.* **Vernon** *listens for a moment.*

Vernon (*half-calls*)   Robert. (*No response. Slight grin.*) I'm taking Sally for a ride. Want to come?

Vernon *goes out.*

Two

Sally *comes in. She carries a freshly laundered shirt.*

Sally (*calls*)   You broke Vernon's windscreen. Dont deny it. He mobiled me at work. (*No answer.*) Must've been you. Who

else would break it? No one round here. Verny's popular.
People like him. Suppose you thought you were being clever.
Well? (*No answer.*) I've got a vandal for a son – that it? (*No
answer.*) Answer me when I speak to you! Verny cant say
enough good things about you. He wants to be proud of you.
He was going to buy you a mountain bike. Even what they
cost! I wont let him after today. Another man would've gone
straight to the police. Not phoned me. I've brought your
clean shirt. – I know you broke the window so why cant you
say so?

Front door rings. **Sally** *puts the shirt on the table. She goes out and
comes back with* **Vernon**. *He wears his suede coat.*

Vernon   He own up?

Sally   He's too ashamed. (*Calls.*) Vernon's here. Tell him
you're sorry.

Silence.

Vernon   You pander to him.

Sally (*irritated*)   What're all the packing cases? The outside
passage is blocked. Cant see over the top. They were
delivered while I was at work. I never ordered anything. Is it
a shed?

Vernon   My surprise. (*Calls.*) Robert there's a surprise
outside. First instalment. For the family. (*Normal voice, to*
Sally.) Not a shed.

Sally   Just tell me! I cant stand any more messing about!
I've enough with him!

Vernon   It's a conservatory.

Sally   Conservatory? (*Slight pause.*) Why?

Vernon   To sit in. – Puts up the value of the house. Never
know – might want to sell it.

Sally   A conservatory! – They cost a fortune. I cant afford that sort of money.

Vernon   No one asked you to.

Sally   You cant just say – (*Slight pause. Bewildered.*) Conservatory.

Vernon   Wanted to do something for you. Make a commitment. Promise you and Robert better days. Shall I send it back?

Sally   Course I'm grateful. But – . A conservatory! Whatever put that in your head? You must've known for weeks.

Vernon   I'm a man of ideas. It's got side panels in coloured glass. Birds. Nature designs. I'm splashing out on the proper furniture. *En suite.* Padded chairs. You can choose from the showroom.

Sally   A conservatory . . .!

She goes out to look. **Vernon** *looks after her for a moment. Then he picks up the shirt. Unfolds it. Stares at it. Hangs it over the back of the chair.*

Vernon (*raising his voice*)   You like good things. Go for bright colours. (*Pulls off a shirt button.*) Button off. (*Shows the button between thumb and index finger.*) I know you can see. You got a hole in the wall. (*Puts the button in his mouth. Sucks it for a moment.*) Tell you what I'll do. I dont like you disobeying your mum. An only child should be more caring. Thoughtful. You get away with this you'll grow up a disappointment to yourself. You own up. Not to me. To her. I want to hear all the words. Mumbling wont do. 'I broke the windscreen on Verny's car.' Seven words. Every one crystal clear. If you dont I put it in the hands of the police. It's my duty. We have to report vandalism. Mum wont like that any more than you do. You have to learn the sort of man you're going to share the house with.

Sally *comes back. She tries to subdue her excitement.*

Sally   It's such a lovely thing! I dont know what I could say.

Vernon   I've made a bargain with Robert. He owns up he broke the windscreen. To you. Not me. He doesnt have to say sorry. I wont charge him for the replacement. Wont bully him. His age I could've done the same. (*Calls.*) It's the principle Robert. You say it so I can hear. We dont want any soft-hearted mums lying to save their boy's skin. You tell mum the truth or it goes to the police. You can speak up like a man.

Silence. **Vernon**'s *tongue plays with the button in his mouth.*

Sally   After all he's done for us! How could you humiliate me like this in front of Verny?

Silence. **Vernon** *spits out the button into his palm. Drops it.* **Sally** *doesn't see this.*

Vernon   You saw the parrot? Did you see the monkey's paw coming out of the foliage to pinch the coconut?

Sally   I didnt bring you up to tell lies! If Verny goes to the police I'll be shown up in front of the neighbours. Verny's right – he knows how to handle you better than I do. He can deal with you from now on. I'm having nothing more to do with you till you own up. And you pay for the replacement. I wont shield you. I'll go to the police myself.

Vernon (*slight pause*)   I'll show you the monkey.

Sally   Thank you Verny. I'd like that.

Vernon   He must've been a real artist. He got the colours just right.

Sally *goes out in front of* **Vernon**. *He follows her.*

Silence.

Robert (*behind the wall*)   Never.

Three

Sally *sits at the table. She sews a button on the shirt.*

Sally   If he goes to the police it wont be just the car window. The vandalism round here – they'll pin all of it on you. The neighbours are fed up with it. They wont give you any sympathy. All you have to do is tell the truth for once. Then it'll all be over. Dont think he's just saying and wont go. I know him better than you. Under all that kindness he can be hard as nails. That's what we all need. Tired of coping on my own. I want to share my life with someone. Now I cant because of a piece of broken glass. *(Sews.)* I play your games. You pretend you're starving yourself. So I make your meals and leave them on the table. I go to work and you come out to eat. I make the meals too big so you can leave some and we can both pretend you havent eaten. 'O poor Robert's starving. My heart's broken.' We cant even get that right in this house. 'I broke the windscreen.' That's all you have to say. It's not the worst crime in the world.

She puts the shirt down. Goes out. Comes back. She brings cutlery and a plate of food. She puts them on the table.

The rest of the meal's on the table. Hotted it up in the micro. I know what it is. You've got a grudge against him. He cant get anything right. Next you'll say he pulled the button off your shirt. I'm sitting here talking to a wall. If it gets cold I'm not hotting it up for you again. *(Silence.)* What am I supposed to believe? Robert I'm asking you to help me. Since your father died I've depended on you for everything. I lived for you till Verny came. That wasnt fair. I put a strain on you. A woman cant depend on a child. It's her job to protect. I'm asking you to help me – perhaps for the last time. Afterwards Verny'll be here to help both of us. I need to know. Perhaps you didnt do it. If Verny's wrong I must tell him. We cant start our life together on a misunderstanding about you. My future's in your hands. Did you break his windscreen? It's the most important question I'll ever ask you.

Robert (*behind the wall*)   Never.

Sally   Stop it! Stop it! Stop it! You're lying you little liar!
What shall I do? Knock the wall down and bury you in it!
Everything's closing round me like a prison. Tomorrow the
men come. The conservatory'll go up. I cant tell Verny to go
when his conservatory's here! If he goes anyway – I'll have to
pay for it! I couldnt face myself otherwise. It's a prison! I have
to carry on with my life when it's not worth living! 'Never.
Never. Never.' Eat. You're good at that. Eat. Eat. You can
come out. I shant stay and watch. Put the clean shirt on. Look
respectable when the police come.

Sally *goes*.

Four

Vernon *alone. He wears his suede coat. He sits at the table. The plate
of food is untouched.*

Vernon   You've done it now. When mum came back and
saw it she was so angry she went for a walk. D'you know, she
was trembling? Couldnt shout. Couldnt talk. You got that
to look forward to. Every pane smashed. Even the monkey.
They'll lock you up in a young offenders. It wont be nice like
your room. You thought you'd got me. Smash my
conservatory – I'd see so much red I'd walk out – if she didnt
chuck me out first 'cause I'm trouble. I dont care about the
conservatory. I'd never sit in it. People stare at you through
the glass. Did you think I'd share this house with you? I
wouldnt live in the same street as you. Thought it'd be hard
work turfing you out. You've done it for me. Did me a favour.
(*Picks at the food with the fork. Swallows a mouthful.*) Dont want this
muck. Wont leave it for you. You dont know what hungry is.
I grew up hungry. Teaches you to look after number one.
You're number one thousand and two. I know your sort.
Your innocent mug is watching me now. (*Lets food drop from the
fork.*) Saw your spy hole first time I came in the room. – The

car's different. I look after my possessions. No one vandalises me and gets away with it. You broke my windscreen.

Robert (*behind the wall*)   Never.

Vernon (*mimicking. Comic*)   Never. Never. – Liar.

Robert (*behind the wall*)   Never.

Vernon (*cold. Menacing*)   Liar.

Robert (*behind the wall*)   Never!

Vernon   I've got witnesses.

Robert (*behind the wall*)   Liar!

The wall collapses into **Robert**'s *shape. He comes forward as the wall-figure.*

Robert   Never!

Vernon   Liar!

Robert   I never broke the windscreen!

Vernon   I suppose you never broke the conservatory? Every pane? Never? Never? (*Silence.*) Well as a matter of fact you didnt. (*Stirs food with fork.*) I did – some of it. A few panes. I knew you'd be blamed after the windscreen. I broke them out of three crates. Three – so it wouldnt look like an accident. I only broke a few. Couldnt afford more – Im not insured. Then you broke the lot. (*Licks tines of fork clean.*) You owe me for that. (*Puts fork down.*) You didnt notice – in your frenzy – some had already been broken. (*Takes industrial gauntlets from side pocket of his suede jacket.*) If you hadnt used these you'd've cut yourself to shreds. Workmen left them. Glazier's mittens. (*Puts on gauntlets.*) I used them before you. Did mine at night. You did yours in broad daylight. Next door saw you. At it fifteen minutes. Did a real job.

Robert   Go to the police! You dont scare me! I'll tell them about you!

Vernon   Go to the police? Last thing I'll do. With my record less I have to do with them the better. I'll tell mum 'I'm not going to the police. They'd put him away luv.' I'll make sure the neighbours go to them. They dont want to live next door to a vandal. Your mum'll think I'm a saint. She'll want to buy me a new conservatory. I wont let her. She can buy me a new car. I'm due for one. Cost more.

Robert   I'll tell her.

Vernon   Even better. She wont believe you. She'd cry and the neighbours'd laugh. No one'll believe anything you say after the windscreen. You broke it. The windscreen was your last chance to tell the truth and be believed. Now you can write it on the wall and no one'll believe you. You'll be like a dog tied on a lead. Tug this way and that. Poor little blighter strangles itself. (*Forks food. Eats a mouthful.*) Your mum's given me the runaround long enough. Had to beg for the key! She'll pay for that. Your dad left her money. When I get my hands on it I'm off. I cant stand her voice. 'Verny love.' Always sounds as if she's in the wrong gear, doesnt she? Tell her I'm a villain. Tell her what I'm saying now. Try. You're out of your league little man. Dont try to play with the big men. (*A mouthful of food.*) You beat me on one thing chummy. You never let me hear you say 'Mum I broke Uncle Verny's windscreen.' I wanted to hear you say that. To help her. Put her mind at rest and so on. She'd've boasted how you came clean like a good boy. That'd've given me real satisfaction. Know why?

Silence. **Vernon** *chews and stares at* **Robert**.

Robert (*flat. Realises*)   You broke the windscreen.

Vernon (*nods*)   I said sorry car and smashed it with a hammer.

Robert's *hand comes out to reach for the plate.* **Vernon** *jabs the fork down at the hand. It sticks upright in the table. He chews in silence for a moment.*

Vernon   Now look what you've done Robert. Ruined the table. You're a real little villain.

He takes a wedge of broken glass from his pocket. In one movement he forces **Robert** *to the ground. Then he stands astride him. Grabs his hand and cuts it with the glass. The blood is not seen.*

Robert   Aow!

Vernon   Cut it smashing the conservatory.

Robert   Aow!

Vernon *rips a strip from the shirt. Grabs* **Robert**'s *hand. Binds the cut.*

Robert   Aow!

Vernon (*harsh*)   Keep still. Not having you bleed to death while I'm here. Be blamed for that. There's always aggro with you. Keep still Robert!

He finishes binding the wound. **Robert** *runs out back to his room.* **Vernon** *sits at the table. Takes off the gauntlets. He flips his hand against the upright fork – it judders and then hums like a tuning fork. He becomes morose and very quiet.*

Vernon   Run away. That's good advice. Anyone can live on the streets these days. No one's bothered. Just keep your wits going. I'll lead your mother a dance. It wont be nice. Dont stay and watch. I dont want to humiliate you. That hurts more than a cut. I suppose you're fond of her. Dont mind her voice. (*He hears the front door.*)

Sally (*off*)   Home.

Vernon *puts the fork on the plate. Inspects his hands. Wipes them on the shirt.*

Vernon (*calls*)   In here luv.

He picks up the gauntlets. Looks around. Chooses a spot. Drops the gauntlets on it. Repositions them with his foot to make them more conspicuous. Walks away. **Sally** *comes in.*

Sally   Did you speak to him?

Vernon   He's been out his room – the meal's touched.

Sally   I dont like to see you upset. A conservatory's not the end of the world. It was a nice idea but – (*Shrugs.*)

Vernon   Now we dont know it's him. People round here are jealous. Next door could've – (*Stops. Stands in front of the gauntlets. Tries to heel them out of sight.*) Could be anyone who –

Sally   What's that?

Vernon (*blocking her view*)   Nothing.

Sally   What is it?

Vernon *picks up the gauntlets. Shows them.* **Sally** *takes them from his hands.*

Vernon   Workmen wear them for fixing glass.

Sally   That's blood. (**Vernon** *doesn't answer.*) What have I got for a son? I'll buy you a new conservatory.

Vernon (*shrugs*)   He'd break it.

Sally   If he gets away with this what'll he do next? I've got a bit of money in the bank –

Vernon   Be throwing it away. Might as well give him stones as a present. A conservatory – it was a stupid idea. There's better things to spend your money on. I wont report the conservatory to the police. (*Takes the gauntlets.*) I'll burn these. In case the police come nosing.

Sally   I knew you wouldnt go to the police. I realised it when I was walking. (*Calls.*) Robert did you hear? Verny's not going to the police.

Silence.

Vernon   I'll leave you to –

Sally   Stay. I want to hear him apologise to you.

She goes to kiss **Vernon**. *He turns away.*

Sally   Please dont be upset. I'll make it up to you. There must be something I can do.

Vernon   I'll be out with the car.

He goes out.

Sally (*calls*)   Now see what you've done. I've never seen him so upset. We dont deserve him.

Robert *comes in as himself. He keeps his bandaged hand out of sight.*

Sally   Surprised you're not ashamed to show your face.

Robert   When you're out he says awful things about you. He doesnt –

Sally   Robert!

Robert   – like your voice! He's after your money!

Sally   Stop it! I wont listen! He's a good man! You heard him say he wont report you to the police! I dont know where you get your wicked lies from –

Robert   He's not good enough for you.

Sally   How do you know?

Robert   You never listen to me!

Sally   You want to listen to yourself. How can a boy know what's good enough? You destroyed the conservatory. You damaged his car. You know how fond of it he is. Sheer spite! But he doesnt hold a grudge. That man's a saint. He wants to be a dad to you and a friend if you'd let him. You're right – I wont listen to you when you lie. Why cant you do what I ask? Do I have to plead?

Robert   No mum – dont!

Sally   Then tell Verny you broke his windscreen. Tell him you're sorry. If you didnt break it who did? Next you'll tell me he did.

Robert   I broke it.

Sally   'And I'm sorry.'

Robert   Sorry.

Sally   Thank you. At last. Now admit you broke the conservatory. I couldnt believe my eyes. All that smashed glass.

Silence.

Robert   I didnt do the conservatory.

Sally   Robert they saw you next door. She called her husband. They stood and watched you do it. For fifteen minutes.

Robert (*gestures pleading with his hand*)   I didnt do it.

Sally   What's that?

Robert (*hides his hand*)   I didnt.

Sally   What's that? (*She snatches for his hand. He tries to pull it away.*) What's that?

Robert   Believe me mum.

Sally (*alarmed, afraid*)   O Robert – Let me look. What is it? (*She unwraps the cut.*) So dangerous, so dangerous. You could've cut your . . . Have you put TCP on it?

Robert   It doesnt matter.

Sally *goes out.*

Robert (*quietly to himself. Rehearsing*)   Believe me. Please. Please. Please. (*Calls.*) Never!

Sally *comes back with a transparent plastic or glass bowl of water, a cloth and a bottle of TCP. She puts them on the table.*

Sally   Let me look. – (*She sits him in the chair. Uncovers the cut.*) You did the bandage well. Like a professional. I'll say that: you look after yourself.

She washes the cut. The water in the bowl reddens.

Robert   Mum.

Sally (*concentrating on washing the cut. Quietly*)   Look at it. You could have done it on purpose. A wonder there's no glass in it.

Robert   I didnt break the conservatory

Sally   Stop it.

Robert   Please mum. Believe me.

Sally (*jerks his hand towards her*)   Keep still. Hold it upright. (*Dips the cloth.*) I'm tired of this nonsense. (*Washes the cut.*) You were seen! Where did this cut come from?

Robert   Please mum.

Sally   Stop it Robert! (*Washing.*) Sick and tired of it. I cant take any more. It's got to stop.

His voice is flat, quiet, tearless, almost monotonous.

Robert   Please mum. Believe me.

Sally   How can I? If there was any possibility I would. I cant.

Robert   Please mum.

Sally   I cant. I want to believe you. Dont ask me like that. Please. You upset me.

Robert   Mum. Mum. Please.

Sally (*washing the wound*)   Stop it! You frighten me. You've no right to keep asking me. It's not right. The devil's got into you. I cant help you. It was never like this in the past. Those days 'll never come back. I wish your father was here. You'd listen to him.

Robert   Please mum.

Sally   I'm crying into your wound. (*Pushes the cloth at him.*) Dry yourself! You can manage that! (**Robert** *lets the cloth fall* *to the ground. Fighting back her tears.*) What'll become of us after this? If I lose Verny what've I got? Nothing. My age I'm lucky to – to get an interest – any interest from a man who's not out of the door as soon as he's got what he wants. Verny's a decent man who wants to take care of us –

Robert   Please mum.

Sally   Could've cut the artery. God knows what – ! I love you Robert. You're my son. If they'd taken you to hospital –

Silence.

Robert (*as before. Quiet. Monotonous*)   Please mum. Believe me. Believe me. That's all there is now mum. It'll be alright then. Like it was. Believe me. Please mum. Please mum.

Silence.

(*Quiet. Monotonous.*) Please mum.

Sally   I cant.

Robert *goes to the wall. Buries his face against it in the crook of his arm. Sobs noiselessly.* **Sally** *watches him. Then she goes to comfort him. Stops herself. Goes to the table. Puts the cap on the TCP bottle.*

Sally   I go to work for you. I give you a home. I feed you. I clean up after you.

Robert *turns to face her. He leans against the wall. Rests the back of his head against it. His eyes are closed. Expressionless.*

Sally   Now you ask me to lie to you. It'd be wrong. Life isnt meant to be easy. (*She looks round futilely for something to say.*) Yesterday you cut your toenails. You left the clippings on the chair for me to clean up. So I did. (*Pause.*) Throw the dirty water down the sink.

Robert *takes the bowl from the table. He leaves – bumps into* **Vernon** *lurking behind the doorway.* **Vernon** *has taken off the suede coat.* **Robert** *and* **Sally** *stare at him.*

Vernon (*scrap of a laugh*)   Caught me listening at the keyhole! Had to − in case there was any − (*Half gestures at* **Robert**.) − you know. Not risk it.

Robert *goes out.* **Vernon** *goes to* **Sally**. *He tries to put his arms round her.*

Vernon   Sorry about that − before. I was a bit − It's getting to me.

Sally (*avoiding him*)   Not now.

Vernon   The clutch is giving me jip. Fork out for a new one.

Sally   I suppose you heard him say he broke the windscreen.

Vernon (*picks up the cloth from the floor. Clicks his tongue in disapproval*)   Tch tch − mess.

Sally   He still says he didnt break the conservatory.

Vernon (*silent for a moment. Then through his teeth with menace*) Sometimes kids want murdering.

Sally   Have to arrange for a special collection with the dustmen. There'll be a charge.

Vernon *lays the TCP bottle on its side. Picks up the table.*

Sally   What're you doing?

Vernon   The new arrangements. Move the furniture round a bit. Make it better for you.

Vernon *takes the table out.* **Sally** *follows him.* **Vernon** *comes back. He stares round the room. With both hands he picks up the chair by its back. He takes it out.*

Five

A city street. A **Girl** *comes on. She has a bundle, a red blanket, an empty dog leash and collar and a whistle pipe. She sits. She spreads the blanket.*

A passer-by comes. She tries to play the pipe: a broken wail. The passer-by goes. She stops trying to play. She shakes. Her teeth chatter in fever. She spreads her hands towards the blanket as if she were warming them at a fire. She sees someone coming. She tries to play: the same wail.

Robert *comes on. He wears an old coat, a knitted cap and scarf. He carries a shopping bag stuffed full with clothes. He stops.* **Girl** *plays. The pipe drops from her hands.*

Robert   You compose that?

Girl   Clear off.

Robert   What were you doing when I came? (*She ignores him.*) Doing something. I watched.

Girl   Clear off. My pals be here soon. They dont like riff-raff gawpers with no money.

Robert   You're on your own.

Passer-by. She snatches up the pipe. Plays: the same wail. Passer-by goes. She stops.

Girl   Hop it. You're bad luck. You scared him off.

Robert (*starting to go*)   Shouldnt be on the streets on your own.

Girl   Got a dog.

Robert   What you call it?

Girl   Angel. Black labrador.

Robert (*stops*)   Where is it?

Girl   Gone.

Robert   Why?

Girl   Couldnt feed her properly. Went to stroke her. She thought I was pinching her bone.

Robert *starts to go again.*

Girl   Ran away. Like you.

Robert (*stops*)   Didnt run. Walked.

Girl   O. Why?

Robert (*explaining*)   Smashed conservatory. They accused me.

Girl   Did you?

Robert   Course. (*Starts to go again. Stops.*) When they accused me – . (*Stops.*)

Girl   Go on.

Robert   Something happened. I felt strong. As big as a – .

He stops. They stare at each other for a moment. **Robert** *goes out.* **Girl** *shakes. Spreads her hands over the blanket.* **Robert** *comes back. Stops some way from her.*

Robert   As big as a wall. I knew I was in the right. Right about everything.

Girl *stares at him. He turns. Goes. Stops when he is almost out of sight.*

Robert   While it lasted I – . Funny – . (*Comes closer to* **Girl**. *Crouches. Tries to explain.*) Everything changed. Everything was in my hands. They couldnt hurt me after that. I could have done anything. I *was* the wall.

She says nothing. He stands. Walks away. Stops. Looks back at her.

It doesnt last – it doesnt have to. I felt it. It happened.

Girl   That why you left?

Robert   No – that was the toenails. (*Starts to leave. Stops again – realises he should explain.*) I cut my toenails and left the bits on the kitchen chair. My mum said I'm not your cleaning person. She was right. I went.

Silence. **Girl** *picks up her pipe. Plays: the same wail.*

Girl   Dont practise enough. (*Tries again.*)

Robert   Shall I teach you to play it better?

Girl   You a musician?

Robert *comes back. Puts down his carrier bag. Takes hold of the pipe.*

Girl (*tugging*)   Get off ! Thief!

Robert   No. No. Blow. Try. Blow.

Robert *holds the pipe to* **Girl**'s *mouth. He stops the holes with his fingers.* **Girl** *blows. A musical phrase.*

Robert   Hear it!

Girl (*little cough*)   I cant make the –

Robert   Give me your fingers. Follow my – . Like this. Blow.

Robert *guides her fingers on the holes. The musical phrase. He backs away. She blows – half-manages the phrase. He squats on his haunches. His arm out straight – points his finger at her. Laughs.*

Robert (*laughing*)   See!

She plays one or two more notes. Stops. Laughs. She copies his gesture. They point at each other and rock with laughter.

Girl (*laughing*)   A wall with toenails! (*She splutters. Her fever returns. Teeth chatter.*) G' – g' – g' – away –

Robert   I cant let you –

Girl (*teeth chattering violently*)   G' – g' – g' – g' – g' – g' – g' – (*She flails the floor with the dog leash. Stops. Exhausted.*)

Robert   Cant leave you here.

Girl   G' – go. 'M alright. Got me blanket. Keep me warm. (*Spreads her hands over the blanket.*) Red.

Robert *picks up his carrier. Goes. Stops. Turns back to her.*

Robert   Red.

Girl (*spreading her hands*)   Colour of fire. Keeps me warm.

Robert (*comes back to her*)   Warm?

Girl   Warm. Lovely. Warm. Right through me.

Robert   A colour doesnt keep you warm.

Girl   It does. It does. This is lovely in the – (*A little spasm of chattering.*) Had a white blanket before. Gave me my cold. (*Draws blanket round her.*) This is –. Lovely warm fire in the –. Warm in the –

Robert (*snatches the blanket away. Very angry*)   No!

Girl   Give me my blanket! It keeps me warm! It does! Give me my – !

Robert   No! No! No!

Girl (*pleading. Teeth chattering*)   Please. Please. Please. Give me my – please –

Robert (*walking away with the blanket*)   No. It doesnt. It doesnt –

Girl (*shaking. Chattering. Stretches her arms, spreads out her fingers towards the blanket*)   Give me my – warm – I'll die of cold –

Robert (*in one swift gesture he throws the blanket round himself*) Then I'll die with you!

Silence. They stare at each other without moving. Then slowly to warm herself she puts her hands in her armpits and hugs her chest.

Girl (*tries to speak, mumbles a few incoherent words. Mutters viciously*) If I could curse you . . .

Robert   It doesnt.

Girl   Sometimes it's so hot – I scald myself – throw it off – walk at night in my bare feet to get cold – dance on the freezing street – people clap –

Robert (*shakily. Trying to explain*)   It's a colour . . . that's all . . . only that. (*Quietly. Desperately.*) A colour cant. It doesnt. Cant.

Doesnt. It's not like the wall. The wall was *in* me. This is – .
A colour doesnt. It cant.

He puts her hand on the blanket. They stare at each other. He folds the blanket.

We'll find a shelter. Go somewhere.

He picks up her things. Gives them to her. Her jaw trembles.

Find somewhere.

He helps her. They go.

A Window

A Triptych

A Window was first staged by Big Brum at Golden Hillock School, Birmingham, on 19 October 2009. The cast was as follows:

Liz   Liz Brown
Richard   Richard Holmes
Dan   Danny O'Grady

Directed by Chris Cooper
Designed by Ceri Townsend

Characters

Liz
Richard
Dan

Setting

City
Now

Room. Door. Window. Chaise-longue. Wooden table and
chair.

The *flat* is in a high-rise block. The window faces the
audience. It is not seen. The table and chair are utilitarian.

Panel One

No one is in the room. The door opens. **Liz** *comes in. She carries a pile of bedding. She goes to the chaise longue. She starts to make up a bed on it. Off, the flat door is heard opening and closing.* **Liz** *goes to the door of the room. Closes it. Goes back to the chaise longue. Makes up the bed. Silence.*

Richard (*off*)   You in?

Liz *doesn't react. Silence. The door opens.* **Richard** *comes in.*

Richard   Did yer 'ear? I called. (*No answer. Sees the bedding.*) We expectin company?

Liz (*making up bed*)   Sleepin in 'ere.

Richard   O no. Not another a' yer things? (*No answer.*) Whass this one about?

Liz   Nothin. It'll be alright.

Richard   Nothin?

Liz   Juss want t' be quiet.

Richard   Yer serious? – yer sleepin on yer own?

Liz   Need t' be quiet.

Richard   If yer ill go t' the doctor's.

Liz   Not ill.

Richard   Seen this comin. Yer bin actin up for days.

Liz   Want a bit a' quiet. Not a crime.

Richard   Quiet!

Liz   Please. I juss need a bit a' space for meself.

Richard   What've I done now?

Liz   Nothin –

Richard   Then what the bloody –

Liz   Please please. I dont want t' row.

Richard   Looks like it! (*Sits at table.*) I come 'ome. Trampin all day. Got nowhere. Yer're turnin the place upside down. Yer dont want t' row?

Liz   Sorry yer day wasnt –

Richard   Dont change the subject! Sorry me day – ? Lot yoo care!

Liz   The flat's in my name. I can do what I like.

Richard   O we're back t' that! So yer want me out?

Liz   No. I tol' yer. I need a bit a' space round me 'ead.

Richard (*elbows on table. Head in his hands*)   Jees. Jees. What've I done t' deserve it?

Liz *goes out. She leaves the door open.*

Richard (*calls*)   I'm takin yer round the doctor's.

Liz (*off*)   I'm not ill. I wouldnt go t' 'er if I was. She'd put me on pills. What use is that?

Richard *stands. Goes out.*

Richard (*off*)   Yer call this fair? If yer got a problem we ought 'a talk! Why didnt yer say before?

Liz (*off*)   Only decided this afternoon. I'm no use t' yer if I'm not – werent meself. 'S only for a little while.

She comes in. She carries a pillow.

Liz   I 'oped yer'd understand for once.

She starts to put the pillow in a pillowcase. **Richard** *comes in.*

Richard   Then it's someone else. (**Liz** *makes a dismissive gesture.*) Yer'd like it if I went off! Vanish God knows where. Ain see me for weeks. I turn up 'n say I juss wanted a bit a' space for me 'ead! More like a bit a' life! Bit a' fun for a change! 'Stead a' the misery a' this place!

Liz   Please please.

Richard   O it'll be great! You in 'ere, me out there. Bump in t' each other. 'O 'ello 'ow's the quiet goin? Okay if I speak?' We still eatin together? – Right! – yer sleep in 'ere till yer 'ad yer bit a' quiet. Then move back next door 'n I'm supposed t' be waitin? Well what if I ain? I'd've thought a bit a' gratitude was in order for once! Yer ain the only skirt round 'ere.

Liz   I thought if I slep in 'ere for a while I'd sort it out for both of us.

Richard   Sort *what* out?

Liz   Please.

Silence.

Richard   So thass it then?

He goes out. **Liz** *lies face down on the bed.* **Richard** *comes in with his jacket.*

Richard   Where's yer 'andbag? Goin down the road. 'Ad enough a' this place. Yer'll 'ave t' give us a sub. Yer know I'm broke. Thass why yer think yer can get away with messin me about. I dont like bein skint! I'll pay yer back. Benny'll drop me a few quid if I give 'im a 'and in 'is yard. (*Silence. He stares at her.*) . . . Quiet? Yer wont get that round 'ere. Never quiet. Cars. Drunks. Street at night. 'Ave t' go a long way out t' get that. . . Yer made yer point. Let's drop it. We goin t' eat? (*Silence.*) What is it?

Liz   I read it in the papers. Some woman – . Yer wouldnt understand.

Richard   Jees.

Liz   'Andbag's by the fridge. Leave me some for the shoppin.

Richard   Read what in the papers?

Liz   . . . The way she said it, as if it was the most natural thing in the. . . as if she juss said it like that yer'd 'ave t' understand what it . . .why she . . .

Richard   Understand why she what?

Liz   She blinded 'er kid.

Richard   O?

Liz   So it'd 'ave t' stay with her. Always be with 'er. When it grew up. Never 'ave t' go out – mix with – never 'ave t' fight its way in the – grovel t' survive – tear itself t' bits. She did it 'cause she loved it. She'd always care for it – look after it – it'd grow up as if 'er 'ouse was its playpen. Be buried in its playpen!

Richard   So? What 'appened next?

Liz   Nothin *'appened next*! She blinded it.

Richard   Thass what the papers – ?

Liz   Yes.

Richard   We ought t' eat. Then yer'll feel – . The papers get it wrong. Bad as telly. Chriss if there's bin 'n accident 'n 'er kid's –

Liz   Wasnt no –

Richard   Can I speak? – so she's upset – blames 'erself – chriss wouldnt yoo be upset, blame yerself, even if it was juss the cat 'oo –

Liz   Get out!

Richard   Dont tell me what t' –

Liz   It wasnt 'n accident!

Richard   Shurrup! A kid's blind? Right. It 'appens. There's mad people about – things 'appen all the time – 'n we got t' tear ourselves t' bits – me kicked out – 'cause *one* child, alright even *one* child but it still dont make it right that I got t' sleep on me own! Does the 'ole world 'ave t' go blind – switch off the telly – creep round bumpin in t' each other – so the kid know we're all sufferin? That make it 'appy? – Chriss life 'as t' go on.

Liz   It wasnt an accident.

Richard   I cant cope with this. Yer need 'elp. Yer bin upset – now yer makin yerself more upset for nothing! 'S mad! Yer trouble is no one never knocked any sense in t' yer! (*Slight pause.*) Was this tart local? God 'elp 'er if she's from round 'ere. She'll 'ave it comin t' 'er. The lads wont put up with 'er caper. I'll give 'em a 'and.

Liz   She did it with some scissors –

Richard   Alright we dont need t' know all the –

Liz   It was both eyes.

Richard   Stop it!

Liz   If she'd done one. If the kid could've talk. Tol' 'er no no please mummy not two mummy leave one so –

Richard   Stop it! I tol yer t' stop it!

Liz   – I can see yer face mummy – she didnt – she took the other one with the – then bang – (*She slaps her hands on to her face.*) she slaps its 'ands on 'er face 'n said feel feel yer can still feel mummy's face – !'

Richard   Stop it!

Liz   Seein it in me 'ead all afternoon

Richard   Stop it! Chriss why're we arguing 'bout this? Look, yer read that – it said all that in the paper – ?

Liz   I can see its 'ands – its little nails – pushin – 'n she still –

Richard *goes out.*

Liz (*voice half-raised*)   It's the way she said it . . . as if yer'd know why the kid 'ad t' be . . . she scared me . . . every bit a' cruelty's like that – every time – dont matter what it is – but no one sees it –

Richard (*off*)   I cant find it! There's no paper!

Liz   – its little 'ands pushin at the . . .

Richard *comes back. He leans in the doorway. Silence.*

Richard   Traffic jam. Bus stuck in the stink. Thought I'd bring up. Chriss I wish I 'ad some money. Move out. Somewhere sane. There's no paper.

He goes to the chaise longue. Scoops up the bedding – one pillow falls to the ground. Goes out with the rest.

Liz (*voice half-raised*)   Tore it up. Didnt want it in the place. Thought I'd imagined it. Keep goin back t' read it on the pieces. Chucked it out.

Richard *comes back.*

Richard   We ought to eat.

Liz   I'm goin t' 'ave a baby.

Richard *goes to the chaise longue. Picks up the pillow.*

Richard (*flat*)   Get rid a' it. Go t' the doctor's in the morning. Get it out the way. Chriss. Yer supposed t' take care a' that side a' it. Cant rely on yer for nothing. 'Ow long yer know? When's it suppose t' be?

He looks at her. She doesn't react. He goes out with the pillow.

(*Off.*) Least thass somethin we dont 'ave t' put up with these days. Go through life with an unwanted brat 'angin round yer neck. Chriss it's quite a day yer set up for me. First the traffic jam. Still smell the stink on the bus. Then the kid in the paper. Wonder she never 'ad twins! Now this. – Go t' the doctor's with yer. Case she asks questions. I can explain the financial situation.

He comes back into the room.

Thass why there's no paper. Yer imagined it. Natural in yer condition –

Liz   Yer sayin I made it up?

Richard   No no but yer let it get t' yer 'stead a juss –

Liz   Yer blind a kid cause yer luv it! – I make that up?

Richard   Yer not thinkin a' keepin it? (*No answer.*) Yer not serious? Yer cant do that! Ain things dodgy enough already? Yer think a kid'd bring us together? Be the nail in the coffin. (*Goes closer. Shouts in her face.*) We cant afford it! (*Goes to the table. Sits.*) What use is a kid? Mess 'n noise. Snot one end, crap the other end 'n piss all over. Clean up after 'em, break yer back, sacrifice yer life – so they can grow up 'n blame yer for bringin 'em in t' the world. Always attackin. 'Other kids've got this, yer never give me nothin.' Well I'm not 'avin some little gangster sponge off me. Kids used t' support their parents. Now it's all want want want gimmee gimmee gimmee 'n the shelves're empty. Kids on the bus today. Dont need their mobile-this-'n-that: yellin their 'eads off, yer could 'ear 'em 'alfway round the planet. No consideration yer spent the day lookin for work 'n end up with nothing. They 'ave all the advantages. Few years time when they 'ave t' fend for theirself they'll end up on the rubbish 'eap. (*Puts his forearms flat on the table.*) Dont want all this. Struggle all me life t' get a roof over me 'ead. Not sharin it now. Cant afford it. If I could I still wouldnt. I knew something 'd 'appen today. Knew by the time it was over things'd be changed. Funny 'ow yer know. Feel it in the pit a' yer stomach . . .

He goes out.

(*Off.*) That kid's a curse on me. Get rid a' it or I'm out.

He comes back. He dangles a black handbag. The top is open. He throws it into the middle of the room.

Richard   Left enough in t' shop for one.

He goes out. The front door is closed. **Liz** *picks up the handbag. Puts her hand in to touch the money. Goes out. Shuts the door behind her.*

Panel Two

Off, the outside door opens and closes. **Dan** *comes into the room. A loose jacket hangs from his shoulders. The hood is raised over his head. He shuts the door. Leans against the wall. Half-raises the right side of his jacket to peer under it. His face is blank. He is tense and tired. He hears a sound. He takes a packet from his pocket. Puts it on the table. Goes to the chaise longue. Sits on the edge.* **Liz** *comes in. She is older, untidy and unkempt.*

Liz (*a bit too brightly*)   O 'ello luv. Thought I 'eard yer. What kept yer? Bin with yer mates?

Dan *gestures to the table. She glances quickly at the packet – doesn't react.*

Liz   Why dont yer take yer jacket off?

Dan   Take it t' yer room.

Liz   I only asked 'cause . . . yoo sittin there. – Did yer eat out? Can I get yer somethin?

Dan   Later.

Liz   Expect yer tired. (*No answer. Goes to the table. Picks up the packet.*) 'Ow much did they . . . ?

Dan   I managed.

Liz   Did they try t' raise the . . . ?

Dan   I managed.

Goes to door. Speaks in the doorway.

Liz (*hurt*)   Dont treat me like a child dear. I worry when yer out.

Dan   Take it t' yer room.

Liz (*stops*)   Yer've no right t' talk ' me as if I . . .

Dan   Made yer wait. Sorry.

Liz   Why're yer sittin in yer − ?

Dan   'S nothing. Juss take it t' yer room.

Liz   I'm not a fool! Something's 'appened.

Dan   I was in a fight!

Liz   O.

Dan   Satisfied?

He pulls the jacket from his shoulders. His right shirtsleeve is soaked in blood. It is almost dry. It is an oddly 'heraldic' image as if the whole sleeve had been dipped in red paint. His hand is almost clean.

Liz (*panicking*)   O God thass knives! Look! Yer bin fightin! I tol' yer no knives! Never take a − ! Yer promised me!

Dan   No knives −

Liz   I tol' yer walk away if they − !

Dan   Didnt fight − !

Liz   This place! I cant cope with any more a' it! Me nerves 're in shreds! (*Sudden panic.*) O God did yer bleed on the stairs? The neighbours'll know if there's blood on our − ! Yer've marked us out!

Dan   Take it t' yer room!

Liz   Dont want it! Take it away! Wont 'ave it in the 'ouse! Couldnt touch it if yer paid me! − not if yer 'ave t'get kill for it! − Did yer bleed on the stairs?

Dan   Take it t' yer room.

Liz   O, it's easy t' say that! (*Tearful self-pity.*) 'Ow can I take it with yer blood on it? If yer'd let me . . . before yer showed me yer arm − I could've − me nerves wouldnt be in such a . . . if yer'd 'ad that little bit a' consideration, no that's too much t' ask . . . – (*Sniffs.*) Yer promise me no knives.

Dan   Promise meself! Not interested . . . –

Liz   But yer –

Dan   Got a cosh. If there's bother I –

Liz   A cosh? One yer – ? . . . Whass goin t' 'appen t' us? I dont see any way out! – nowhere t' turn . . . Sometimes I wish I'd never bin born – .

Dan *eases the sleeve away from his arm. Half-winces.*

Liz   O God! – Yer sit there 'n let me talk 'bout my troubles – . (*Puts packet on table.*) It's got t' be wash.

Dan   Not deep – scrape the skin off the top – made a mess –

Liz   Wait. Stay there. O God!

Liz *goes out.* **Dan** *rolls up the sleeve on his arm. It is not as bloody as the sleeve. He moves his hand and flexes his fingers. He bows his head in exhaustion.* **Liz** *comes back with a bowl of water and bottle of TCP. She puts them on the table.*

Liz   Sit 'ere. (**Dan** *goes to the table. Sits on the chair.*) Leavin it like that. Not sayin. (*She looks at the cut.*) Thank God it's the arm – a few more inches 'n – (*Realises.*) Cloth! Didnt bring a – !

Liz *goes out.* **Dan** *remains bowed over the table.*

Liz (*off*)   No bandages in this 'ouse!

She comes in with a sheet.

Never anythin when yer want it. (*She starts to tear a strip from the sheet.*)

Dan   Dont spoil the –

Liz   'As t' be – cant leave it – ! (*She tears a piece from the sheet. Dips it in the water. Washes the cut.*) Shirt ruined. More expense. Not that I begrudge. – 'Old that.

Dan *holds the cloth against his arm.* **Liz** *tears another strip from the sheet.*

Dan (*grabbing at the sheet*)   Dont ruin it − I'll find somethin in the −

Liz (*tugging*)   Still! Wander round drippin all over the − . Yer mother cant neglect a cut like that − (*She jerks at the sheet. Knocks over the bowl. The water sloshes.*) Damn! Now look what yer made me − ! Me nerves − the sight a' blood − ! I'll never forgive meself if anythin − I shouldnt let yer go but yer insist − (*Stops.*) Was anyone 'urt when yer − anyone else − ? (*Sudden panic.*) The police! − was the police involve −

Dan   No one −

Liz   O God! − the water's runnin! (*She picks up the packet.*) 'As it wet the − ? (*Relief.*) No, it's − . I'll put it out the way in me room. Cant let it get wet − after yer took the risk − (*She starts to leave. Takes the packet with her. In the doorway.*) Never could 'andle blood.

She goes out. **Dan** *washes his arm. Mops up the spilt water.*

Dan (*half raises his voice. Factually*)   It was Arnie. We'd got the stuff −

Liz (*off*)   Arnie?

Dan   'E asked me t' give 'im the lot.

Liz (*off*)   'Oo's Arnie?

Dan   Arnie. Yer know Arnie! 'E comes with me when we buy the − . Two a' us in case − . On the way back 'e asked for the lot. Tried t' grab it. 'E 'as t' give 'is girl − 'arf 'is family. 'E was high. Tell 'im not t' take nothin when we're out. No one listens. Wouldnt give 'im it. 'E drew 'is knife on me. (*His voice sinks.*) No police. (*Squeezes bloody water from the cloth.*) Me mate did this t' me.

Liz *comes back. She brings nail scissors. She is drugged.* **Dan** *bandages his arm.*

Liz   O. Yer managed . . .

Dan   Go back t' yer room.

Liz   Must mop up the –

Dan   Done it.

Liz   Yer never let me 'elp –

Dan   Im goin t' lie down.

Liz *starts to cut the sheet with the scissors.*

Dan   Leave that.

Liz   Too small. (*Drops scissors on table.*) Need bandages –

Dan   I bandaged it.

Liz (*tearing strips*)   Need more. 'Ave t' change the –

Dan (*half-heartedly tries to stop her*)   Leave it.

Liz (*pulling away*)   Why're yer so stubborn?

Dan   I want t' lie down.

Liz   I'm not stopping yer. Didnt I offer t' get yer something
t' eat? Wouldnt let me. Wouldnt let me wash that. Wont let
me do the bandage.

She tears more strips from the sheet. **Dan** *watches in silence. The
strips litter the floor.*

Dan   Yer ruin our lives.

Liz   'Oo's Arnie?

Dan   We need 'elp.

Liz   Yer sound like somethin in the papers.

Dan   Yer got t' give it up.

Liz   I cant. I know meself. Yer got t' let me understand
meself. At least allow me that. Some people start on it easy,

they're the ones 'oo give it up easy. I didnt want t' start – it was 'ard. Thass why I cant give it up. Wish I was different. This is 'ow I'll always be. Too late t' change.

Dan   Ow much did yer take?

Liz (*still tearing strips from the sheet*)   Please dont argue with me . . . Let me enjoy the benefit after yer took the risk . . .

Dan   I dont do yer any good.

Liz   Yer do. If I could give it up it'd be 'cause yer ask me to.

Dan   I'm not fetchin any more.

Liz (*giggles. Tearing.*)   Yer said that before. Yer only sayin it now cause yer bin scratch.

Dan   I could leave. Not stay 'ere 'n watch yer fall apart. If yer was on yer own yer'd 'ave t' make an effort.

Liz   . . . Yer father ran away.

Dan (*almost to himself. Ignoring* **Liz**)   Dont like goin out in the streets no more. Used to. Now they dont lead anywhere. Sun juss shows up the dirt. Takeaways drop in the gutter – bits a' animal bodies 'n 'uman sick. Want me own life while I'm still young enough t' do somethin with it. (*To* **Liz**.) I mean it – not fetchin no more.

Liz (*contented. Tearning*)   Yer will, yer will.

Dan   Today was the last.

He curls up on the chaise longue. Pulls his jacket over his head. Silence.

Liz   Try some. (*Takes package from her pocket.*) Some kids 're born with a 'abit. Their mothers pass it on. If they dont get it they shrivel up 'n die. (*Goes closer to him.*) Try it. Then yer'll understand. It takes the worries off yer. Yer wouldnt get the 'abit. Yer not the sort. Yer safe – yer dont even get angry. (*No response.*) Never let yer seen me do it. Go t' me room. Too ashamed t' show. I look at the needle when I stick it in. Want t' pull it out. Stab it in me chest. Stab. Stab. All I got left a' me self-respect is the shame. I cling to it. When it goes there's nothing. (*Lifts the cover.*) Asleep. Drop off like a child. Thass all 'e is, a child. (*She walks away.*) I know where yer get the money. Yer not discoin when yer say. Yer out on the street muggin some poor sod so yer mum can – . One day it wont be yer arm. (*She goes back to shake him awake. Instead she wrings her hands over his head.*) Dont go. Dont go. If yer dont go I'll 'ave t' stop it! Dont go! (*No response. She goes back to the table. Tears strips.*) Yer 'ate me! See it in yer eyes! Yer think it's luv! It's 'ate. Yer dont know the difference – yer too young. Yer father'd teach yer. (*She sees the scissors. Picks them up. Tries again to cut the sheet with them. Cant. Puts them back on the table.*) The woman 'ad a kid. She took out its eyes. (*Tearing strips.*) It was in the paper. I never tol' yer. Yer too clever – yer'd understand too much, know why she did it. – Yer ain bin cut. Aint no Arnie. (*Malice.*) Yer cut yerself t' punish me. T' see me suffer. Yer turn'll come. Seen yer smirk in yer new clothes 'n I ain got rags fit t' die in. The blood wont run out yer arm. Run round 'n round inside yer burnin yer up with yer own 'ate! Scaldin inside! (*Tearing.*) Yer'll suffer like the rest a' us. She carried its eyes t' the toilet. They was in a saucer. 'Ad to, 'ad to. The eyes said no mummy not the toilet. Not the water. She flushed 'em down the toilet with its tears. 'Cause she luv it. Cared for it. Always look after it. Yer'll never leave me. I couldnt live 'ere on me own. (*Picks up the scissors. Goes to* **Dan**.) The neighbours 'd drive me out on the street. I'll look after yer. Always take care a' yer. Luv yer. I promise. See the needle in me 'and. I got the skill. (*Holding the scissors motionless over his eyes.*) Stab. Stab. Stab. I cant . . . (*Vague.*) I cant – in yer sleep – yer'd never know it was the last light yer saw before yer . . . I cant – yer'd know the truth. She said she did it so she'd always look after it. Not true. She didnt know 'erself. She did it so it'd never get away from 'er. She'd never be alone. They took it away. Put it in a 'ome. Where is it now? Tap tap tap on the street like a clock. It's better t' know yerself. (*She goes to the table. Puts the scissors on it. Tears more strips.*) I wish I could comfort 'er. Wash 'er 'ands. Not judge or condemn. (*Suddenly brusquely picks up the chair. Takes it further into* *the room. Thumps it down. Goes back to the table. Ties strips together to make a rope.*) That day I went out in the street. The kids playin. Waggin their thumbs. The women 'd told 'em it was in the papers. They'd drew the kid's eyes on their thumbs. Makin a game. Waggin their thumbs 'n laughin. (*She ties a noose in the rope.*) I didnt go t' the shops. Turned back. Went 'ome. Thass why I cant go out now. (*She puts the noose round her neck. Goes to the chair. Stands on the seat.*) Cant take 'is eyes out. Done that already. 'Undreds a' times. When yer went fetchin. When I shouted at yer. When I cursed yer. When yer looked at me wrinkled – . When yer saw me 'ands shakin. When yer cried. Thass 'ow yer grow up t' be a man. (*She reaches up with the rope. Tries to hitch it overhead.*) Yer see it every day. Famine. Kids' bones wrap up in old skin. War. Fightin. Tanks bouncin in the dust – clouds a' it. A piece a' bread in the street. The long streets with a piece a' bread drop in 'em for the fillin. The city's a stone sandwich. I seen enough – got the right t' die. (*Looks down.*) The world's under the chair. Fall into that. That far. I cant (*She climbs down. Kneels by the chair. Rests her head on the seat.*) Who's Arnie? Praps 'e'll get drugs for me. (*Sleeps. Wakes.*) Death's the best drug. A knife's the map of a street. I understand now. (*She climbs back on the chair. Lifts the rope overhead.*) Cant feel anything. Be good t' be dead. (*Shuffles her feet.*) Look I made a space for yer on the seat. Stand by me. 'Elp me. Push me off. I wouldnt 'ave t' jump . . . 'S asleep. (*Little whine.*) Eeee . . . be quick or the sickness'll come back, I'll be alive. (*Tries to attach rope. Lets it fall. Silence.*) Cant – not in front of 'im. Be ashamed. 'E woke up 'n saw – 'e'd close 'is eyes – never open 'em again. (*She steps down from the chair. Goes to **Dan**. Uncovers his head. Looks at him.*) I'm at peace now. Like looking down at a pool a' water. (*She covers his head. Goes to the table. Takes a music player from the drawer. Turns it on. Dance music.*) Got nothing t' leave yer. – (*Takes the packet from her pocket.*) Give yer the drugs. Yer wont take em. But yer'll know I thought a' yer. Mustnt linger 'ere. Go t' me room.

The noose is round her neck. She picks up the end of the rope. She goes out. The music plays. Strips litter the floor, others hang on the chair.

Off, a crash. After some seconds **Dan** *stirs. Slowly sits up. Opens his eyes. Vaguely aware of the crash. He looks at the chair and the strips. Slowly stands and begins to collect them. He dances. Strips dangle from his hands. He weeps. Dancing and weeping he cleans the table. Picks up the bowl, TCP, packet, scissors and player. Goes out. Closes the door behind him. The music plays a little longer. Silence.*

Panel Three

The room. The chair is where **Liz** *put it. Off, the doorbell rings. Slight pause. The door is opened.*

Dan (*off*)   'Ello.

Richard (*off*)   'Ello.

Dan (*off*)   Wasnt expectin yer yet. Yer office said they'd fix a time.

Richard (*off*)   Sorry. Now I'm 'ere . . . ?

Dan (*off*)   Yeh. Come in.

Richard (*off. Slight pause*)   On yer own now . . .?

The answer isn't heard. The door opens. **Dan** *ushers* **Richard** *in.*

Dan (*at the door*)   If yer wait in 'ere. Be with yer.

He goes. Closes the door. **Richard** *looks round. Listens a few seconds. Goes to the table. Opens the drawer. Looks in. Shuts it. Moves away. Waits.* **Dan** *comes in.*

Dan   They said they'd send a woman.

Richard   Social service? – always busy – . Yer know why Im 'ere?

Dan   See 'ow I'm copin.

Richard   Wan' t' talk about it? (**Dan** *shrugs slightly.*) Talkin 'elps. 'S interestin.

Dan   Didnt like it in the papers. Private. Nothin t' do with them.

Richard   Mind if I sit? (*He moves the chair closer to the table. Sits.*) Yer was on yer own at the time? Must've bin a shock? Yer didnt 'ear – ?

Dan   Slep.

Richard   Why dont yer sit? (**Dan** *sits on the edge of the chaise longue.*) Neighbours said yer bang on their door so 'ard they thought they was on fire.

Dan (*flat*)   It'd juss 'appened.

Richard   She say anything before?

Dan   Dont understand it. (*Realises* **Richard** *has spoken.*) What?

Richard   Say she was contemplatin?

Dan   Contemplatin? No.

Richard   People dont juss . . . Was there a lodger? Boyfriend?

Dan   No. It was the two a' us. She chuck me father out before I was born. Yer mustnt think bad a' 'er. I'd never blame 'er. She did everythin for me. – Wasnt sudden. Built up over the years. 'Er situation wore 'er out.

Richard   A bit on the side?

Dan   What?

Richard   Could 'a kep it off yer t' –

Dan   No – I tol' yer –

Richard   Dont get upset.

Dan   Dont know why they sent yer. Office said it'd be a woman.

Richard   Yer're my concern, not 'er. I came t' see *yoo*. My way a' thinking, it's wrong what she done t' yer.

Dan   Yer never met 'er. If yer 'ad yer'd know different. When me father went 'e took every man out a' 'er life with 'im. Wouldnt let a man in the 'ouse t' read the meter if she could 'elp it. There was something evil about 'im. 'Urt 'im t' do a good turn. She said 'e was 'n iceberg crushed in a teacup.

Richard   Woman talk. Yer never met 'im. If yer did yer'd think different.

Dan   Never met 'im – done better: I dreamt 'im. Thass all I remember when I was a kid: 'im in me 'ead at night. Since she's gone 'e's come back. 'E's the sort a' man 'oo 'as worms crawlin on 'is face while 'e's still alive. If 'e come through that door I'd know 'im straight away. I'd kill 'im. Take 'im t' where she 'anged 'erself – kill 'im on that spot. 'As t' be justice somewhere.

Richard   Yeh. Well. 'S 'ard work understandin people.

Dan   Yer wouldnt meet many a' 'is sort even in social work.

Richard   Like father like son – so it's said. Better 'ave a look round. Make me assessment.

Dan (*stands*)   I'll show yer –

Richard   No you sit there. Yer upset. I know where I am – matter a' fact feel quite at 'ome. All these flats're the same.

Dan *sits.* **Richard** *goes out. Shuts the door.*

Dan (*calls*)   Bit untidy. No time t' sort it out yet. (*He stands. Goes to the window. Stares down at the street. Half-loud.*) People in the streets. One way, then the other way. They dont know where they're goin. Spend their life walkin t' reach a blind corner. (*He realises* **Richard** *has come back. Lowers his voice.*) They dont know whass be'ind it.

Richard *stands just inside the room. His arms are full of a large bundle of* **Liz**'s *clothes. Some are still on their hangers.* **Dan** *turns. Stares at him.*

Richard   Shift these for yer. (*A clothes hanger falls.*) Oops. (*He stoops to pick it up.*)

Dan   Thass 'er things.

Richard   Emptied the wardrobe. Dispose 'em t' a suitable –

Dan   Put 'em back.

Richard   We got lists a' charities where we – in the office –

Dan   Dont want 'em disposed of. If they – I'll choose charities *she'd* want –

Richard   Dont bury yerself in the past. Memories're bad things. For a start, yer in a place too big to be in on yer own. Yer should get a –

Dan   Not gettin no one! Ain lettin no strangers in where she . . .

Richard   Where she what? She should've thought a' that. I'll loan the canvas 'old-all in the kitchen. Didnt come prepared. Not that it's 'ardly worth 'andin out free. Be 'n insult. – We got some immigrants 'oo grab at anythin if it saves 'em the bother a' goin thievin. (*Looks down at the clothes.*) Surprises me – thought she'd 'ave better stuff. Used t' be a smart woman. Knew 'ow t' dress.

Dan   I said put it back.

Richard   Keep calm sonny. Yer doin alright so far. Natural yer upset. I'll put in a good report for the –

Dan   'Ow d'yer know 'ow she used t' dress?

Richard   Neighbours tol' me.

Dan   Neighbours?

Richard 'Ad t' knock 'em up t' find the right flat. Yer know neighbours! Once they start yappin –

Dan Right flat? – We got a number! Yoo the police?

Richard Dont think yer want the police round 'ere! – Not accordin t' yer neighbours.

Dan (*yanks the clothes from Richard's arms*) Get yer 'ands off 'er! (*Throws the clothes on the table.*) Where's yer identity?

Richard Identity?

Dan Yer from the social yer got n' identity!

Richard Yer want me identity? Lucky I ain the police. I know why she 'ang 'erself. They tol' me next door.

Dan Tol' yer? Lies! Gossip!

Richard Drugs.

Dan Lie.

Richard She was so high they 'ad t' deliver 'er mail t' the moon. I know 'oo kep 'er supplied. Next door used t' see yer scuttlin up the stairs clutchin mummy's ruin in yer 'ot little 'ands. Yer so useless it showed on yer face: guilt – 'cause yer knew yer was puttin 'er in 'er grave.

Dan Lie. If I got – . Anythin I got was for me. Not 'er. She was clean.

Richard The coroner'll know better when he cuts 'er up. She'll be full a' it. She'll tell the truth now she's dead – shame she left it late.

Dan 'Oo are yer?

Richard Yer dad – the one yer recognise soon's 'e come through the door.

Dan Ain got a dad. Went before I was born.

Richard Wrong – I ain got a son. Yer ain the sort a son any man 'd choose. I *know* I lie. Yer like 'er – yer lie 'n believe

it! – I learnt that already. Yer'd like me t' lie now n' say I
come t' get a glimpse a' yer. I came for the pickings. The loot.
Get me own back now she's dead. I *know* I'm 'ere, struttin
about in 'er place. She dont know. Cant. Never will. Thass
the real satisfaction: I know 'n she dont. Yer too young t'
understand that. Yer'll learn it later. (*Pokes at the clothes.*) 'Oped
for somethin better. (*Shrug.*) Fetch a few bob in a boot sale.

Dan *is half-sprawled on the chaise longue.*

Dan   She never lied. Always said the truth. Yer dont
understand 'er.

Richard   Lad – I juss give yer yer identity. All yer can do is
talk about 'er! – Show a bit a' initiative. Ask yer dad for yer
share a' the loot. Yer'll 'ave a 'ard life. – Did she tell yer
about the kid with the eyes? No? Funny. 'Er big story. She
read it in the papers. Woman blinded 'er kid with a pair a'
scissors. She went on about it all the time she was carryin yoo.
I left. Couldnt take no more. I come back t' give 'er another
chance. She got worse! – Woman – kid – scissors. None a' it
'appened. Never in the papers. In 'er 'ead. Thass why I left.
She's screwed. – Funny she never tol' yer. She buried it under
'er snakes.

Dan (*low*)   Go away. Get out.

Richard (*picking up the clothes*)   'E thought I was social service!
Me! – do I look that thick?

Dan   Get out.

Richard   I'm goin. Seen enough 'ere. I tol' 'er t' get rid 'a
yer. Flush yer down the toilet. She done that she couldnt a'
turned yer in t' 'er druggie pimp and she'd still be alive. (*Stops.*)
Yer said I 'ad worms on me face. She 'ad snakes inside 'er.
Thass 'ow druggies end up, feedin their snakes t' get a bit 'a
quiet. (*Starts to go to the door again.*) Things I could tell yer. Yer
think yer money kep 'er 'abit goin. What yer petty crime
brought in werent 'arf enough t' feed 'er snakes. When yer

was out muggin she was out sellin herself on the streets. Plyin 'er trade as they say. Thass the sort a' mother yer 'ad.

Dan *gets up. Stands between* **Richard** *and the door.*

Dan   'Oo tol' yer that?

Richard   Now dont do any –

Dan   'Oo? 'Oo? 'Oo tol' yer?

Richard (*drops the clothes on the ground*)   Yer wanted the truth! – yer got it. Now get out a' my –

Dan   'Ow long did it go on?

Richard   Ask next door – they'll tell yer.

Dan   'N they was laughin be'ind me back . . .?

He falls on the chaise longue. **Richard** *looks at him.*

Richard   Yer'd've found out in the end anyway. 'Ad a right t' know. I'm sorry. Yer never 'ad a mother. Not a proper one. Yer cant call 'er that.

Dan   Dad.

Richard   Yer can sort it out for yerself. Teach yer not t' be so cocksure. – Dont call me dad. Too late for any a' that. We'll keep out a' each other's way after this. (*Picks up the clothes.*) I 'ave t' – no work nowadays – get 'ard up. 'Ave t' screw what yer can if yer wan' t' live.

Dan   Take it. Dont want it in the 'ouse. Now yer said. She 'ad some bits 'n pieces a' jewellery. Watches I'd – Bits a' chains. Take it with yer. Dont want it 'ere.

Richard   I can take it off yer 'ands – if yer sure yer dont –

Dan   In 'er wardrobe. False bottom. 'Ave t' pull it up.

Richard *puts the clothes on the table. He goes out.* **Dan** *goes to the clothes. Picks them up.*

Dan   Lie. Lie. Lie (*Hugging the clothes.*) Not true. Yer never. Never. We'll kill 'im. We'll kill 'im.

He throws the clothes to the chair. Some drape over it, some fall to the floor. He goes to the chaise longue. Turns it over. The floor underneath is strewn with a heap of strips torn from the sheet. The chaise longue lies on its back. The four bare wooden legs stick up in the air.

Richard (*off*)   Not 'ere. Did yer say floor? (*His voice jerks as he tugs.*) Dont shift.

Dan (*calls*)   Try the back.

He stands by the door. Flattens himself against the wall. Takes a black cosh from his pocket. Waits. **Richard** *is seen through the doorway.*

Richard   I tried the floor – it dont – (*He comes into the room. Catches a glimpse of the strips.*) What – ?

Dan *coshes him from behind. He falls.* **Dan** *moves with a mugger's skill. Throws* **Richard** *on to the upturned chaise longue. Ties him to it with the strips.*

Dan (*to the clothes*)   Yer see! Yer see! (*Pulls clothes up from the floor. Throws them on the chair. Some fall down again.*) Sit up! See better from there! Watch! Watch! Yer'll see! (*Goes back to* **Richard**. *Shakes him.*) Wake up! Wake up!

Richard (*groan*)   Wha' . . .? (*Gasp.*) Wha' . . .

Dan (*to clothes*)   See! See! 'E's comin – ! (*To* **Richard**.) Liar! Liar! What yer said – every word! Liar! Yer drove 'er – left 'er – drugs – 'ang 'erself – (*To clothes.*) Yer 'ang cause a' – look at 'im! – tell 'im! (*Burst of tears.*) She cant! She cant! She's sufferin still! (*To* **Richard**.) She 'ung 'erself 'cause 'a yoo!

Richard (*dazed*)   Dont – dont – son – son –

Dan   Ain yer son! Yer said! Tell 'er yer lie!

Richard   Son – son dont – too far – too far – there'll be terrible trouble – yer angry – dont –

Dan   Tell 'er the truth!

Richard   I 'ave!

Dan   The truth! Yer said she went on the street!

Richard   She went on the street!

Dan   Liar! Liar! She never –

Richard   She never – she never –

Dan   Then why did yer say she – ! Liar! Liar!

Richard   She did! – I tell yer the truth –

Dan   Liar! She never went out! Couldnt!

Richard   – n' yer say – liar! She did! She did! Tell me! Tell me! What is it? What shall I say?

Dan   The truth!

Richard   What truth? – what truth d'yer want me – ? Tell me – I'll say it – !

Dan   Yer said she went on the –

Richard   She did!

Dan   Liar!

Richard   When yer was muggin!

Dan   Liar! Liar! Ain bin – !

Richard   Muggin! Yer did! Yer went! Yer know it! Yer paid for the stuff she –

Dan   Liar!

Richard   Muggin! Muggin! It's the truth!

Dan *leaves* **Richard***. Goes towards the chair. Turns to face* **Richard***.*

Dan   Liar!

Richard   Yer cosh! Broke people's 'eads! Yer know it! Dont 'ave t' tell yer!

Dan   'Oo said? 'Oo told yer?

Richard Yer mates! The street! Everyone knows it!
Nothin's kept quiet! They all know she was on the –

Dan 'E's said it again! Liar!

Richard 'E asks for the truth! I say it! 'E rages!

Dan Liar!

Richard Arnie! Yer mate! 'E tol me! Believe 'im! She was
on the street!

Dan Liar! Liar!

Richard Ask 'im! Yer mate! Yer mate!

Dan No mate! Not my! – Liar! Dont want none a' the – !
All a' yer liars! All a' yer!

Richard I saw 'er! Dont I believe me eyes?

Dan Liar!

Richard One night! – I stood in the doorway!

Dan (*hugs clothes*)   Dont listen!

Richard Watch 'er! She's toutin the cars!

Dan Dont listen!

Richard Slow down – look – drove off – better slags up the
street! –

Dan No! No!

Richard 'E asks for the truth! I tell 'im! 'E rages!

Dan Not true! Liar!

Richard I go – cross over – acost 'er – pick 'er up – yer
mother – !

Dan (*goes to Richard*)   Liar! Liar!

Richard Whass wrong? She'd bin my woman! Go with 'er!
Ain wrong! In the doorway! I pay 'er! She dont know me! –
thass whass wrong! She dont know me! Full a' the drugs yer
got 'er!

Dan (*to clothes*)   Yer never! Tell me 'e ain true!

Richard   Yer want the truth!

Dan (*to clothes*)   Please! Please! Tell me!

Richard   I was in this room before yer was born! I got the
right t' speak it! Yer cant push me so far I'll lie for yer! I lie
for me! – my sake not yern! Yer make me savage! Kill me?
Yer cant! Yer never met me! Never seen me! Look at me
bundled 'ere! All yer see's what she sees! What she tells yer t'
see! Yer kill me – yer'll be killin 'er! Killin what's in 'er 'ead!
Listen – not my son – juss as a 'uman bein – be that for now –
believe me! – I ain make the truth – it 'appens! I tell it! 'E
rages!

Dan (*holding up the clothes, hugging them*)   Look at 'er! Tell 'er!
Ain 'er – only 'er clothes! All thass left! Tell them! She made
the ropes yer tied in. Sheet off 'er bed. She should 'a slep
there in peace. She tore it up 'n 'ang 'erself in it! Now yer tied
up in it! Y ain' got away from 'er! Tell 'er yer sorry! Tell 'er –
yer can see 'er – !

Richard   Son son dont – yer 'arm yerself – no one's there –

Dan   I know! Ain mad! 'S all thass left! Tell 'er!

Richard   Sorry sorry sorry –

Dan   Look at 'er – say it!

Richard   O God why did I come – for a few bloody rags –
sorry sorry –

Dan   Look at 'er! – 'cause yer goin t' lose yer eyes! Thass
why yer come 'ere! Why yer come in this room! So I can put
the room right! Yer goin t' lose yer eyes!

Richard   No no son – please please –

Dan   Too late! Both eyes – like the – if I 'ad a saucer – !

Richard (*twisting away*)   Dont dont – yer mad son – 's the
truth – believe me – I'm tellin the truth – yer'll do terrible –

undo the – let me 'elp yer – take care a' yer – there's no
reason for this – look after yer –

Dan *lurches to the chair. Takes it to* **Richard**. *Sets it down. Puts
the clothes on it. They scatter.*

Dan   Look! Thass all that yer left me! Still ain enough! Yer
come t' sell 'er clothes in the gutter!

Richard   I cant go on – cant say – what shall I say – what
d'yer want me t' – please – please – tell me – I'll say it –

Dan *stamps across the floor.*

Dan   Stamp! Stamp! Stamp! Bang! Bang! For all the – !
Stamp! Stamp! Stamp! (*Goes to* **Richard**.) Look! Look! (*He
stamps close to* **Richard***'s head.*) Look! – what did the kid see –
what did its 'ands do – (**Richard***'s hands rise. Jerking. Shaking.
Still tied in the strips.* **Dan** *stamps.*) – when it saw the – (*Stamp.*)
when it saw the (*Stamp.*) comin –

Richard *gets a hand free. Grabs* **Dan***'s foot. Wrenches.* **Dan**
topples. He slashes down at **Richard** *with the edge of his heel.*

Dan   Slash! Slash! Slash! What did the kid do with its 'ands –
what could it – could it – ! Aaaaaooghghgh!

He gets to his feet. Throws the chair and the clothes across **Richard**.
Richard *is struggling free.* **Dan** *backs away. Staggering. Groaning.
Crying.*

Dan   Sorry – sorry – sorry – (*Turns away from* **Richard**.) –
slash – slash – sorry –

Richard *gets to his feet. Grabs the chair as a weapon. Clothes
scatter. Strips are caught on his foot and the chaise longue. He backs.
The chaise longue thumps across the floor towards him.* **Richard**
kicks himself free. Backs to the door. **Dan** *is turned away from him.*

Richard (*dry with panic*)   Mad. Mad. Police.

Dan   For the kid.

Richard *backs out of the door.* **Dan** *goes to the window. Stares down at the street. Silence.* **Richard** *comes back in the doorway. Stares at* **Dan**.

Richard (*low*)   Mad. Mad.

He comes gingerly into the room. He gathers some of the clothes. Reaches for another piece. Its too near **Dan** *– gives up. Backs to the door.*

Richard (*silently mouthing*)   Mad. Mad. Mad . . .

Richard *backs out through the door.* **Dan** *stares down at the street.*

Dan   For the kid. For the kid.

The Edge

For Chris

The Edge had not yet been performed at the time of going to press (September 2011). The company for Big Brum's planned touring production was made up of:

Stranger	Richard Holmes
Ron	Danny O'Grady
Sal	Liz Brown

Directed by Chris Cooper
Designed by Ceri Townsend

Characters

Stranger
Ron
Sal

Setting

Now
City

Street
Flat

One

Deserted city street at night. The **Stranger** *comes on from the right.
He is elderly and grey-haired. His jacket and the rest of his clothes are
dark and scruffy. He stops. Stands still. Drops to the ground. Lies
motionless. Silence. A teenager comes on from the left. He has been
celebrating. He passes the* **Stranger** *without seeing him. He stops.
Turns back. Looks at the* **Stranger**.

Ron Hey up. (*Pauses. Goes back to the* **Stranger**. *Stands looking
down at him.*) You alright? Can yer 'ear me? (*Crouches beside
man.*) Alright grandad? (*No response. Stands. Pushes the*
Stranger's *leg gently with his foot.*) Bin drinkin. On yer own.
Shouldnt drink on yer own. No one t' carry yer 'ome. Sleep it
off there. Cheaper 'n a doss 'ouse.

Ron *goes out. Pause. The* **Stranger** *doesnt move.* **Ron** *comes
back. Stops some way from the* **Stranger**. *Looks at him. Goes to
him. Squats by him. Puts his hand inside the* **Stranger**'s *jacket.*

Ron Ticker working. (*Stands.*) What yer wan' t' do that for? –
End up like that? Bin celebratin? Sit up grandad. I'm off
t'morra. 'Arf way round the world. 'Ope we dont get lost eh?
Law find yer there they'll run yer in. D'yer want an ambulance?
Sit up. (*He sits the* **Stranger** *up. The* **Stranger** *leans against
him.*) Cant 'ang about with you. 'S late. Cop it when I get
'ome. (*Annoyed.*) State yer in. What yer wan' t' get like that?
Your age. Anyone come they'd rob yer skint . . . I'm off
t'morrow. 'Arf way round the world. Did I tell yer? (*Stands.
The* **Stranger** *falls back.*) Jeees. (**Ron** *walks away to look down the
street.*) Bloody street. Always empty when yer want someone.
(*Goes back to the* **Stranger**.) Get on yer – . (*Pulls the* **Stranger**
to his feet.) Walk a few steps it'll wake yer up –

The **Stranger** *falls and ends on floor on top of* **Ron**.

Ron Get off! Yer stupid bloody – ! Get off! Bloody 'ell!
(*Stands. Kicks the* **Stranger**.) Yer lie there mate if yer want –
dont drag me down t' yer gutter! (*Brushing himself.*) Muck me
gear up! Kick yer bloody 'ead in! (*Walks a few steps away. Squats.*)

Chriss – liftin 'im took me puff – I drank too much. Get 'ome. Why dont no one come? (*Calls.*) 'Ello! – Old geezer needs someone t' – . (*Silence.*) 'Arf way round the world . . . (*To the* **Stranger**.) Thought yer was a trick – one a' me mates lyin in the road playin dead. (*Looks up at the sky.*) Thought I'd walk 'ome quiet. Last time. See me own sky at night. Be different down there. (*Stands. Brushes himself.*) Muck. (*Looks down at the* **Stranger**.) Yer' trash pop. (*Is going to kick him. Doesn't.*) Trash. Ain soil me boot on yer. (*Walking right.*) . . . Get away from it.

Ron *goes out right. Slight pause. The* **Stranger** *stirs. Looks round. Sees* **Ron** *down the street. Half points at him. Pauses a moment. Stands. He goes out right.*

Two

The living room in a flat. A door right to the hallway and (not seen) the front door. Another door left to the rest of the flat. A table and two chairs. One end of the table is laid for a simple meal – plates, cutlery. On the other end a backpack. It is three-quarters full. Beside it a small pile of clothing – socks, underwear, a grey jumper.

Sal *sits in a chair. She stares into space. She gets up and begins to pack clothes into the pack. The sound of the front door being opened. She stops packing. Sits and waits. Noises in the hallway.* **Ron** *comes in.*

Ron   'Lo.

Sal   Nice time?

Ron (*flat*)   Yeh. (*More enthusiastically.*) Yeh yeh. Good lads. (*Slight pause.*) Didnt think yer'd be up.

Sal   Have yer eaten?

Ron   Yer know. Somethin at the bar.

Sal   That wont do yer no good. Meals they serve yer on planes wont feed yer.

Ron   No – 'ad somethin.

Sal I was out shoppin.

Ron Dont want yer workin in the kitchen this time a' night.

Sal It's in the micro. Just switch it on. – Thought we'd 'ave a last family meal.

Ron Eat late it keeps me awake.

Sal If yer'd said I neednt 'ave bothered.

Ron The lads. Wouldnt let me get away. I've known 'em since – Paul went all through school with me. Known Liz since – . . . Lashed out. Wouldnt let me pay for anythin. – Eat the meal tomorrow. Save yer a bit a' work.

Sal It's for two.

Silence.

Ron We goin' t' 'ave a row?

Sal Not unless you start it.

Ron That's alright then.

Silence

Sal Yer didnt pack enough. I put out some socks 'n undies.

Ron Dont want t' carry too much.

Sal Ain lettin yer go 'f yer not decent.

Ron Get stuff out there.

Sal Why pay when yer got it 'ere? Yer never know what yer'll need yer money for out there. (*Slight pause.*) Stays 'ere just clutter the place up. I didnt interfere with yer toiletries. Dont forget t' pack yer razor in the mornin.

Ron What's that?

Sal Jumper.

Ron I know what it is. What's it doin' there?

Sal It's yer father's –

Ron   It's summer down there.

Sal   I thought we'd 'ave our meal 'n then I'd give it t' yer as a farewell.

Sal *goes to put the jumper in the pack.*

Ron (*stopping her*)   I wont take it.

Sal   It's yer father's.

Ron   It's yourn. Yer kept it till now. I'd think I was robbin yer.

Sal   I *want* yer t' 'ave it.

Ron   It belongs 'ere.

Sal   I washed it. Wasnt cheap. Yer father always 'ad the best. 'E'd want yer t' take somethin a' –

Ron (*low*)   Your father. Your father. Your. Your. Your. 'E's your 'usband. Why dont yer say that? 'E's got a name. Why cant yer use it? . . . Yer make him sound like some foreigner – 's if yer 'ave t' keep remindin me who 'e is.

Sal   Sometimes yer 'ard t' please. (*Slight pause.*) – In a bad mood yer last night . . .

Silence.

I didnt try t' stop yer. Yer cant 'old that against me. When yer came out with it I 'ad no idea what'd been goin on in yer 'ead. Yer'd already made all the arrangements. I'm not told till it's been settled. Not a word. I thought when yer left school you'd find a proper job. Settle down. That's what yer father taught me to expect. It's not like that now. You kids 'ave t' be different. In yer father's day – (*She stops.*)

Ron   It's too late to say that now. Yer should've said it before. It's my life. I'll do with it what I want.

Sal   That's what I want. Why else d'yer think I've always given yer a good 'ome? I've nothing to criticise meself for in that line. Fair's fair yer've always been grateful. I want what you want. Yer father'd never stood in your way.

Ron   Sorry. I should've left the lads earlier.

Sal   Yer can 'ave the meal for breakfast. Set you up for the – but I dont understand why yer cant take the jumper.

Ron (*bangs palm on table*)   It's too late for all this! Yer dont mind? Yer do! Yer dont want me to go! Yer think I'm walkin out on yer!

Sal   I wont row. (*Puts jumper in the pack.*) It's in now. Take it out in the mornin if yer want. It'll be your hands do it not mine.

Ron   I knew yer'd start this. Yer've been looking forward to it. That's why I stayed out. If yer must know I left the lads early. By then they'd forgotten I was there. I didnt exist. They just wanted t' get on with their own lives. I went for a walk. Crime! An' tomorrow I'm goin 'arf way round the world. I dont know if I'll ever come back. If yer asked me now, it'd be no. I could've avoided this – took the jumper – when I'm round the corner drop it in the neighbour's wheely-bin. *That's* what obedience is! That the sort of son yer want? Just leave me alone! (*He takes the jumper out of the pack.*) I 'ave t' tunnel through ten brick walls t' get out of this 'ouse. (*He goes left to the door. Stops.*) Yer make a meal, we dont eat, we row. Why? It ain healthy. They say talk – it solves everythin. It dont. I'm tired. I've got to get some sleep. – It's good we said this. We dont 'ave t' say it in the mornin. We can say our goodbyes in a proper way.

Sal   When yer talk to me like that yer make me feel so small – I can feel meself shrinkin in this chair. I wanted tonight t' go well – so yer could go away 'n not worry about me – I did the meal so –

Ron   There's nothin t' say.

He goes out through the door left. **Sal** *picks up the jumper. She is going to pack it. She hesitates. She lays it on top of the pack. She picks up one* *plate and cutlery. She goes towards the door left. The front doorbell rings. She stops. Goes right. Hesitates. Looks over her shoulder at the door left. Then goes out through the hall door. Brief silence. The hall door bursts open. The* **Stranger** *comes in. He stops in the middle of the room. Rapid glance round.* **Sal** *comes through the hall door. She still holds the plate and cutlery.*

Sal   What d'yer want? Who are yer? (*The* **Stranger** *stares at her.*) Yer cant barge in without a – ! 'Ow dare yer! What d'yer want?

Stranger   'E knows.

Sal   Who knows?

Stranger   The lad –

Sal   What lad?

Stranger   – 'e lives 'ere.

Sal   Who?

Stranger   Followed 'im!

Sal   Who are yer?

Stranger   You 'is mother?

Sal   Tell me what yer want?

Stranger   Know 'e live 'ere! Saw 'im goin in? Fetch 'im!

Sal   What for?

Stranger   Fetch 'im!

Sal   You dont leave I'll fetch the police.

Stranger   No yer wont. I'll call 'em! Yer know what it is. Not the first time is it? 'Is usual!

Sal   Tell me what yer want!

Stranger   (*goes to door left*)   'E in there?

Sal   What's 'appened? If yer dont tell me 'ow can I know what yer talkin about? If yer've got a reason t' see 'im wait outside on the doorstep 'n I'll –

Stranger   Not movin till it's sorted. You fetch 'im.

Sal   If yer dont go I'll call me neighbours next door. (*Turns towards the hall door.*) Call 'em anyway.

Stranger   'E stole me wallet.

Sal (*stops short*)   'E didnt.

Stranger   Ask him. Fetch 'im. 'E cant deny it now 'e knows I know where 'e lives!

Sal   'E didnt steal yer – . 'E'd never take anythin that's not 'is.

Stranger   Yer'll see.

Sal *puts the plate and the cutlery on the table.*

Sal   Yer accusin 'im of stealin yer property?

Stranger   Wouldnt come 'ere if 'e 'adnt! – dont make a 'abit a' burstin in t' strangers' 'ouses!

Sal   When?

Stranger   What?

Sal   When did 'e steal it?

Stranger   Just now.

Sal   Please tell me what's 'appened. Why should my son take anythin of yours? If yer've lost yer wallet I'm sorry. 'E hasnt took it. Yer could've drop it.

Stranger   Where's 'is room?

Sal   Wait! Whatever 'e says yer're not goin t' believe 'im. (*Thinks a moment.*) I wont 'ave 'im upset – another night I wouldnt tolerate this for one minute –

Stranger (*derisive hoot*)   Hoo-hoo!

Sal   If there's been some bother – 'is mates larkin about 'n it went too far –

Stranger   No mates!

Sal   – I'll sort it out. 'E'll tell me if 'e's done anythin –

Stranger   'E took me wallet.

Sal   – 'n I'll explain it for yer –

Stranger   Dont need explainin. Want me wallet.

Sal (*calming him*)   Yes but he wont say anythin in front a' you. Go outside 'n –

Stranger (*sits on chair*)   Not leavin this –

Sal   Wait in the 'allway. Listen when I ask 'im. It's a misunderstandin. My son wouldnt rob an old man.

Stranger   Yer'll let 'im out through the window.

Sal   If there's been trouble I want it sorted out more than you. Yer came in 'ere 'n made accusations. They could land yer in trouble. A slangin match with you an' 'im wont get yer anywhere. If 'e's done wrong I'll see yer get satisfaction. 'Ide in the 'all or I'll fetch me neighbours.

Stranger   Ain wait long. Give yer a couple a' minutes. That's all.

The **Stranger** *gets up and goes out through the hall door. Closes it but leaves a gap.* **Sal** *picks up the jumper. Puts it down. She goes to the hall door. Half closes the gap. She goes left.* **Stranger** *looks out from the gap.*

Stranger   See yer through the gap if yer make signs t' tell 'im I'm 'ere.

Sal   Trust me.

The **Stranger** *goes out of sight behind the hall door.* **Sal** *goes to the door left. Opens it.*

Sal (*calls*)   Ronnie you asleep? (*No answer.*) I need a word love.

She sits in a chair. **Ron** *comes in. He has removed his shirt and is in his vest.*

Sal   Yer werent asleep love?

Ron   No.

Sal   Did yer get in a state – upset – 'cause I . . .? (*No response.*) It's yer last night. I dont want yer t' go t' sleep on a misunderstandin.

Ron   It's late.

Sal   I only need a minute. Yer can spare me that.

Ron *sits in the other chair.*

Sal   I'm glad yer went out t' enjoy yerself. If I give a different impression I'm . . . (*No response.*) I didnt want t' spoil yer evening by –

Ron   I'd've asked yer t' come but yer wouldnt've enjoyed it. It was just the lads.

Sal   Did they walk yer 'ome?

Ron   I told yer. I left 'em at it.

Sal   They might've followed yer love. Got up t' some trick for yer last night. Yer can tell me what 'appened.

Ron   Nothin.

Sal   Yer came straight 'ome? At your age yer dont mean any 'arm but things get out of 'and.

Ron   Mum what is it? Yer think I been with a tart while yer was waitin for yer dinner.

Sal (*slight silence*)   I worry about yer.

Ron   I can 'andle meself. – I'm glad yer've 'ad yer little say.
Ends it on a nice note. (*Stands.*) Let's turn in. We'll both sleep
okay now.

Sal   In the old days yer felt secure. Nowadays people do
things when there's no reason for it. I dont understand me
own life – 'ow can I be expected t' understand me son? Who
can yer trust? Yer wouldnt go off 'n leave me a mess t' sort
out when yer –

Ron (*going towards the door*)   Nighty-night.

Sal   If yer short yer could've asked me for money. I've got a
bit put by in the bank. Yer'r welcome t' it.

Ron   Mum stop it. The sooner I'm out a' this 'ouse the
better. We need a break from each other. We'll sort it out
when I'm there. It'll be easier when there's a distance . . . Yer
need yer money. I dont want it. Jeees! I'd feel I was robbin
yer! 'Ow could she think I'd take 'er money? (*Goes to door left.
Stops.*) Let's stop it. We'll say things we'll be sorry for.

He goes out. The **Stranger** *starts to open the hall door.*

Sal (*gesturing*)   Wait! If 'e lied 'e'll come back. 'E wouldnt
leave me with a lie in 'is mouth.

Pause. **Ron** *comes back. He stares at* **Sal***. She stands.*

Ron   It's the jumper. I'm not takin it. I know it's a silly
stupid petty little thing but I'm not takin it! That's what I
decided 'n yer'll 'ave t' accept it okay! It's petty but I dont
care! I've a right t' – ! (*He grabs the jumper and throws it at her.*)
No! I dont want it!

Ron *goes out left. Door slammed. The jumper lies on the floor. The*
Stranger *opens the hall door.*

Stranger   Yer never asked!

Sal   What?

Stranger   Yer never asked 'im!

*The **Stranger** goes towards the door left.*

Sal   Leave us alone! Yer 'eard 'im! I offered 'im! – *offered!* –
'e said rob! 'E wouldnt take money from no one –

Stranger (*banging on the door*)   Come out! I know yer're 'idin
in there!

*The **Stranger** backs from the door. Stands facing it. **Ron** comes
into the room.*

Stranger (*pointing*)   It's 'im!

Ron (*staring*)   What's . . .?

Sal   'E's goin –

Ron   Wait! – what's 'e . . .? 'Ow did 'e get in 'ere?

Stranger (*pointing*)   'Im!

Sal   'E 's just –

Ron (*to **Sal***)   Wait. Wait. (*To the **Stranger**.*) Are yer lost?
What're yer – ?

Stranger (*pointing*)   'Im!

Sal   It's alright! 'E's goin! I told 'im yer –

Ron   Wait! – for God's sake . . . (*To the **Stranger**.*) Why've – ?
What yer doin 'ere?

Stranger (*pointing*)   Followed 'im! 'E run. Run. Chased
after. Lives 'ere. Watch out in the street. Got the key 'ere. Yer
aint get away! Chased after – coughed me lungs up – phew! –
if I 'ad a 'eart attack that'd be you too! Yer'd 'ave a murder
on yer 'ands. Robbery 'n murder!

Ron   'E's mad! Why did yer let 'im in?

Stranger (*pointing*)   It's 'im!

Ron (*calm*)   Listen chummy sit down 'n give yerself a chance
t' –

Sal   Yer took 'is wallet.

Ron   I took 'is – ?

Sal   That's what 'e says.

Ron   Listen yer poor old – . Yer was lyin in the street. I asked yer was yer alright. Yer didnt answer –

Stranger (*pointing*)   Yer took me wallet.

Ron   If yer wallet's gone it went before I was there. I should've called an ambulance. Anyway yer didnt need it – yer lively enough now. If yer lost yer wallet did yer go back t' look for it? I never took it. No one did. If yer bin rob it'd show. Jacket torn or somethin. Not a scratch on yer. Yer was legless. (*Drinking gesture.*) Glug-glug. That's what toppled yer. So dont come in t' people's 'ouses 'n make accusations yer cant –

Stranger   Give me me wallet! 'S all I 'ad. If I 'ad anythin else yer'd've took it! – your sort do! (*Holds out his jacket flaps.*) Empty. (*Picks at his shirt.*) Thin yer can see me ribs through it. Yer took all I 'ad 'n left me lyin in the street! That's yer son!

Ron   Yer shouldnt 've bin lyin in the street.

Stranger   Took a nap! 'S long day. Man my age needs 'is kip – yer'll find out one day!

Ron   Then 'ow d'yer know I rob yer?

Stranger   What?

Ron   If yer was asleep?

Stranger   Woke up when I felt yer 'and rummagin inside me –

Ron   Did yer put up a fight?

Stranger   No no course not –

Ron   Shout 'elp?

Stranger   – lay there dead! Seen yer face! – yer a
dangerous maniac. Git me throat cut I offer resistance. Police
tell yer. Dont offer resistance!

Ron   Yer never 'ad no wallet!

Stranger (*to* **Sal**)   Where's 'e 'ide 'is stuff? (*Going towards door
left.*) 'S under 'is bed. Place they usual put it!

Ron *slams the door shut. Stands in front of it.*

Sal   Dont upset 'im – !

Ron (*bewildered exasperation*)   What yer let 'im in for? 'E's a
nutter!

Sal   – we got 'a sort this out so yer –

Ron   Let the police sort it.

Sal   If 'e accuses yer –

Ron   Of what? 'E ain got a shred of evidence! Who'd
believe a senile old bugger off 'is rocker like 'im –

Stranger   Senile? Off me rocker? Yer wont say that when I
stand up in court 'n denounce yer – I fought for this country –

Ron   I'm callin the police.

Sal   Yer cant!

Ron   I bet 'e's got a record! Yer often do this? –

Sal   Yer cant go t' the police?

Ron   – make a 'abit a' enterin strangers' 'ouses 'n accusin
'em a' –

Sal   They'll 'ave t' investigate. If 'e accuses yer the police
cant let it drop!

Ron   O heck!

Sal   They wont let yer on the plane in the mornin – stop yer
leavin the country till it's cleared up –

Ron   Jeeees! –

Sal   – no matter 'ow innocent yer are!

Ron   Jees! Jees! – Why didnt I come straight 'ome? Went for a walk! – as if I was in a free country! Need me 'ead testin! Go for a walk in a mad'ouse yer bound t' bump in t' a lunatic – !

Sal   What was in yer wallet?

Stranger   What?

Sal   What was in yer wallet? 'Ow much?

Stranger   'Ow much?

Sal   'Ow much was in your wallet? 'Ow much money did yer lose?

Stranger   Why?

Sal   I'll pay yer.

Ron   Pay 'im? Yer cant!

Sal   'Ow much?

Stranger   I'll 'ave t' do some calculatin – I made some purchases in the mornin – then I 'ad a flutter on the three-thirty – 'e'll begrudge me that – !

Sal   Well 'ow much did that leave yer in yer wallet?

Stranger   . . . er 'ow much d'yer think I was likely t' 'ave . . .?

Ron   Yer pay 'im I'll look guilty! Yer'll never get rid a' 'im! 'E'll be round all the time askin for more!

Sal   Leave this t' me! I'll settle it! If yer was stupid enough t' get mixed up with someone sleepin in the street –

Ron   What was I suppose t' do? Walk by?

Stranger   Yer did walk by! – yer only stop long enough t' pinch me wallet – !

Ron   Jeees! It's almost funny. (*Sits in a chair.*) Yer goin round the world in the mornin? No yer not – ain even allowed on the plane! 'N old fool stops yer in the street 'n everythin goes in the bin! They take yer life over! 'N for what? Does 'e look the sort a' man who ever owned a wallet? I ask yer! – I never touch yer wallet!

Stranger   Yer stole me wallet! Rob me! Even if yer didnt makes no difference. Yer cant wriggle out a' it that way! I been rob all me life! Everythin I ever 'ad's bin stole! Always! Yer young take everythin! I lived in proper places – not digs yer wouldnt keep a dog in! Put out on the streets t' make room for families with too many kids! 'Ad good jobs! Please the boss! Then a kid turns up – says grandad's past it – cant keep up the pace. I'm out! I used t' dress! Went out in the best! Good gear! Sharp! Kids follow yer in the street – look at grandad in 'is night shirt! They steal the laces out yer shoes t' see yer trip up! I 'ad wheels. A Morris Minor. Yeller. Pink chrome. Gilt on the dashboard. Pinch off the street! All stole! Take take take! I 'ad wallets stuffed with money! Bulgin! Young come scroungin – give us a sub grandad. When I forked out – I was brought up t' do charity! We went t' Sunday school them days! – they put their fist in yer face 'n say it aint enough! Now they dont even ask – they steal! If yer ain got me wallet it's 'cause some other young bleeder got it first! Nip round the corner 'n share it with 'is mates before yer yell stop! Look under 'is bed – be full a' me wallets 'e stole! 'E's got me stuff under these floorboards! Yer kids take everythin – an' if it aint the kids the grown-ups take it for 'em t' stuff 'em till they're fat 'n spend the rest on trash t' keep 'em quiet! When did I last swaller a meal that did me any good? When's the last time yer slep on the streets? I bin drinkin? Yer'd drink if yer 'ad my misery! Yer laughed! Yer'll come to it. Yer young – but the younger ones are on the way up. Rut rut! (*He doubles over gasping for breath.*) Run round the world ten times yer wont get away – it'll catch yer! Look at me! – yer'd never think I ruled the world! It'll come t' yer! Yer'll live in ruins worse 'n the ones I lived in!

Ron   . . . 'E was be'ind the door when yer questioned me.
Yer 'ad 'im 'id with 'is eye at the key'ole. Yer turn me 'ome in
t' a police station. 'Yer know I care son. I worry for yer love.'
She can whinge like that in front of a stranger? Yer call that
trust? Then yer offer to pay 'im off so yer can buy me respect!
I dont want t' go round the world. Ain far enough. I want t go
t' another planet.

He stands and grabs the **Stranger**. *Propels him towards the hall
door.*

Ron   The street mate! Out! That's where yer belong! Down
there!

Stranger   See! I got evidence! That's what 'e done! – Grab
me 'n rob me wallet! Get yer 'ands off!

Sal   Stop it! Stop it! I wont 'ave violence in my 'ouse. Yer
want t' fight go 'n do it in the street! The pair a' yer!

Ron *lets the* **Stranger** *go and goes out through the door left. He
leaves it open.*

Stranger (*shouting after* **Ron**)   I'll 'ave bruises t' show the
law!

Sal (*calls*)   Yer cant put 'im out. E'll be down there shoutin
all night. Yer'd 'ave the 'ole street up.

Stranger   Look at the luxuries 'e lives in! All stolen goods!
That's why' 'e's off! – goin in t' 'idin!

Sal (*calls*)   If yer'd come straight 'ome like yer said none a'
this would've 'appen!

Ron (*off*)   O yes I'm guilty! I knew it'd be me.

Stranger   Someone 'as t'pay for the life I bin dole out! It's
goin t' be'im!

Ron *comes back. He is putting on his shirt.*

Ron   I'm goin up the end of the street 'n back. I want 'im
out when I come through the door.

Stranger   'E's goin' t' 'ide me wallet outside!

Ron (*to the* **Stranger**)   Out! When I come back I dont want yer loiterin round the corner or in no doorway. Be out the 'ouse. Out the street. 'N out the city if yer wan' t' stay in one piece.

He goes out through the hall door right. He shuts it.

Stranger   O the violence! The violence! 'E wont come back! Aint see 'im again! 'E's run off with the evidence!

Sal   'E 'as t' come back. 'Is rucksack's 'ere.

Stranger   'E wont bring the wallet! 'Ide it in the street! Stop 'im! You're 'is mother. You're responsible for 'is conduct.

Sal   What can I do? 'E dont listen t' me! 'E dont listen t' no one!

Stranger (*sits on the floor*)   Ain leavin without me wallet!

Sal   Yer dont know 'im when 'e gets in 'is states. Yer say 'e took yer wallet. I dont know if 'e did or 'e didnt. Anyone could've took it while yer slep.

Stranger   I never slep.

Sal *stoops to pick up the jumper from the floor.*

Sal   'E wouldnt take yer money. If 'e took yer wallet e'd drop it down a drain. Wouldnt even open it. That'd appeal t' 'im. I dont know what's got in t' young people. They do things 'cause they know they're forbidden. I cant talk t' 'im. I start out nicely 'n it ends in rows. I dont even know what they're about. 'E takes offence if yer look at 'im. They wont tolerate it abroad. If 'e's out there 'n cant make 'is way 'n starts gettin in t' 'is states . . . I bin t' the travel agents. Enquired about a flight – didnt dare book it. If I turned up 'n said it's just t' see yer settlin in – got a good place – 'e'd accuse me a' followin 'im. I'd 'ave t' stay in another part a' town – watch me son from a distance. There's somethin between us. I cant 'elp 'im. I love 'im 'n I'm 'is worse enemy.

Stranger   Did yer 'ear 'im run down the stairs? Jumpin four or five at a time. Showin off! Let 'em break their necks if they want to – not break the stairs for other people t' fall down.

The **Stranger** *looks at* **Sal**. *She hasn't heard him – she is lost in thought.*

Stranger   Poor woman – it's got t' yer early: the young cause sufferin, it's always been the way . . . It's not the jobs – the places t' live – the fancy clothes . . . look at me arm . . . wrinkled . . . no meat left on the bone under the skin . . . they stole it . . . they take it off yer bit by bit while yer asleep or thinkin a' somethin else so yer dont notice . . . starts with the little tots . . . when they grow where'd they get their bodies from? . . . they steal 'em from yer, yer skin 'n 'uman-flesh – where else they get it? . . . there's nowhere else in nature . . . they take yer blood, water it down till yer cold 'n they run off with their 'ot faces . . . they take out yer things inside so yer get pains 'n cramps . . . take yer 'air 'n stick it on their bodies . . . take yer breath 'n jump 'n dance 'n yer pant standin still . . . they take the sight out yer eyes, oh they got sparkling eyes, all yer see's grey as dust . . . they take yer voice so yer whisper 'n they 'oller – they take the ideas out yer 'ead 'n spread it out, spread out yer thinkin so clear it's a map they can live off 'n yer cant remember who yer are . . . 'n then they take yer bones so yer go stoop 'n bent as if yer lookin for a 'ole t' lie in . . . I 'ave this taste in me mouth while I tell yer this, the taste a' me own dust . . . (*His arm stretches out towards the hall door.*) Yer arm stretch out, look shakin, tryin t' get back what they took . . . last thing they take is yer time . . . (*His palm turns upwards in a begging gesture.*) Spare me a little time, yer got so much . . .

Silence. **Sal** *notices it and looks at the* **Stranger**.

Sal   I can give yer twenty-three quid. (*He turns to stare at her.*) Cant do more. 'S all there is in the 'ouse. If there was more in yer wallet yer'll 'ave t' come back with receipts.

Stranger Receipts?

Sal The purchases yer said. Receipts'll give me 'n idea a' yer standard a' livin then I can tell what yer 'ad in yer wallet. Why yer sat on the floor?

Stranger Cant fall down from 'ere. Cant be push off.

Sal Twenty-three. I'll fetch it. Then yer go. (*Going.*) Get off the floor.

She goes through the door left. The **Stranger** *stretches out on the floor. He lies as he did in the street.*

Sal (*off*) Cant give yer more without receipts.

Pause. Off, the front door opens. **Ron** *comes in from the hall. He stares at the* **Stranger**.

Ron Jees.

Sal *comes in left. She carries a black handbag. It is open.*

Ron 'Ow long's 'e bin like that?

Sal I dont . . . 'E was ramblin somethin about . . . – . Get a doctor.

Ron 'E dont need a doctor.

Sal I ain 'avin no one dyin on me kitchen floor.

Ron 'E can die where 'e likes as long as 'e stays dead when 'e's done it.

Sal *takes twenty-three pounds from her handbag and waves them under the* **Stranger**'s *nose. No reaction.*

Sal Twenty-three. (*No reaction.*) Quid. (*No reaction.*) 'E dont react – get doctor –

Ron Yer payin 'im!

Sal What am I supposed t' do? He's lyin there in –

Ron I told yer not to!

Sal   If you 'adnt stole 'is wallet –

Ron   I didnt steal 'is wallet!

Sal   I said if –

Ron   Yer said if I hadnt! That means I 'ad!

Sal   Well did yer?

Ron   Jesus! Jesus! Jesus!

Sal   'E said yer took 'is 'air so I thought –

Ron   I took 'is 'air?

Sal   – 'e got mixed up 'n meant yer wallet – ! Why'd 'e accuse yer if –

Ron   'Is 'air! I took 'is 'air? Jees! – what do I do? Chriss! Cancel the flight! Pay the penalty for cancelling! Tell me mates sorry I change me mind! – me mum invited a lunatic in the 'ouse 'n 'e upset me plans – took me life over!

Sal   Please dont 'ave one a' yer – !

Ron   One a' me whats?

Sal   We 'ave t' get a doctor.

Ron   For 'im or me? – Yer payin 'im cause yer dont want me t' go!

Sal   I want yer t' go!

Ron   Yer want me t' go 'cause I bring lunatics in the 'ouse! Not because I – I – I – want t' go!

He starts to pull the **Stranger** *to his feet.*

Ron   Get up yer senile ol' duffer!

Sal   Careful with 'im!

Ron (*slaps the* **Stranger**'*s face*)   Wake up! Yer goin walkies! Long walkies grandad!

Sal Careful! If yer bruise 'im they'll use it as evidence yer took 'is wallet − !

Ron (*lets the* **Stranger** *fall*)   I never took 'is wallet!

Sal I never said yer took 'is wallet!

Ron Yer did! Yer said − (*To the* **Stranger**.) Didnt she say I − ! (*Remembers the* **Stranger** *isn't conscious. Slaps his forehead.*) Jeeesus!

Sal I said the bruises'd be evidence yer did!

Ron *goes round the room clutching his head.*

Ron Jesus! Jesus! Jesus!

He kicks the **Stranger**'s *leg.*

Ron Get up! Get up! Yer batty ol' nutter!

Sal (*collapses over the table*)   The bruises! 'E'll get fractures! There's no first aid in the 'ouse!

Ron (*jerks the* **Stranger** *to his feet*)   Up! Yer senile ol' basket case −

He shakes the **Stranger**. *Something flies from the* **Stranger**'s *jacket and crosses the room. It lands on the floor.* **Ron** *goes to look at it. Stops.*

Ron (*points. Horror*)   Urrgghh.

Sal (*looks up from the table*)   What is it?

Ron *points at the object. He tries to speak but cant.* **Sal** *goes to him. They stare at the object as if it were a snake.*

Sal 'Is wallet!

Ron Jees. Urgh. (*He gently touches the wallet with the side of his shoe.*) Cunnin ol' so-'n-so. 'Id it in 'is linin.

Sal *and* **Ron** *look at the* **Stranger**. *Then back at the wallet.* **Ron** *stoops to pick it up. Peeps inside.*

Ron (*awe*)   'E's loaded! . . . Got 'undreds. 'Undreds! 'E won the three-thirty! – I'm goin t' the airport.

Sal   What?

Ron   I'm goin t' the airport. Now. I'll 'itch a ride! No! – (*Waves wallet.*) I can afford an all-night cab!

Sal   Yer cant use 'is money! It's not yer –

Ron   It's mine! Woooo-eeee! (*Tries to count the notes.*) 'Undreds! I'm rich! That'll teach 'im! 'E said I took it! Accuses me! – so I'll take it!

Sal   Yer cant! It's found now! We're in the clear – there's no need t' – !

Ron   No need? In the clear? If I stay 'ere 'e'll say I give 'is wallet back t' stay out a'prison but I stole 'arf 'the dosh before I give it back!

Sal   I'll tell 'em yer didnt!

Ron   'E'll tell 'em I did! 'E'll twist 'em round 'is little finger the cunnin ol' – ol' – ! 'E gets 'is wallet back 'e'll accuse me a' somethin else! There'll be no end a' it! I'll be the iceberg that sank the Titanic!

Sal   Yer cant go! When 'e comes round, what do I – I cant cope with 'im on me own! – 'elp me! – stay! – please!

Ron   No! (*Goes towards the hall door. Stops.*) I've done all that just now when I thought I was trapped – went all through it: I'd stay 'ere the rest a' me life (only it'd be over) – work till I'm old – 'n all the junk they throw at yer t' shut yer up ain worth pickin off the floor – I'd 'ate yer for 'oldin me back – 'n one day I'd 'ave t' bury yer – 'n then spend the rest a' me life learnin t' 'ate meself. It 'appens . . . I dont fit in. Yer know that. Yer a widow. Yer brought me up. Yer got experience. If yer was 'onest yer'd tell me t' get out. Let me go.

Sal   Why're yer so selfish! Yer'll leave me t' clear up yer mess? That what yer intend?

Ron   I been accused. That 'urt! 'Urt! That lump a' crap degraded me . . . I dont like accusations when I done nothing wrong. 'N yer believed 'im.

Sal   No –

Ron   Yer believed 'im against yer son.

Sal   No I didnt know what t' believe – I said I believed yer –

Ron   Yer *said* – but yer *believed* 'im –

Sal   Ow could I know? – 'E burst in – 'n yer was awkward – in one a' yer –

Ron   I'm goin –

Sal   Please – I cant cope with it – the police'll come –

Ron   Yer should've thought a' that. It's yer mess. Yer encouraged 'im. Yer 'id 'im be'ind the door. Yer cheated me. Yer lied.

He goes to the hall door. **Sal** *pulls at his clothes.*

Sal   Dont go – stay till the mornin – then we'll sort it out – please!

Ron   Too late!

Sal   I need yer! Please!

Ron   Get off!

Sal   Is that all I'm worth?

Ron   Yer lied t' me!

Sal   Would yer leave me lyin in the street!

Ron   Yes! (*Shocked silence.*) Yes! – Get off me!

He goes out through the hall door. **Sal** *follows him. Off, he slams the front door. She comes back into the room. She is crying. She goes to the table and buries her face in her arms. The* **Stranger** *stirs.*

Stranger   . . . Someone weepin . . . me mother wept long ago . . . been weepin all these years . . . (*Sits.*) Am I in the 'ospital? (*Half rises – rests for breath. Looks at* **Sal**.) Weepin dont 'elp . . . yer cant change it . . .

Sal *looks up at the* **Stranger**. *She tries to speak but bursts into tears again.*

Stranger   It's got dark. Or is that in me 'ead?

Sal   Yer alright now?

Stranger   What is this place?

Sal   Yer were upset.

Stranger   O? Why?

Sal   My son upset yer. 'E's gone.

Stranger   Dont cry. Yer dont need a son.

Sal *is hunched over the table. The stranger pulls up the other chair. He sits and puts his arm round her.*

Stranger   All kids is trouble.

Sal   'E's the only thing I got left t' show for all these years – 'n I drive 'im away. 'Is dad died too early. When 'e was a kid I used t' 'ear 'is dad's voice in 'is baby babble. I knew 'e'd go. 'E's bin wantin to for years. I dont want t' live without 'im. I dont see any point. (*She tries to calm herself*.) – Yer passed out on the floor.

Stranger   The tiredness comes over me. I dont 'ave nightmares when I'm asleep. I wake up 'n see nothin's changed 'n 'ave a nightmare . . . I was somewhere empty 'n there was drops a' water splashin in a puddle . . . I woke up 'n it was you cryin inside me. Yer son stole me wallet. Let 'im go 'n contaminate the people where 'e's goin. That's what the young do – fly off on cheap 'olidays 'n spread their poison round the world. They call it livin. 'Ope 'is plane comes down. Good riddance. I'd kill 'im for yer.

Sal   Yer shouldnt say that.

Stranger   'E's killin you. Cryin like that costs yer. It wears yer out. If 'e was dead yer'd cry a bit but afterwards yer time'd last longer. 'E wont come back but yer wont stop pinin for 'im. What use is that? A son like 'im – yer cant be 'appy till 'e's dead.

Sal   Yer dont mean it.

Stranger   I do. When he rob me I felt 'is 'and scuttlin in me jacket like a rat – cunnin – pulled me wallet out bit by bit so I wouldnt notice – but I was wide awake. Let the rat perish.

Sal   Who looks after yer?

Stranger   What?

Sal   'Ave yer got anywhere t' go?

Stranger   Know a 'ouse that lets out beds.

Sal   Yer better stay 'ere tonight. Yer'll be comfortable in the chair. I'll make some tea.

She goes out left. She leaves the door slightly open. The **Stranger** *stands. Goes quietly to the door. Calls through.*

Stranger   I 'ave two sugars. It's prescribe for me condition.

The **Stranger** *listens for a moment. He quietly closes the door. He fetches a chair and jams the back under the door handle. He goes to the table. Searches in the side-pockets of the backpack. A few packets. A clasp knife. He opens the top and rummages inside. He takes out a T-shirt. Holds it up. Glances at the door left. Opens the clasp knife. Stabs the T-shirt – drags the knife through it. Stops midway – thinks he's heard a noise. Goes to the hall door. The knife in one hand, the ripped T-shirt dangling from the other. He goes out into the hall. Comes back. Shuts the door. Crosses the room. Throws the ripped T-shirt on the table. Goes to the door left. Takes the chair from under* *the handle. Opens the door and goes through with the knife. Shuts the door behind him.*

Silence.

Ron *comes in slowly through the hall door. He stands in the room. He is surprised no one else is there. Pause. The* **Stranger** *comes through the door left. He is empty-handed. He closes the door behind him. He stares at* **Ron**.

Ron   Where's me mother?

Stranger   Gone.

Ron   Where?

Stranger   Out.

Ron   Out?

Stranger   Lookin for yer.

Ron   'Ow long ago?

Stranger   Went t' find yer in the street.

Ron   'Ow long?

Stranger   Just now.

Ron *goes towards the door left.*

Stranger   Go 'n find 'er.

Ron   What?

Stranger   She'll be lookin everywhere.

Ron   She say anythin – about . . .?

Stranger   Went t' tell yer yer'd left yer luggage. (**Ron** *stares at the clothing scattered on the table.*) I was lookin for me wallet.

Ron *looks at him for a moment. He goes to the table and sits on a chair with his back to it. He is hunched and stares in front of him. The* **Stranger** *starts to go to the hall door. As he passes the backpack he is tempted and puts out a hand. Stops himself. Goes on towards the door.*

Ron (*staring into space*)   She said I forgot me backpack.
Doesnt want me stuff in 'er 'ouse.

The **Stranger** *stops in the hall doorway. Watches* **Ron***.*

Ron   I get angry. Clench me fists. Want t' 'it someone.
Knock 'em down. – Cold in the street. Can yer get a 'eart
attack my age?

He reaches for the jumper. Holds it. As he talks the **Stranger** *comes
back to the table. Quietly pulls the backpack towards him and searches
in it.*

Ron   Frightened meself out there. Ran. 'Eart started t'
bang. Loud. Stood still. Bangin got worse. Shook me ribs.

The **Stranger** *sorts* **Ron***'s clothes. Rejects some, chooses others.
Puts them on over his own clothes.*

Ron   Wanted t' shout out lad in the street's got a 'eart
attack. Couldnt. Voice whispered. (*He puts on the jumper.*) No
one would've come. Open a door. Light in a window.

The **Stranger** *pulls the ripped T-shirt over his own shirt.*

Ron   Me chest bobbin about. Could've been drownin. Sea
roarin in me 'ead. Could' ve died. It'd been over.

Stranger   The young always cause sufferin.

Ron   Why've I come back? If I tell 'er sorry it'd be a row.

The **Stranger** *pulls a pair of Bermuda shorts over his trousers.*

Stranger   I could kill 'im now.

Ron   Cant leave 'er like that. Walk out shoutin. She dont
deserve that.

Stranger (*puts on a baseball cap*)   Kill 'im.

Ron   She wants me father 'ere not me. It's 'is 'ouse.

The **Stranger** *ties a pair of footballer's socks round his legs.*

Ron   She tried t' make me talk like 'im.

The **Stranger** *stands behind* **Ron** *with the knife.*

Stranger   Why dont yer kill 'im?

Ron   Couldnt do 'is voice. Couldnt remember it. Too little when 'e died.

Stranger   Shall I kill yer?

Ron   Say it proper or yer wont get yer sweetie.

Stranger   I should kill yer. Make some use a' me life while I still got it. Like t' see a shadow lyin in the floor. Yer wouldnt even know. (*Puts the knife on the table.*) Now I can do it, it dont seem right. (*Wanders to the hall door.*) Kill 'im. Go back 'n kill 'im.

Ron   The dead dont go away.

Stranger   Tell me why I shouldnt kill yer.

Ron   'E's in this 'ouse. I 'ave t' go.

Stranger   There 'as t' be a reason not t' kill yer. All these years 'n I never found it. 'Elp me. Tell me.

Ron   She'll never forgive me for me father's death.

Stranger (*at the hall door. Quavering*)   Tell me. Please.

Ron   A scaffolder by trade. Accident at work. Fell from 'is ladder. It could still've gone well. 'E'd've fell out of the sky 'n 'it the bottom. Broke 'is ankle. Concussed 'isself.

Stranger (*starts to shuffle back to* **Ron**)   Tell me why I shouldnt kill yer.

Ron   'Arf way down the fall 'e reach out for the ladder. Grab the sides. 'Is chin struck a rung. Bang. Broke 'is neck. 'E's stuck up on the ladder. 'Angin in the air.

The **Stranger** *reaches* **Ron**. *He picks up the knife. He raises it over* **Ron**'s *back. The knife shakes violently.*

Stranger   Tell me why I shouldnt kill yer.

Ron   When 'is mates carried 'im down 'e was dead.

Stranger   It 'as t' be.

The **Stranger** *lunges the knife at* **Ron***'s back.* **Ron** *leaps up. Chair sent flying.*

Ron   No! No! No! Dont! Dont! Dont! Stop 'er! Stop 'er! She's killin 'erself! Where did she – ? Which way? Which way? Which way? Where did she – ? (*Lurches to the hall door.*) She's killin 'erself! (*To the* **Stranger**. *Frantic.*) Went out t' kill 'erself! Which way did she – ? (*Turns back to the door.*) Stop 'er! Stop 'er! She's –

Sal *comes through the doorway left. She holds a mug of tea in front of her.* **Ron** *sees her.*

Ron (*howl*)   Aaah! She's dead! Killed 'erself! Poisoned the – ! (*Grabs the mug. Hurls the tea away.*) What did yer put in the – ? Killed yerself! Put in the tea – !

Sal   Ronnie! Ronnie! Ronnie! What is it?

Ron   Yer killin yerself! Dont! Dont! Dont!

Sal   Ronnie! Ronnie!

Ron   Dont die! Dont die! Dont die!

Sal   No! Ronnie! Ronnie!

Ron *collapses against her. Falling. Crying. She bends over him. Clings to him.*

Sal   Wont die! What is it?

Ron (*against her*)   I love yer.

Sal   Ronnie what is it? What is it?

Ron (*gripping the cup as if he is trying to bury it in himself*)   Yer was poisonin – in the cup –

Sal   No! No!

Ron   Because I left yer! Went off! Shoutin – shoutin at yer – !

Sal   No! No! I didnt – the cup was – there's nothin –

Ron (*whining howl*)   Sad. Sad. Sad. Sad. Sad.

Sal   I havent! I havent! It's alright!

Ron   I thought I saw me father here! Then it was you! It's mixed up! Mixed up!

Sal   Ronnie Ronnie Ronnie dont cry. I wouldnt kill meself. I wouldnt do that to 'urt yer. I wouldnt. Dont. Dont. When yer left yer 'urt me – listen – the pain was you cause I love yer – I loved the pain – yer gave me the pain t' remember yer –

Ron   Ive come back. No pain. I wont leave. Wont go. It's alright. It's bin mix up. I couldnt leave yer like – I was cruel – cruel –

They notice the **Stranger**. *He is watching them. He is grotesque.* **Ron**'s *clothes are like a child's clothes on top of an old man's. He is chewing the bar of chocolate he found in the backpack.* **Sal** *takes the cup from* **Ron**. *She puts it on the table. She strips* **Ron**'s *clothes from the* **Stranger** – *it is like a mother undressing a child.* **Ron** *watches.*

Sal   Yer mustnt wear 'is things. They're not yours. Bad. Dont belong.

Sal *finishes taking the clothes from the* **Stranger**. *She picks up the backpack. She holds it open to* **Ron**.

Sal   'Elp me.

Ron   Yer neednt pack now.

Sal (*packing*)   'E soiled some. Yer ave t' get 'em laundered.

Ron   I'm not going.

Sal (*straightening the backpack in his hands*)   'Old it steady.

Ron   I'm staying.

Sal (*packing*)   Yer cant. (*Stops packing. Looks at him.*) Yer 'ave t' go. (*Packing.*) 'Itch a lift t' the airport.

Ron   I want t' be 'ere.

Sal (*the backpack*)   Keep it steady. (*Packing.*) Yer cant stay. Look at this, look around yer. – I need yer t' go.

Ron   Not now – in the middle of the night –

Sal (*packing*)   In the mornin we'll get it wrong again. It's your life. Take your chance now.

Ron   Cant leave yer with 'im.

Sal   'E's a child. I can manage 'im. 'E'll sleep in your bed tonight. In the mornin I'll arrange somewhere for 'im t' go. You'll be far away. Somewhere safe.

Ron *reaches to hold her.*

Sal   No. Dont touch me. I'm not strong enough for that yet. One day. Yer held me just now. I'll remember it. Always feel yer.

Ron *takes the wallet from his pocket. Throws it to the* **Stranger**. *It lands at his feet. He doesn't look at it.* **Ron** *holds the backpack by the straps. He goes to the hall door.* **Sal** *follows him. He goes out.* **Sal** *stays in the room. She closes the hall door. The outside door is heard closing.* **Sal** *crosses the room and goes through the doorway left. The* **Stranger** *is alone. Chocolate is smeared round his mouth. He holds the remains of the bar in his hand.*

Stranger   I'll die in 'is bed.

Five Theatre Poems

The Bear

I saw theatre once
A bear danced on the mountainside in snow
It was moonlight
It stamped its brutish feet
Waved its heavy paws armed with claws
Spittle shook from its sabre teeth
No tamer or organ-grinder
Only the stars in the black sky
And a whimper of wind from the strip of pines
Theatre is always at war
The great actor faces his enemies
Fights
And is soon dead
The great actress raises her hands wet with tears
Rails at her lover
Slaughters her children
There is horror and – suddenly – knowing
In tragedy the heroes and heroines commit their crime
    to prove they are innocent
The gods scamper away in fear
Their heels catch in the hem of their skirts

1957

It is Manifest

For days snow fell
And now in the full moon's light the silent night is as bright
    as day
And the untrodden snow a new world where even the
    black gnarled withered oak is clad in seamless white

We live in a savage age
The pre-catastrophe time
Savages destroy things before they are made
Fanatics stamp on the bars of their treadmills
And we plunder the earth to nurture the parasites that will
    devour our children

We have spent our patrimony – legal moral creative –
Towers and domes and dwellings fall and the bricks lie like
    broken hands that clutched at the grass as they fell
We have sold our birthright to furnish our grave
Then let us write of the stage – the court of justice we build
    so that our lives and our cities may prosper

What is theatre? – in theatre the audience mocks itself – laughs
    at its weeping and weeps at its laughter – then satisfied
      goes away
It forgets that the price of the ticket is less than the debt all
    who live in this world must pay

What is drama ? – it is simple and simply said: humanity
Drama knows the secret self each one of us hides from our self
    out of pity and dread
And the acts of rebellion we were too young to commit though
    we are bound to commit them from the hour we are born –
      but instead left to lie in wait for us as chaos and crime in
        the years ahead

The actors tell us these secrets and show us this chaos
And bear for us the pity we dread to bear and the dread that
    is pitiless
And wipe out these secrets and crimes with the sky as if
    it were a towel from our kitchen or a sheet from our bed
So that the ageless tragic paean of freedom is sung
It is as simple as that and as simply said: the actors have
    empathy for the audience

December 2010

The Towers of Ilium are Fallen

So reason doesn't make us human
By itself it makes us barbarous
Only the imagination can make us human
That is the origin and work of drama

Fiction is the source of our reality
In drama imagination makes reason rational and brings
    understanding
In drama what is measured changes the measuring rod
    and the measurer
That is the logic of humanness
Its paradoxes spin through time and confound history

Again mere anarchy is loosed upon the world
We have spent spent spent our patrimony in a waste of shame
There is no health – no truth – in us
And fanatics slouch in-step towards the cities
When faith usurps the place of drama imagination cannot
    make reason rational
Instead reason is mad and makes bombs
As long as there is a God we will make nuclear weapons
That is the logic of humanness

We have no drama – only the trickling sump of theatre
We must make drama but have no stage
In the city there is an empty space – a cicatrix of bone –
    and the Tragic figures of our time wander around it in
        darkness howling our names

Where shall we begin?
Return to the origin – the origin of tomorrow
To the craft and art of Ibsen and Chekhov and their kind
To the lucid frenzy – the forensic violence – of the Greeks

My blood spoke to me as it gurgled down the sink and said
    rebel make drama

November 2010

The Boom-Boom Man

See when it happened yeah
Like boom – it was like a kinda quick ting – like boom
Went down the road – come back up
Boom-boom – finished – boom – ghost
Yer get what I'm sayin?
The police secret recording of a young killer shortly after
   his gang had knifed to death a stranger
Precise terse summary and expansive
Shakespearian – from the kitchen table to the edge of the
   universe
You see a traveller in rags on that dark journey
No poets laureate use language so well – they have no need
Instead the rattle of teacups on saucers – the clink of glasses –
   the tea leaves of sawdust words
But the poets kill no one?
No but they must go to the street where the body is broken
   and blood wells and seeps – must see the gaping eyes and
     mouths and be knocked down by the pounding feet
Only there can lyric and stone houses have meaning
The poet must unravel the city's entrails and lock the gates
   of hell

November 2009

The Question

(The Drama Teacher)

I dream of the young child in a distant land
Who one day woke to play but met a bomb instead
And in that instant lay living among the dead
With both his arms blown off
My sleeping self said wake
I wake and in that instant know
To change one centimetre of the world I must change all of it
And I have slept too long and wake too late
Is the child howling in the city gate and raging with a knife
The story of our common human fate or of lost hope and
    wasted human life?
And I have slept too long and wake too late
And as I rise and leave my bed
And wash and dress and break my bread
And go to face the day and set about my task
Deep deep deep are the questions I must ask
Must I cut off the hand that holds the knife to take the knife
    away?

2008

Methuen Drama Contemporary Dramatists
include

John Arden (two volumes)
Arden & D'Arcy
Peter Barnes (three volumes)
Sebastian Barry
Dermot Bolger
Edward Bond (eight volumes)
Howard Brenton
   (two volumes)
Richard Cameron
Jim Cartwright
Caryl Churchill (two volumes)
Sarah Daniels (two volumes)
Nick Darke
David Edgar (three volumes)
David Eldridge
Ben Elton
Dario Fo (two volumes)
Michael Frayn (three volumes)
David Greig
John Godber (four volumes)
Paul Godfrey
John Guare
Lee Hall (two volumes)
Peter Handke
Jonathan Harvey
   (two volumes)
Declan Hughes
Terry Johnson (three volumes)
Sarah Kane
Barrie Keeffe
Bernard-Marie Koltès
   (two volumes)
Franz Xaver Kroetz
David Lan
Bryony Lavery
Deborah Levy
Doug Lucie

David Mamet (four volumes)
Martin McDonagh
Duncan McLean
Anthony Minghella
   (two volumes)
Tom Murphy (six volumes)
Phyllis Nagy
Anthony Neilsen (two volumes)
Philip Osment
Gary Owen
Louise Page
Stewart Parker (two volumes)
Joe Penhall (two volumes)
Stephen Poliakoff
   (three volumes)
David Rabe (two volumes)
Mark Ravenhill (two volumes)
Christina Reid
Philip Ridley
Willy Russell
Eric-Emmanuel Schmitt
Ntozake Shange
Sam Shepard (two volumes)
Wole Soyinka (two volumes)
Simon Stephens (two volumes)
Shelagh Stephenson
David Storey (three volumes)
Sue Townsend
Judy Upton
Michel Vinaver
   (two volumes)
Arnold Wesker (two volumes)
Michael Wilcox
Roy Williams (three volumes)
Snoo Wilson (two volumes)
David Wood (two volumes)
Victoria Wood

Methuen Drama Student Editions

Jean Anouilh *Antigone* • John Arden *Serjeant Musgrave's Dance*
Alan Ayckbourn *Confusions* • Aphra Behn *The Rover* • Edward Bond
Lear • *Saved* • Bertolt Brecht *The Caucasian Chalk Circle* • *Fear and
Misery in the Third Reich* • *The Good Person of Szechwan* • *Life of Galileo* •
Mother Courage and her Children• *The Resistible Rise of Arturo Ui* • *The
Threepenny Opera* • Anton Chekhov *The Cherry Orchard* • *The Seagull* •
Three Sisters • *Uncle Vanya* • Caryl Churchill *Serious Money* • *Top Girls*
• Shelagh Delaney *A Taste of Honey* • Euripides *Elektra* • *Medea*•
Dario Fo *Accidental Death of an Anarchist* • Michael Frayn *Copenhagen*
• John Galsworthy *Strife* • Nikolai Gogol *The Government Inspector* •
Robert Holman *Across Oka* • Henrik Ibsen *A Doll's House* • *Ghosts*•
Hedda Gabler • Charlotte Keatley *My Mother Said I Never Should* •
Bernard Kops *Dreams of Anne Frank* • Federico García Lorca *Blood
Wedding* • *Doña Rosita the Spinster* (bilingual edition) •*The House of
Bernarda Alba* • (bilingual edition) • *Yerma* (bilingual edition) • David
Mamet *Glengarry Glen Ross* • *Oleanna* • Patrick Marber *Closer* • John
Marston *Malcontent* • Martin McDonagh *The Lieutenant of Inishmore* •
Joe Orton *Loot* • Luigi Pirandello *Six Characters in Search of an Author*
• Mark Ravenhill *Shopping and F***ing* •Willy Russell *Blood Brothers*
• *Educating Rita* • Sophocles *Antigone* • *Oedipus the King* • Wole
Soyinka *Death and the King's Horseman* • Shelagh Stephenson *The
Memory of Water* • August Strindberg *Miss Julie* • J. M. Synge *The
Playboy of the Western World* • Theatre Workshop *Oh What a Lovely
War* Timberlake Wertenbaker *Our Country's Good* • Arnold Wesker
The Merchant • Oscar Wilde *The Importance of Being Earnest* •
Tennessee Williams *A Streetcar Named Desire* • *The Glass Menagerie*

Methuen Drama Modern Classics

Jean Anouilh *Antigone* • Brendan Behan *The Hostage* • Robert Bolt *A Man for All Seasons* • Edward Bond *Saved* • Bertolt Brecht *The Caucasian Chalk Circle* • *Fear and Misery in the Third Reich* • *The Good Person of Szechwan* • *Life of Galileo* • *The Messingkauf Dialogues* • *Mother Courage and Her Children* • *Mr Puntila and His Man Matti* • *The Resistible Rise of Arturo Ui* • *Rise and Fall of the City of Mahagonny* • *The Threepenny Opera* • Jim Cartwright *Road* • *Two & Bed* • Caryl Churchill *Serious Money* • *Top Girls* • Noël Coward *Blithe Spirit* • *Hay Fever* • *Present Laughter* • *Private Lives* • *The Vortex* • Shelagh Delaney *A Taste of Honey* • Dario Fo *Accidental Death of an Anarchist* • Michael Frayn *Copenhagen* • Lorraine Hansberry *A Raisin in the Sun* • Jonathan Harvey *Beautiful Thing* • David Mamet *Glengarry Glen Ross* • *Oleanna* • *Speed-the-Plow* • Patrick Marber *Closer* • *Dealer's Choice* • Arthur Miller *Broken Glass* • Percy Mtwa, Mbongeni Ngema, Barney Simon *Woza Albert!* • Joe Orton *Entertaining Mr Sloane* • *Loot* • *What the Butler Saw* • Mark Ravenhill *Shopping and F***ing* • Willy Russell *Blood Brothers* • *Educating Rita* • *Stags and Hens* • *Our Day Out* • Jean-Paul Sartre *Crime Passionnel* • Wole Soyinka • *Death and the King's Horseman* • Theatre Workshop *Oh, What a Lovely War* • Frank Wedekind • *Spring Awakening* • Timberlake Wertenbaker *Our Country's Good*

For a complete catalogue
of Methuen Drama titles
write to:

Methuen Drama
Bloomsbury Publishing Plc
50 Bedford Square
London WC1B 3DP

or you can visit our website at:

www.methuendrama.com